The Depoliticisation of Greece's Public Revenue Administration

Dionyssis Dimitrakopoulos • Argyris Passas

The Depoliticisation of Greece's Public Revenue Administration

Radical Change and the Limits of Conditionality

Springer

Dionyssis Dimitrakopoulos
Department of Politics
Birkbeck, University of London
London, UK

Argyris Passas
Department of International
European and Area Studies
Panteion University of Social and Political
Sciences
Athens, Greece

ISBN 978-3-030-23212-2 ISBN 978-3-030-23213-9 (eBook)
https://doi.org/10.1007/978-3-030-23213-9

This Springer imprint is published by the registered company Springer Nature Switzerland AG.
The registered company address is: Gewerbestrasse 11, 6330 Cham, Switzerland

Despite being classified as an advanced economy by virtue of its euro area membership, by all accounts Greece's institutional capacity in the judicial process, tax administration, expenditure control, and statistical services was below that in practically any other European economy

(Kopits 2016, 24)

'We spend a lot of time on the revenue administration, trying to drag it out of the 1930s' (statement made at a meeting held in London in January 2018 under the Chatham House rule)

'We certainly cannot say that these people (i.e. the EU and IMF staff) came here to destroy paradise' (interview, Athens, 9 November 2016)

'I must say that, were it not for the Troika's major pressure, it might have never materialised' (interview, Athens, 2 June 2017)

We dedicate this book to Katerina Papakonstantinou, Maria Zampara and, in particular, Alkis A. and Yiorgos A. Passas hoping that at least the latter two will experience Greece as a country where paying and collecting tax fairly will be the norm. If that happens, it will be in no small part due to the reform that we examine in this book.

Preface

When we started working on this project, we had no idea we would end up making a book out of it. Our much more timid objective was to write an article for an academic journal and even that felt like a bit of a stretch for two political scientists who do not normally write about public revenue administrations. What sparked our interest in the reform of Greece's public revenue administration was the fact that, as President Obama's chief of staff rightly noted, 'you never want a serious crisis to go to waste', i.e. a crisis 'is an opportunity to do the things that you think you could not do before' (Emanuel 2008). As anyone who has encountered the modern Greek state's apparatus would testify, at the onset of the crisis it was in desperate need for reform, but the country's public revenue administration in particular stood out in that respect. Having grown accustomed to reading, hearing or even experiencing stories about its legendary ineffectiveness, heavy-handedness, opacity and corruption (all of which are sociopolitical constructs), coupled with our deeply held belief that paying and collecting tax fairly is first and foremost a basic civic duty, a matter of social justice—since none of the public goods that need protecting and none of the resources and opportunities that need to be redistributed in unequal societies can be protected, funded or redistributed without tax justice—we decided to try to look into it by participating in the annual competition for small research grants conducted by the Hellenic Observatory at the European Institute of the London School of Economics and Political Science.

We did so after reading the surprising (to us at least) news in the press that the Greek government was going to establish an independent public revenue authority that was meant to operate at arm's length from the government of the day. To us, this sounded like nothing short of a revolution since we were aware of the Greek political establishment's aversion to genuinely independent authorities, the problems that extant authorities were facing, the academic literature on Greece's limited reform capacity as well as the pervasive view amongst Greeks that acknowledges the need for deep reforms 'because the country could not go on as it was' as long as these reforms start from other social groups first.

When we decided to participate in the Hellenic Observatory's competition, we did so with a degree of trepidation that was due not only to the highly competitive nature of the process. The reasons for our trepidation were threefold. First, we believe that independent authorities pose particular challenges to democracy. Detachment from the exigencies of the electoral cycle implies that voters are necessarily as unwilling to hear unpopular truths being said as unwilling politicians vying for office are to tell them. Although it is true that far too many citizens in advanced liberal democracies either take democracy for granted—as the rampant rise of populism shows—or construe democracy only in terms of rights, we do not believe that the use of independent authorities across the board is always as necessary as their proponents purport it to be while they remain rather silent (often deafeningly so) with regard to the material lures of the market as well as the problem of 'revolving doors'. As for the meaning of independence, if one takes a sociological perspective, one will notice that in many cases the senior officials of these authorities have rather similar backgrounds in terms of class, education, gender, etc. to those of many leading politicians. The strength of isomorphism is significant, as are its pitfalls. One of the most significant pitfalls is the potential for blame avoidance. Independent authorities offer this potential especially in a country such as Greece where politicians (and senior officials) often show excessive aversion to the very idea of resigning from office.

Second, shifting the focus of political accountability from intra-departmental hierarchies to accountability to parliament poses particular challenges in the case of Greece since the Greek parliament is characteristically docile. Its key weakness, which is also one that permeates the country's entire political system, is aversion to evidence-based debates. This is unsurprising since gathering and interpreting evidence is a cumbersome and challenging activity and Greek parliamentarians are not accustomed to it. This is not due to the lack of means (itself a political construct). Their offices remain handsomely funded by the state budget. Rather, they are culturally keener on the use of slogans, as are much of the Greek press and body politic. The final reason for our trepidation was our fear—based on past experience—that the interview-intensive nature of this research project would be undermined by the relative absence of the culture of research interview from large segments of both the political and administrative *élite*. On that front, and with only a handful of (anyway telling) exceptions, we ended up being pleasantly surprised.

Carrying out this research project would have been impossible without the financial support provided by the Hellenic Observatory. We are grateful for it. We are also grateful to Ms Eva Katakalou, doctoral candidate at Panteion University of Social and Political Sciences, for the excellent research assistance that she has provided; the 34 individuals who have agreed to be interviewed for the purpose of this project and for help with tracking down obscure documents; as well as Georgette Lalis, Nikos Erinakis and Michalis Psalidopoulos for the help they have provided in tracking down key officials. Our work has benefitted from the comments offered by Tryfon Alexiadis, Nikos Karavitis, Fragiskos Koutentakis, Georgette Lalis, Antonis Papayannidis, Philippos Sachinidis, Calliope Spanou, Harry Theoharis and Theodore Tsekos during the presentation of an earlier paper at the Jean Monnet Chair's workshop on administrative reform in Greece at Panteion University, Athens, on 5 April 2017. We have also benefitted from the comments made by Dr Ali Burak Güven, Professor Deborah Mabbett, Professor E. C. Page FBA, Dr David Styan and Professor Theodore Tsekos in the context of the 'book club' of Birkbeck's Politics Department. The usual disclaimer applies. Dionyssis G. Dimitrakopoulos gratefully acknowledges the research funding and time off from routine duties granted by Birkbeck's Politics Department while working on this project. We would also like to thank the team at Springer, especially Johannes Glaeser, for the professional handling of the production process.

London, UK
Athens, Greece
April 2019

Dionyssis Dimitrakopoulos
Argyris Passas

Contents

Acronyms and Abbreviations

ADEDY	Anotati Dioikisi Enoseon Dimosion Ypallilon (Supreme Command of Civil Servants' Unions)
ASEP	Anotato Symvoulio Epilogis Prosopikou (Supreme Council for Personnel Selection)
ANEL	Aneksartitoi Ellines (Independent Greeks)
CEO	Chief Executive Officer
DIMAR	Demokratike Aristera (Democratic Left)
DOY	Demosia Oekonomiki Ypiresia (Local tax office)
ECB	European Central Bank
EDP	Excessive deficit procedure
EFF	Extended Fund Facility
EFSF	European Financial Stability Facility
ELSTAT	Hellinki Statistiki Arkhi (Hellenic Statistical Authority)
EMU	Economic and Monetary Union
ESM	European Stability Mechanism
ESY	Ethniki Statistiki Ypiresia (National Statistical Service)
EU	European Union
GDFS	General Directorate for Financial Services
GGPS	Genike Grammateia Pliroforiakon Sistimaton (Secretariat General for Information Systems)
HQ	Headquarters
HMRC	Her Majesty's Revenue and Customs
HR	Human resources
IAPR	Independent Authority for Public Revenue
IFI	International financial institutions
ILO	International Labour Organisation
IMF	International Monetary Fund
IRS	Internal Revenue Service
IT	Information technology
LAOS	Laikos Orthodoxos Sinagermos (Popular Orthodox Rally)
MoF	Ministry of Finance

MoU	Memorandum of Understanding
MEP	Member of the European Parliament
MP	Member of Parliament
ND	Nea Dimokratia
NMI	Non-majoritarian institution
PASOK	Panellinio Sosialistiko Kinima (Panhellenic Socialist Movement)
PM	Prime Minister
PSI	Private sector involvement
QUANGO	Quasi-autonomous non-governmental organisation
RA	Revenue authority
SBA	Stand-by arrangement
SDOE	Soma Dioksis Oekonomikou Egklimatos (Financial Crime Squad)
SG	Secretary General/Secretariat General
SGPR	Secretariat General for Public Revenue
SYRIZA	Synaspismos Rizospastikis Aristeras (Coalition of the Radical Left)
UNECE	United Nations Economic Commission for Europe

Chapter 1
Introduction

The purpose of this book is to analyse how Greece has come to 'depoliticise' its public revenue administration, i.e. how the body that is responsible for collecting taxes has ceased to be a part of the Ministry of Finance operating under the direct control of the minister of finance and has become an independent authority that (a) operates at arm's length from the government of the day and (b) is accountable directly to parliament. This is arguably the single most significant institutional reform that came about as a result of the three 'bailout' agreements of 2010, 2012 and 2015 involving the International Monetary Fund (IMF) as well as the Eurozone countries. In exchange for the provision of vitally needed funding without which the country would have gone bankrupt, successive Greek governments agreed to an evolving series of policy and institutional reforms, including the depoliticisation and broader modernisation of the country's public revenue administration. This 'exchange' is the essence of conditionality, i.e. the cornerstone of the adjustment programme, of which the reform examined in this book is an emblematic example.

The depoliticisation of the public revenue administration was not even mentioned in the first memorandum of understanding (MoU) that was signed in 2010. However, during the decade that followed (2010–2019) this issue has come to occupy a central role in the Greek adjustment programme. This book focuses on how this happened and, in particular, how a key reform that had extremely limited support within the Greek political establishment has come to be not only enacted but also successfully implemented in a country that is reported to have a rather limited reform capacity. Researching this reform is made even more worthwhile (and remarkable) by the fact that it relates directly to one of the purely domestic causes of Greece's crisis: lax tax collection. It is a 'success story' in an adjustment programme that has been marked by many crises, starts and stops. The aim of this introductory chapter is to set the scene for this study by providing a discussion of its basic parameters.

The depoliticisation of Greece's public revenue administration is very significant because of (1) the central role of deficient tax collection in the pre-crisis management of Greek public finances (alongside the country's highly problematic budgeting processes and problems with official statistics) and (2) Greece's problems with tax

D. Dimitrakopoulos, A. Passas, *The Depoliticisation of Greece's Public Revenue Administration*, https://doi.org/10.1007/978-3-030-23213-9_1

collection since the establishment of the modern Greek state in 1830. The first two sections of this chapter present (a) the scale of these problems and (b) the nature and basic characteristics of Greece's public revenue administration at the onset of the crisis. The reform that we set out to examine in this book is, as we will show in the following chapters, radical in nature in comparison to (1) the status quo ante as well as (2) much of Greece's public administration. Yet it came about in a country that, according to the prevailing wisdom, has limited reform capacity (Featherstone 2011: 195; Featherstone and Papadimitriou 2008; Kalyvas et al. 2012; Spanou and Sotiropoulos 2011) or at least it has a highly problematic 'reform technology' (Monastiriotis and Antoniades 2009). The nature of this limited reform capacity and the barriers to reform are examined in the third section of this chapter. Moreover, this change took one of the several forms that it could have taken. The fourth section presents the landscape of the main models of public revenue administrations as they exist in Organisation for Economic Co-operation and Development (OECD) countries. The final section brings together the key elements of the previous sections and outlines the book's puzzle and central argument. Briefly put, the question that we seek to answer is this: what accounts for the switch from the previous model of direct ministerial control to an independent authority that operates at arm's length from the government in a country that has limited reform capacity? How did reform-averse Greece come to enact and implement this radically different model—indeed one whose effectiveness and efficiency are not certain (OECD 2015: 30) and is used by a minority of European Union (EU) member states? Our argument is that while conditionality—in particular the power asymmetry between Greece and its international partners—explains the choice of the direction of travel (i.e. less ministerial control) as a response to a real problem, it does not account for how far the reform went. We argue that the extent of the reform is best understood as a result of not only (a) the priorities of the government in the final stages of the negotiations but, more importantly, (b) successive Greek governments' reactions (and subsequent loss of credibility) to pressure for reform. These reactions arguably exacerbated the problem of credibility and lack of trust in the eyes of the country's international partners.

The next section outlines Greece's enduring problems with tax collection.

Tax Collection in Greece: The Magnitude of the Problem

Tax collection has been an enduring problem for the modern Greek state since its establishment in 1830. Although no European state can claim to have a perfect tax collection record, the magnitude of the problem in Greece was very high in the run-up to the onset of the crisis. Greece's tax gap—the difference between the amount that the public revenue administration is expected to collect on the basis of legislation in force and the amount that it actually collects (Khwaja and Iyer 2014)—was huge. The magnitude of the tax gap and the onset of the crisis have been attributed to Greece's historically very low public revenues.[1] Indeed, according to one view, in 2009 Greece's real primary deficit was 10%, i.e. seven percentage points above the Euro area's average, but six of the seven percentage points of the difference were due to lower Greek public revenues in comparison to the Euro area's average.[2] According to the European Commission's estimates, 'uncollected tax revenue in 2006 amounted to 30% (or 3.4% of GDP)' (Featherstone 2011: 196). In the run-up to the crisis, the magnitude of the system's ineffectiveness was demonstrably known to at least the government of the day. We know that because that government commissioned the IMF report which noted that in June 2005 (i.e. after several years of significant economic growth), the total tax debts owed amounted to 18 billion euros, i.e. more than 40% of the previous year's tax collections (which is the standard international comparator), whereas the aim of most developed public revenue administrations is approximately between 5 and 10% (Perry et al. 2005: 13–14). Even as late as 2011 the OECD was reporting that

> if Greece could collect VAT, social security contributions and corporate income tax with the same efficiency as its main partners do, it could boost tax revenues by about 4¾ per cent of GDP per year (OECD 2011: 85).

In terms of value-added tax (VAT), the gap was estimated to be as high as 33.7% in 2009, i.e. approximately 7.5 billion euros, while (1) the figures for the comparable case of Portugal were 14.5% and just over 2 billion euros respectively and (2) in the United Kingdom—a country where the public revenue administration was already operating at arm's length from the government—the VAT gap was 13.4% (Center for Social and Economic Research 2015, Tables B6 and B7).

Between 1995 and 2011, the average total tax receipts in Greece were 21.3% of gross domestic product (GDP) while the EU average was 26.6% and if one includes social security contributions the average total was 31.9% while the EU27 and Euro area average was 40% of GDP (Anastasatou n.d.: 20). As regards the tax rate, while the nominal rate (when it comes to income and consumption) is high, the corresponding tax take has historically been comparatively low despite some convergence observed in the post-2009 period. In 2012, the implicit tax rate (which takes account of the real tax take) on consumption in Greece was 16.2% (nominally at 23%) while in the EU28 it was 19.9% (Ernst and Young 2017: 31–32).

---

[1]This does not mean that tax evasion is evenly distributed across social groups. Pensioners and salaried workers would normally find it difficult or impossible to avoid paying income tax when paid via payroll. On the contrary, path-breaking new research estimates that '43–45% of self-employed income goes unreported and thus untaxed. For 2009, this implies 28.2 billion euros of unreported income, implying forgone tax revenues of over 11 billion euros or 30% of the deficit' (Artavanis et al. 2016).

[2]This is the view of Prof. Euclid Tsakalotos (Minister of Finance in the post-2015 Tsipras administrations) and Fragkiskos Koutentakis, an academic economist who was also one of the Tsipras administration's top officials in the Ministry of Finance and subsequent head of the Hellenic Parliament's Budget Office (Tsakalotos 2010: 10, Figs. 2 and 3; Koutentakis 2018).

In terms of ranking on the basis of the ratio of tax effort in relation to actual tax collection,[3] Greece was classified as medium ranking (Khwaja and Iyer 2014: 20, Table 3) while a former government minister argued that tax collection in Greece was the costliest amongst OECD countries (interview, Athens, 19 July 2016). Economists have also highlighted the electoral dimension of tax collection. It has been estimated that between 1982 (the year after Greece's accession to the then European Communities) and 2007 (5 years after its adoption of the euro) deviation from budgetary[4] provisions was much higher and—in particular—the tax intake often dropped considerably in election years (Hardouvelis et al. 2006: 10–13) because—as former Finance Minister George Papaconstantinou reportedly acknowledged—'The first thing a government does in an election year is to pull the tax collectors off the streets' (Lewis 2011: 49). More recent research—co-authored by another Greek former finance minister and covering the 13 elections between 1972 and 2009—shows that around election times 'tax revenue is reduced by changes in tax authority auditing patterns and by intentionally more relaxed enforcement of tax laws' to the tune of 2.34% of GDP in 2008 figures (Skouras and Christodoulakis 2014: 544, 550). All this points in the direction of a highly ineffective public revenue system. Its key characteristics at the onset of the crisis are presented in the next section.

Greece's Public Revenue Administration at the Onset of the Crisis

At that point in time, as subsequent developments have clearly confirmed, Greece's entire set of public financial management institutions was highly problematic. This applies to budgeting (Rapanos 2007; Rapanos and Kaplanoglou 2014), official statistics (European Commission 2010) but above all the collection of taxes. More than 6 years into Greece's adjustment programme, a senior official said that what is being attempted is 'to drag the country's public revenue administration out of the 1930s'.[5] This may sound like a hyperbole but it is not one. As a ministerial adviser (and former employee of the Ministry of Finance) put it, Greece's international partners cannot be accused of trying to destroy paradise; rather, on some issues 'we were in total hell' (interview, Athens, 9 November 2016).

The Greek public revenue system was highly problematic before the onset of the crisis. Its problems were well known. Many of them had been mentioned in the IMF's report of 2005 commissioned by the conservative Nea Dimokratia

[3]The two measures relate to the level of taxation and the extent to which a country's public revenue administration performs close to, above, or below its potential.

[4]An average of approximately 1.83 percentage points has been added to the country's public deficit every election year between 1974 and 1993 (Thomadakis 1997: 55).

[5]Statement made at a meeting held in London in January 2018 under the Chatham House rule.

government and—as George Papaconstantinou acknowledged (Papaconstantinou 2016: 103)—were also applicable in the autumn of 2009 when he took over as finance minister of the centre-left PASOK (Panhellenic Socialist Movement) government. First, much like the remainder of the Athenian bureaucracy, Greece's public revenue administration was both highly hierarchical[6] and centralised at the ministerial level. In terms of autonomy, at the time, i.e. before the onset of the crisis, the Greek public revenue administration was similar to the French and German ones in a range of issues (OECD 2007: 27–31, Tables 1–5), key amongst which is the incorporation of duties to various directorates within the central Ministry of Finance, which also implies the predominant role of the corresponding politician(s). This translated into repeated interference in operational decisions, as staff had repeatedly claimed (interview, Athens, 13 February 2017; see also POE-DOY 2012) and as the country's central bank too noted (Bank of Greece 2010: 174). However, this does not mean that tax collection was a major political priority in Greece. Quite the opposite is true for any Greek prime minister at least since the restoration of democracy in 1974, both when public borrowing was expensive and when (as is the case of the period after Greece's adoption of the euro in 2002) it was cheap. In fact, quite remarkably and unlike several of his predecessors, upon taking office in the autumn of 2009, George A. Papandreou did not even appoint a junior minister in charge of public revenue collection—a decision that a senior official of that administration acknowledged had been a mistake (interview, Athens, 2 June 2017). George Papandreou's decision appears to be even more remarkable in light of the fact that (a) he had campaigned on an anti-austerity platform summarised in the slogan 'the money is there' which implied improvements in the management of public finances partly via the fight against corruption and (b) he was aware of the scale of the task relating to Greece's public finances well before the 2009 elections since the German Finance Minister Peer Steinbrück (a social democrat) saw to it (Steinbrück 2010: 121–122).

Second, this laxity was mirrored at the administrative level in the form of the Finance Ministry's (and its political masters') chronic inability reliably to forecast public revenues during the pre-crisis period (interviews, Athens, 19 July 2016 and 15 February 2017). While the old adage that the best predictor of this year's budget is last year's budget may well apply in normal times—as the incrementalist school of thought in the study of public budgeting sees it (Wildavsky 1975)—the point here is that civil servants did not possess this knowledge and their political masters did not care about ensuring they did, opting instead for arbitrary 'forecasting' (for a detailed analysis of the problems in pre-crisis Greece's budgeting see Rapanos 2007, esp. 45–60). This is remarkable also because several of Greece's pre-crisis finance ministers were economists, including some academic ones.[7] The rationalisation of public budgeting was a key element of the first MoU and technical assistance played

[6]On its structure at the beginning of the crisis, see Nanopoulos (2010).

[7]Two examples from the 2000s (pre-crisis) are Professors Nikos Christodoulakis and George Alogoskoufis. Two examples from the post-2008 period are Professors Yiannis Stournaras (currently Governor of the Bank of Greece) and Ghikas Hardouvelis.

a key role in this improvement (interviews, 19 December 2016 and 15 February 2017; see also Iordanoglou 2011). In addition, the public revenue administration's 'point staff'—i.e. the tax inspectors whose job it is to ensure tax compliance amongst firms and individuals—were rather aged: more than half were above the age of 50 including 26% aged 55 or older, as the IMF and the European Commission noted as late as 2013 (Story et al. 2013: 21). This means that at least a quarter of tax collectors were not unlikely to have been recruited before the enactment in 1994 of the Peponis Law, which introduced recruitment to the civil service on the basis of competitive written examinations in an effort to put an end to decades of pervasive clientelism involving recruitment in the civil service in exchange for votes. The need for competent and better-trained staff was widely known to have been held amongst senior officials inside the public revenue administration (Telloglou 2012). Indeed, after having been forced to resign (see Chap. 4) a former head of the public revenue administration noted that several cases could not be prosecuted because staff are poorly trained or lacking or because their superiors had made politically motivated arrangements with the relevant individuals (Handelsblatt 2015). Moreover, changing senior officials (e.g. directors or even heads of individual tax offices) in the public revenue administration to suit the wishes of a newly appointed finance minister was commonplace.[8] As a former finance minister noted—after leaving office—

> high rank [sic] bureaucrats in tax authorities have intimate party affiliations and have even been candidates for various elected government posts in the same constituencies as those for which they were responsible for collection (Skouras and Christodoulakis 2014: 537).

The ruling politicians' grip on the public revenue administration was also demonstrated by the fact that traditionally, one of the first key appointments made by any incoming prime minister was the head of the Financial Crime Squad (*Soma Dioksis Oekonomikou Egklimatos*—SDOE). An emblematic example is the case of Prime Minister Antonis Samaras who went as far as to appoint to that post a former tax inspector who was, reportedly (Ta Nea 2012b), also a boyhood friend and a close confidant of his (Kathimerini 2012). The list of SDOE heads who were widely known to have been appointed on the basis of personal and/or party political links (even after the onset of the crisis) is long (Tsoukas 2012). SDOE was seen as an instrument in the government's hands that could be used to further political causes at least in relation to unfavourable political influence of large domestic business interests.[9] More broadly, the practice of party political influences in key—especially personnel related—decisions produced a politicisation spiral also encountered in

---

[8]One telling example is the replacement of all heads of units, deputy directors and directors in the public revenue administration in October 2012. To do so, Finance Minister Yiannis Stournaras in the 'Grand Coalition' government led by PM Antonis Samaras changed the selection process and replaced it with one that required only his decision for these appointments to take place (Ta Nea 2012a). He was not the first one to try to do so even after the onset of the crisis (Hadjinikolaou 2011).

[9]Indeed, a former government minister went as far as to cite the specific example of Andreas Papandreou who allegedly ordered tax inspections against media companies as a reaction to unfavourable coverage (interview, Athens, 15 February 2017).

countries of Central and Eastern Europe (Meyer-Sahling 2004: 76). Knowing that the previous government had placed its own trusted individuals in key posts of the public revenue administration, any new government had a strong incentive to replace them with officials of its own choosing.[10]

Third, the Greek public revenue administration was perceived as both inefficient and ineffective to such an extent that one former minister said it was 'rotten and crumbling' (interview, Athens, 20 July 2016) while a seasoned parliamentarian said that, in terms of the management of public finances more broadly, Greece was 'a third world country' given the absence of control systems and mechanisms (interview, Athens, 9 November 2016). Even the country's central bank noted the problem of corruption, highlighting the fact that interference in operational decisions came not only from 'high up' but also from the 'outside' (Bank of Greece 2010: 174 esp. where reference is made to 'έξωθεν (και άνωθεν) παρεμβάσεις'). It is worth noting that comparative research shows that (a) the recruitment of civil servants on the basis of merit exerts 'a significant influence on curbing corruption' (Dahlström et al. 2012: 665) and (b) in the eyes of civil servants too, 'merit recruitment is associated with less corruption, while politicisation is associated with more corruption' (Meyer-Sahling and Mikkelsen 2016).

Fourth, at the administrative level, the public revenue administration was using antiquated methods of work, some of which were a hotbed for corruption. For example, tax inspections were personalised—in the sense of involving direct contacts between tax inspectors and taxpayers though (tellingly) many of these contacts were not taking place in the revenue administration's offices. Rather, they were being held in the inspectee's premises—a recipe for corruption. In addition, the internal distribution of personnel was highly problematic. As the IMF indicated in its report of 2005, whereas in modern tax administrations about 25% (ideally 30) of staff perform audit (inspection) functions, reliable figures were absent in Greece, but (a) even the highest numbers suggested were clearly inadequate and (b) the corresponding staff were also loaded with additional duties such as answering taxpayers' inquiries, and making checks that related to tax amnesties (Perry et al. 2005: 49). The Greek public revenue administration was making very limited use of (in any case highly fragmented, sometimes outdated) information technology systems whose reform was riddled with problems and many reported starts and stops. In 2005, the IMF noted that

> while there is a wealth of raw data gathered by the tax administration and included in computerized databases, there is nonetheless a dearth of actual information that would permit either effective management, or appropriate analysis of the real risks to tax compliance in Greece. (Perry et al. 2005: 10)

---

[10]Appointments to key posts in the public revenue administration were not only based on party political criteria. A range of other influences that were not in the public interest applied. For example, a former government minister mentioned the influence of senior officials of the Greek Orthodox Church in some parts of the country (interview with former government minister, Athens, 15 February 2017).

Decisions as to which taxpayer's tax affairs ought to be inspected were not based on standard international practice, i.e. objective risk analysis techniques, while some inspectors chose to inspect taxpayers who were known to be willing to make corrupt payments in exchange for favourable treatment (interviews, Athens, 20 and 23 July 2016). The aforementioned IMF-authored report commissioned by the conservative Nea Dimokratia government underlined the absence of broader strategic plans or organisational statements highlighting the fact that in 2005 there was

> no specific plan to address, in a coordinated way, all of the various aspects of the administration's functions, which bear either directly or indirectly on compliance levels. The current annual work plans focus mainly on setting simple numerical targets—generally revenue based—and do not appear to the mission adequately to reflect the current broader compliance demands of the tax system. (Perry et al. 2005: 21)

Fifth, as a result of these problems, there was some demand for reform and—up to a point—some plans for reforms. These plans ranged from 'back of an envelope' type of ideas to government-commissioned IMF-authored plans. Nevertheless, little reform activity followed although the country's high administrative costs and, consequently, barriers to investment were well known (World Bank Group 2016). Indeed, shortly after taking over as Greece's Finance Minister in October 2009, George Papaconstantinou discovered at a meeting with IMF staff whom he had invited to advise the new government on reforming Greece's tax policy and administration that the previous government had commissioned and obtained from the IMF (but never acted on) a plan (Perry et al. 2005) to reform Greece's public revenue administration (Papaconstantinou 2016: 102).

Finally, like much of the rest Greek administrative and legal system, tax law was highly complex, opaque and couched in a multitude of texts, coupled with favouritism and lack of transparency (Sotiropoulos and Christopoulos 2016). A typical example of its real operation that also displays several of the aforementioned characteristics of Greece's public revenue administration was the use of tax amnesties. In a country where formal penalties for tax avoidance and evasion can be severe, enforcement was often lax and dogged by the public revenue administration's limited real capabilities, corruption, complex tax law under the pressure imposed by the requirements of the statute of limitations. Despite the system's multiple problems, all returns had to be audited within 5 years. Although this was practically impossible, ministers and legislators did not dare eliminate this formal provision because of the public outcry that would follow. So, this provision remained a dead letter. The need for public revenue in the short term and the near-total absence of real strategic thinking on the part of the administration and successive governments led ministers to the recurring use of tax amnesties. These amnesties entailed the collection of a fraction[11] of the tax that was formally due in exchange for a formal certificate of compliance, thus further undermining the already fragile compliance ethos amongst those taxpayers who are not subject to payroll taxes. This kind of short-termism demonstrated both that (a) the systematic and efficient collection of

[11]This was calculated on the basis of sectoral coefficients (Perry et al. 2005: 49).

taxes was not a high priority for ministers and legislators and (b) few, if any, cared about credibility. As a result, the IMF had urged ministers to end this practice, abolish the requirement for the audit of all returns within 5 years and opt, instead, for 'more effective and targeted audit of tax payers actually posing a revenue risk' (Perry et al. 2005: 49).

Greece's Limited Reform Capacity

For most of the period since the end of the dictatorial regime in 1974, Greece has had single-party governments enjoying comfortable parliamentary majorities, aided by the enforcement of party discipline and respect for internal party hierarchies (Sotiropoulos 2012: 12). In addition, Greece is certainly not immune to change[12]—especially during periods of growth (Christodoulakis 2012: 113)—or lacking in potential.[13] Yet, before the onset of the crisis, a seasoned observer of its politics argued that, in a number of areas it is a *société bloquée*, borrowing Michel Crozier's concept, which Featherstone defined as 'a political setting of stalemate between contending veto points' (Featherstone 2005: 226). Just a few years later, right at the onset of the crisis, a Bertelsmann Foundation study found that it was in great need for reform and had the lowest reform capacity of the 30 member states of the OECD (cited in Featherstone and Papadimitriou 2012: 32–33).

Existing literature highlights several characteristics of the Greek political system, economy and society that operate as effective barriers or hindrances to reform. The first point on which there is widespread agreement is the impact of the notion of 'political cost'—understood in terms of popularity, especially in the run-up to elections—which even former government ministers acknowledge as an enduring barrier to reform (Sotiropoulos 2012: 17). For example, in his quantitative analysis of market reforms between 1990 and 2008, Christodoulakis shows that both privatisation and the reduction of public debt are negatively correlated with elections, i.e. these reforms are likely to be postponed so as to minimise conflict ahead of elections. He also argues that parliamentary strength is negatively correlated with both controlling corruption and improving regulation (Christodoulakis 2012: 112–113).

However, existing analyses go beyond that elementary point and highlight the relevance of a range of economic, social, cultural and political barriers. Greece's

---

[12]Indeed, several examples demonstrate the opposite and include the modernisation of family law (including the introduction of civil marriage) in the 1980s, the liberalisation of banking, the partial privatisation of public utilities and the establishment of an array of independent agencies in the 1990s. In his examination of reform between 1990 and 2008 Christodoulakis finds a strong and positive correlation between growth on the one hand and market reforms on the other (Christodoulakis 2012: 113).

[13]The 'Greek paradox' is the difference between promise and performance (Allison and Nicolaïdis 1997).

belated and weak industrialisation and reliance on the diaspora and foreign investment generated a vacuum that the state has sought to fill (Mouzelis 1978). This involved not only the introduction of wide-ranging rules, forms of protectionism as well as subsidies, but also their particularistic application (based on the corresponding group's close links to the ruling party) because the state was subject to extensive rent-seeking[14] in Greece's underdeveloped capitalism[15] where much depended on the outcome of competition between sectional interests for favours (Pagoulatos 2003). The impact of this arrangement has been very enduring. Efforts to promote privatisation in the early 1990s suffered a backlash from those who were benefitting from the status quo, including public sector suppliers (especially in telecommunications and construction) as well as other private firms that feared the consequences of privatisation-induced competition in their respective industry and it is quite telling that the Federation of Greek Industries did not act as the vocal champion of privatisation (Lyberaki and Tsakalotos 2002: 108).

Though omnipresent and often overbearing,[16] the state has historically been also quite weak. This weakness takes two meanings. First, it denotes the inability to assert state authority (Featherstone 2008: 17) but this is not an accident. The nature and extent of the state's presence in the economy is directly linked to clientelism which it was intended to serve while populism provided the link between the two (Tsoukalis 1997: 165). The mechanisms utilised for state intervention in the economy also had a dark side, namely their use in the interests of political favouritism (Thomadakis 1997: 51). The fact that successive governments have failed to stump out the endemic problem of illegal building by 'land-grabbers' (i.e. often well-connected individuals who build private property on public land) is a good example which is associated with corruption too.[17] Second, weakness also means lack of capacity—including capacity to change—as (a) Greece's low ranking in international comparisons of government capabilities indicates (Bertelsmann Stiftung 2011) and (b) the emblematic as well as enduring saga of the country's still incomplete land registry shows. Both the (in) ability to assert state authority and the lack or presence of capacity are, of course, sociopolitical constructs.

The state's formal omnipotence and omnipresence go hand in hand with a weak civil society,[18] which is more often than not subsumed by the state, i.e. the ruling

[14]On the concept of rent-seeking, see Krueger (1974).

[15]Greece has never had a productive middle class (Kondylis 2011). The local 'comprador' bourgeoisie directed foreign capital not towards manufacturing but services (e.g. shipping, commerce and banking) and sat next to a large agrarian sector and a myriad of labour-intensive, low added-value family-owned and family run small and medium-sized firms as well as a large black market (Mouzelis 1978: 20–21; Zambarloukou 2006: 215).

[16]This is so not only in the economic sense but also in terms of civil liberties in a country that was a democracy only in formal terms until 1967 (Tsoukalas 1969).

[17]Featherstone notes the example of the transfer of a senior official of the state's land service in Aitoloakarnania, as a result of the pressure exerted by illegal builders on the Ministry of Finance in July 2007 (Featherstone 2008: 17).

[18]A good example is the lack of a genuinely autonomous trade union movement.

party.[19] This weakness follows decades of authoritarian rule[20]—or 'illiberal parliamentarism', as Mouzelis put it, in a triarchy also involving the Crown and the armed forces with the King being at the apex of the latter two (1978: 126)—but also mirrors other enduring features of modern Greece. Together, they reflect a particular conception of democracy which combines an emphasis on the unmediated exercise of power (as opposed to valuing the mediatory role of institutions), is distrustful of the active role of civil society, promotes clientelism—often couched in divisive political discourse—and entails an instrumental view of the political process (Diamandouros 1994; Lyberaki and Tsakalotos 2002: 99).

Clientelism is not a new phenomenon in Greece. It dates back at least to the mid-nineteenth century pre-capitalist Greece: when local oligarchies realised that state expansion was inevitable, they tried to control the state from within, a task that a malfunctioning parliamentary regime would help in a country where the state was linked to society not via collective institutions but through 'purely personal clientelistic networks' which later on, with the advancement of what Kondylis appositely called 'clientelist parliamentarism' (2011: 35), tried to control the expanding central bureaucracy so as to compensate for the loss[21] of regional autonomy (Mouzelis 1978: 16, 101, 143). Clientelism's impact was also evident in the Greek party system's response to the crisis (Afonso et al. 2015).

Seen from the perspective of the 'varieties of capitalism' literature, Greece is—as Featherstone points out (Featherstone 2008: 14)—akin to what Molina and Rhodes defined as 'mixed market economies'[22] (MMEs) (Molina and Rhodes 2006). This means that trade unions and employers' organisations are more fragmented and find it more difficult to articulate their interests than in coordinated market economies, although their organisational structures are stronger than in liberal market economies. They have the capacity to block reforms but lack the ability to deliver collective goods and coordinated action in collective bargaining (Featherstone 2008: 14). The enactment and effective implementation of reforms is extremely hard and operates as a constant test for the government's ability or willingness to pay

[19]An emblematic example is the close link that tied the socialist PASOK with ADEDY (Ανώτατη Διοίκηση Ενώσεων Δημοσίων Υπαλλήλων—Supreme Command of Civil Servants' Unions), the country's peak trade union in the public sector.

[20]This goes some way towards explaining the Greeks' mistrust of the state, which several previous generations had experienced as little more than an apparatus that oppressed them. This perception seems to confirm Rothstein's argument that highlights 'the importance of impartial, un-corrupt and fair government institutions for generating social trust' (Rothstein 2013).

[21]Initial attempts at state building through the centralisation of power tried to reduce the power of local elites but the establishment of captive democratic institutions ended up reinforcing it (Kalyvas 2015: 53).

[22]The introduction of liberal market elements aiming to improve Greece's competitiveness under the bailout agreements, the argument has been made that the country is left with the worst of both worlds, that is, suboptimal economic performance as well as diluted social cohesion (Kornelakis and Voskeritsian 2014).

the corresponding political cost, at least in the short term. This is unsurprising given the low levels of trust[23] and low social capital found in Greece (Jones et al. 2008).

Indeed, it has been shown that 'for more than a decade, Greece has consistently ranked last in Europe on almost all indicators for trust and confidence' (Theocharis and van Deth 2015: 64). During the crisis, trust in impartial institutions has dropped even further in a country that started from a very low base (Ervasti et al. 2018). How this lack of trust affects policy and institutions is exemplified well by Zambarloukou's study of collective bargaining, and attempts to reform employment arrangements and the social security system through social pacts in Greece in the late 1990s and early 2000s. She has shown that the failure to achieve tripartite policy consensus was the result, in part, of the lack of trust between the social partners as well as the absence of a dialogue- and consensus-promoting culture[24] (see also Ioannou 2000). Instead of using official consultation fora, social actors were used to exerting influence on the state via particularistic ties with political parties. This was in addition to the deleterious effects of the traditional fragmentation of Greek trade unionism along party lines (Zambarloukou 2006: 221).

It is important to note the huge contradiction between institutions that require or are meant to promote consensus and the culture of political polarisation (an expression of which is the inflammatory political discourse) that permeates the Greek political system since before the onset of the crisis. On the one hand, since 1974 the electoral system has been reformed in a way that has moved it towards the proportional end of the spectrum, various types of independent agencies—largely as a result of EU requirements—have been introduced and accompanied by the appointment of their board members on the basis of super-majorities in parliament. On the other hand, the major political parties seek coalition partners only when forced to do so. Their daily political rhetoric is littered with inflammatory language[25] as if to prove there is a reason why *hyperbole* is a Greek word. That rhetoric seeks to play to the gallery—divorced as it often is from the content of the reforms[26]—by denouncing political enemies (not opponents) instead of focusing on alternative solutions to problems. When they think it is expedient for their short-term political aims, they turn consensus-based institutions into veto points.[27] Consensus-orientated or consensus-based institutions sit uncomfortably side by side with a

[23]Low trust also helps explain the prevalence of very small, family-run firms in Greece (Lyberaki and Tsakalotos 2002: 101).

[24]Lavdas uses the term 'disjointed corporatism' to describe Greece's system of interest intermediation (Lavdas 1997).

[25]One example from the immediate pre-crisis period is the treatment meted out to former Prime Minister Costas Simitis (a socialist) when he warned the ND (Nea Dimokratia) government in 2008 that the country's public finances were in need of deep reforms in the absence of which the IMF would need to be called in.

[26]The reform of pensions is a case in point (Tinios 2012: 127).

[27]A case in point is ND's effort to veto the appointment of the board of Greece's National Broadcasting Council so as to prevent the SYRIZA-ANEL (Coalition of the Radical Left/Independent Greeks) government from radically reforming TV channel licensing.

prevailing ethos of polarisation and a winner-takes-all mentality that corresponds to majoritarianism. More often than not, this logic of reform as a zero-sum-game is encountered in other societal actors (the medical profession is a good example; see Mossialos and Allin 2005). But this is not the only contradiction or expression of dualism that affects the country's reform capacity.

This dualism—i.e. the uneasy coexistence of and recurring conflict between institutions of modernity and the antiquated practices of Greece's past—is also present in the actual operation of one of the most significant reforms introduced in the country's civil service since 1974, namely the Supreme Council for Personnel Selection (ASEP), the independent authority that operates at arm's length from the government and since its establishment in 1994 is in charge of recruitment in the public sector. It has become synonymous to the end—via the emblematic written examinations that are so common to all European states—of the corrupt practice of clientelistic (jobs for votes) recruitment for the bulk of permanent posts.[28] This system, which is often described as rigid but transparent, coexists with various exemptions whose purpose is to serve patronage (Spanou 2012: 189). This happens to such an extent that an authoritative assessment of the reform of Greece's Napoleonic model concluded that politics is 'still too present in routine administration and personnel management, with recruitment being the most visible part' (Spanou 2008: 168). Indeed, recent comparative research covering 22 European, Latin American and African countries shows that Greece has one of the highest levels of party patronage (only Argentina, Paraguay and the Dominican Republic have a higher score) and behind the large scope of party patronage lies the intention to control policy and its implementation as well as the willingness to reward the ruling party's faithful (Kopecký et al. 2016, Figs. 1, 421 and 426).

In their contribution to the literature on Greece's limited reform capacity, Monastiriotis and Antoniades have made another claim, by going beyond the aforementioned points about blockages, resistance and contestation. They have argued that several reforms have failed in Greece because 'they were ill-thought, ill-prepared, and poorly substantiated and designed' (Monastiriotis and Antoniades 2009: 8). This, they argue, is a conception-related problem, not one that concerns the communication, negotiation, or implementation of the reforms. Rather, their claim focuses on the problematic engagement of policy makers on the one hand, with communities of experts on the other, which is particularly prevalent in Greece. Politicians either do not engage systematically with the communities of experts, or when they do so, they tend to ignore or even contradict expert advice and consequently, 'more often than not, reform proposals are drawn with little reference to a solid evidence-base and with very little attention to contextualisation' (Monastiriotis and Antoniades 2009: 26). Their evidence relates to several areas of public policy including employment (e.g. the Koukiadis report), pensions (the 'Analytis report', the 'Spraos report', the 'Giannitsis committee's' report) and tax (report of the

[28]Clientelistic recruitment has played its part in undermining the first socialist government's attempt to place public enterprises under 'social control' (Lyberaki and Tsakalotos 2002: 104).

'Georgakopoulos committee'). These are cases where either the government[29] that commissioned a report unceremoniously shelved it or made major decisions without even considering evidence but the key point is that Greece's 'reform technology' is highly problematic because it does not involve the systematic engagement with experts and real evidence (Monastiriotis and Antoniades 2009: 12–17, 20–21, 25; cf. Ladi 2005). The point about evidence is particularly apposite and relates also to the management of Greece's public finances. Using evidence from the marginal role of accounting in the development of the Greek National Health System (i.e. one of the biggest spending items in the annual budget of the state) Ballas and Tsoukas have argued that politicisation in the Greek political system is so intensive and pervasive that it has 'tended to over-shadow the economic-cum-managerial dimension of running public bureaucracies, favouring overtly political evaluation criteria of organizational and individual performance' (Ballas and Tsoukas 2004: 661). The lack of systematic engagement with experts and disdain for evidence has another important implication. As a seasoned observer of Greece's public administration noted in relation to administrative reform,

> [v]alues like merit, impartiality and objectivity that entered the common heritage of western bureaucracies almost a century ago, dominate the political discourse in Greece, but have lost any content in the light of their inflationary use (Spanou 1996: 119).

This disdain for evidence, in turn, is linked to two key features of the political debate in Greece. One is its formalistic–legalistic nature which means that, more often than not, attention is shifted away from the substance of the issue at hand, partly because 'debate' operates either at a very high level of abstraction with frequent references to lofty principles or is intensely competitive and personal in nature but, either way, it ends up maintaining the status quo (Mouzelis 1978: 134). The other is the relentless use of language (especially slogans) as if it had the character of actions.[30] Greece's polarised political system has two by-products. First, public institutions operate in a personalised manner coupled with the coexistence of formal rules and informal practices and processes indicating low levels of legitimacy and institutionalisation. Second, the culture of verbality is prevalent and takes precedence over the use of texts and evidence. This culture reflects short-termism, is heavily conjunctural, and individualised for it mirrors the exigencies of the electoral cycle. Attitudes couched in individualism prevail over the feeble sense of collectivity. The individual prevails over the institution. On the contrary, written text is programmatic and more long-termist in nature. For organisation theory written text (a) is a means that gives stability to an organisation and thus facilitates organisational change and (b) separates organisational (i.e. collective) realities from individual or conjunctural ones (Anderson 2004; Putnam and Cooren 2004). Written text and evidence act as tests of political conflict and facilitate convergence and the establishment of consensus.

---

[29]The examples relate to both PASOK and ND administrations, that is, the two parties that have governed Greece almost uninterruptedly between 1974 and 2015.

[30]This is what philosophers call 'speech acts' (Green 2017; Smith 1990).

The flipside of speech acts in Greece is the typical absence of concrete plans for reform (or the ability to make such plans) both amongst the major political parties and the civil service. As regards the major political parties, they are little more than sloganeering, vote-gathering devices[31] in the sense that little, if any, attention[32] is paid to thinking through their policies and how they can be put into practice. This would not be a major problem if Greece had the tradition of civil service reliability and independence that exists in other European states. However, Greece's civil service lacks this ability (Sotiropoulos 2012: 25). This is due to (a) the pervasive influence of party politicisation (Sotiropoulos 2001; Spanou 1996) which meant that allegiance to the ruling party was a key criterion for recruitment and promotion,[33] and (b) the overbearing role of politicians and the enduring presence of ministerial advisers who serve a particular minister and leave the ministry when she does (see, e.g. Pappas and Assimakopoulou 2012: 156). In these conditions, and in a climate of subservience (which paradoxically exists alongside and despite security of employment) little room is left, in reality, for central government to develop the capacity to think on its own in spite of the recruitment by *concours*—as opposed to corrupt practices—of well-qualified civil servants since the mid-1990s and the training they receive in the National Centre for Public Administration and Local Government. A good example of the combined impact of limited bureaucratic capabilities and excessive centralisation of power at the political level is the highly problematic attempt to promote privatisation in the early 1990s. The dominant role of ministers, very senior political appointees and advisers was coupled with the distrusted (and fearful) bureaucracy's (1) isolation from the radical change of government policy and (2) consequent inability to serve the new policy (Pagoulatos 2001: 133). Heavy and extensive reliance on ministerial advisers may serve the minister in the short term, but fails the public in the medium and longer term. This is just one example of the country's prevailing culture of short-termism too.

The flipside of this is bureaucratic inertia. This translates not only into slowness—especially when, as is the norm in Greece, the implementation of a new reform enacted by parliament, requires the adoption of a bewildering myriad of decrees that give concrete meaning to it, e.g. by interpreting its provisions, and

[31]Just like many other collective endeavours in Greece, most of them do not operate democratically; rather, they are dominated by the image or reality of a charismatic leader, a figure to be treated like a Messiah. Clientelism operates within these highly personalist parties too, not only between parties and voters (Bermeo 2002: 219). PASOK under Andreas Papandreou is a good example (Spourdalakis 1998).

[32]This is not due to the lack of funding. In the run-up to the crisis, all major parties were receiving significant amounts of money from the state, bank loans and other (not always legal) sources. An indication of how much money had been channelled to the two largest parties (Nea Dimokratia and PASOK) is the fact that, together, they owe more than 400 million euros to various Greek banks.

[33]This is the core definition of politicisation too (Peters and Pierre 2004: 2).

issuing guidance to implementing agencies—but also, on occasion, the bureaucracy's unwillingness to act in accordance with the spirit of the law.[34]

Another barrier to reform is the legalistic culture of the administration (Spanou 2012: 190). Far greater attention is paid (often in a defensive[35] manner) to process than to outcomes, as indicated by the fact that attempts to modernise the administration between 1974 and 2009 have focused on institutions rather than performance (Spanou 2012). This may well mirror the Napoleonic model, but is certainly also a reflection of a prevailing culture in (a) courts (with some courts issuing, even after the onset of the crisis, rulings that directly affect the country's public finances but without bearing any relation to their objective condition, also ignoring the fact that under the country's constitution, the executive, not the courts are responsible for economic policy[36]) and (b) parliament too. Far too often politicians—especially ministers, a plurality[37] of whom traditionally are lawyers, as are the country's legislators (Kountouri 2018: 570)—believe that they have solved a problem once a law they have sponsored has been enacted. They pay much less attention to the subsequent action that is needed to put it into effect, e.g. by allocating resources and ensuring it remains a priority for the relevant implementing agency.[38] The problematic allocation of attention to policy problems that require sustained effort—a key reason why the reform of the state's territorial organisation has not progressed as much as it could (Spanou 2012: 189)—is not unique to Greece but its intensity is. It mirrors a political culture where merit is not—to put it mildly—a top priority for the allocation of political posts in the cabinet and the shadow cabinet. Politicians may spend years learning the ins and outs of their brief while serving in the opposition benches or the shadow cabinet, only to see their party leader allocate the corresponding portfolio to somebody else once in government. Ministerial and government turnover is also comparatively high by West European standards.[39] A quasi-institutionalised aversion to meritocracy means that ministers are often chosen not on the basis of expertise and ability but for all sorts of other reasons including loyalty to the leader, the preservation of a façade of unity of purpose, the perceived need to have as many as possible of the country's regions represented in cabinet. The other implication of the legalistic

---

[34]For one example that relates to decentralisation (see Sotiropoulos 2012: 20). The aforementioned example of privatisation is another one (Pagoulatos 2001: 133–134).

[35]This means that the emphasis of administrative action is not on problem solving but how the relevant officials can tick the box and avoid being accused of not acting as they should in terms of the requisite formalities.

[36]As a leading constitutional lawyer points out, Greek courts have been too eager to stretch the notion of unconstitutionality of some legal provisions in a way that has blocked reforms, though it is fair to say that some provisions of the MoUs are highly problematic from the legal point of view (Alivizatos 2010).

[37]Between 1843 and 2001 the percentage of ministers who had a law degree fluctuated between 29.4% (1936–1941) and 68.2% (1946–1967) (Sotiropoulos and Bourikos 2002, Table 7b, 187).

[38]Administrative reform is a good case in point (Spanou 2012: 190).

[39]Koutsoukis has counted 589 ministers between 1946 and 1976 (cited in Sotiropoulos and Bourikos 2002: 157).

culture that prevails both within the political system and the Greek public administration is that it perpetuates the hegemony of lawyers and legal experts for only they (are deemed to) know the way to find solutions or deal with constraints[40] even in the myriad of policy areas that require substantive expertise and involve techniques—such as cost-benefit analysis—which lawyers are not trained to provide.

Finally, one can mention the culture of resistance that permeates key (and powerful) segments of society—in particular liberal professionals. Their presence spans the public and private sectors, in a country where the ethos of avoiding conflicts of interest is almost absent. Examples include journalists working for private media as well as the press office of a ministry or one of the myriad of public agencies that exist in Greece; lawyers and medical doctors who hold private practices while also working for (sometimes several) public institutions (e.g. hospitals, state-owned banks, and public agencies) as well as private ones and—in the most egregious cases—teaching in the country's public universities (Sotiropoulos 2012: 27).[41]

Against this backdrop of the country's low reform capacity on the one hand, and the state of its highly politicised and very ineffective public revenue administration on the other, the question arises as to the *actual menu of options* from which policy makers could choose while reforming Greece's public revenue administration. The next section outlines extant models.

Models of Public Revenue Administrations

The OECD has been active in monitoring the public revenue administrations of both its member and non-member states in the context of its Forum on Tax Administration in an effort to identify and promote practices that enhance efficiency,

[40]This happens in a country where draconian laws coexist with lax enforcement or as Tsoukalas notes, a country where laws are not always seen as limits that ought to be respected but as obstacles that need to be overcome (Tsoukalas 1993: 23). No wonder a major international comparison of the transposition of EU employment law has classified Greece in the 'world of neglect' (Falkner et al. 2005). This attitude towards the law is one of the signs of uncivic culture, alongside a hierarchically organised public life and corruption (Putnam 1993: 115).

[41]A recent example of their self-serving attitude as well as power even during the crisis is quite telling. Since 1997 all academic doctors who teach in Greek public universities while also working in their own private practices are obliged to pay into their employing university's research account a 7% levy on their private practice's gross turnover. Those teaching in dentistry schools have been refusing to do so and even went on strike—causing major problems for their students—claiming that after nearly two decades of failing to pay the levy, the corresponding amount had become very big, exceeding 100,000 euros in some cases. Education minister Costas Gavroglou in the SYRIZA-ANEL government practically caved in (so as to bring about the end of the strike) and agreed to drop the claims regarding the first 15 years of the law's operation and offered them the possibility of paying the remainder in instalments. However, Finance Minister Euclid Tsakalotos (himself an academic, like his colleague in charge of education) vetoed this arrangement partly because other groups of academics (medical doctors) with private practices had already paid the levy (Lakassas 2018).

effectiveness and fairness in tax administration. In that context, it has been publishing informative regular reports[42] since 2004. Just before the onset of the crisis, it noted the existence of four types of public revenue institutions, namely

> *[s]ingle directorate in ministry of finance (MOF)*: Tax administration functions are the responsibility of a single organizational unit (e.g. a directorate) located within the structure of the ministry of finance (or its equivalent).
>
> *Multiple directorates in MOF*: Tax administration functions are the responsibility of multiple organizational units (e.g. directorates) located within the ministry of finance.
>
> *Unified semi-autonomous body*: Tax administration functions are carried out by a unified semi-autonomous body, the head of which reports to a government minister.
>
> *Unified semi-autonomous body with board*: Tax administration functions are carried out by a unified semi-autonomous body, the head of which reports to a government minister and oversight body/board of management comprised of external officials. (OECD 2009: 12)

Over time, and in light of further details uncovered by its surveys, it has reported a slightly revised, more detailed and expanded version of this typology:

> *[s]ingle directorate in ministry of finance (MOF)*: Tax administration functions are the responsibility of a single organizational unit (e.g. a directorate) located within the structure of the ministry of finance (or its equivalent).
>
> *Multiple directorates within the MOF*: Tax administration functions are the responsibility of multiple organisational units (e.g. directorates) located within the ministry of finance (often sharing necessary support functions such as information technology and human resources).
>
> *A unified semi-autonomous body*: Tax administration functions, along with support functions (e.g. IT and human resources) are carried out by a unified semi-autonomous body, with the head reporting to a government minister.
>
> *A unified semi-autonomous body with a management/oversight board*: Tax administration functions, along with necessary support functions (e.g. information technology, human resources) are carried out by a unified semi-autonomous body, the head of which reports to a government minister and oversight body/board of management comprised of external officials.
>
> *A category of "Other"*: Other setups not covered by the abovementioned. (OECD 2015: 27)

The key distinguishing point in this typology relates directly to this book's focus, namely the autonomy of the public revenue administration as indicated by its institutional location, within or outside of each country's ministry of finance. The difference between the two is, in fact, significant. When the public revenue administration is part of the ministry of finance, its staff (including its head) are subject to orders that emanate from the minister who is (a) expected to put into effect the ruling party's election manifesto (or a coalition agreement) and (b) directly accountable to parliament. This means that the minister may—directly or indirectly—steer the public revenue administration towards decisions that favour certain groups or individuals. When this is done on the basis of the routine rules of the democratic process—e.g. through legislation—democracy's usual checks and balances apply. Opposition parties can voice their views, public opinion can be informed by the independent media and so on. But things are much more complicated when ministers

[42] This is the 'Comparative Information Series'.

or even the prime minister seek(s) to steer the public revenue administration's decisions in a covert, undemocratic or even corrupt manner. Of course, not all civil servants are corruptible, nor are all politicians prone to corruption but the issue goes beyond the human characteristics of specific individuals. As we will see in the remainder of this section and (in greater detail) in the next chapter, increasing the distance between the locus of political power on the one hand and the locus of administrative power on the other is the key response given to this major issue. How this is done can take various forms. Table 1.1 presents that state of play in the member states of the OECD in 2008, i.e. at the onset of the crisis.[43]

The table indicates that while just over half (17) of the OECD's member states had some kind of semi-autonomous body, 13 had opted for a structure operating within their ministry of finance. The picture is different if one concentrates on member states of the European Union: an absolute majority (15) were using a structure within their ministry of finance, while 11 had opted for a semi-autonomous body. There is no clear North–South divide since 6 of the 15 countries that have followed the traditional model are in the North and 4 of the 11 that rely on semi-autonomous bodies are in the South. However, more than half (6) of the EU countries that use semi-autonomous bodies became members of the EU in 2004 or 2007. The other half (5) of the countries that acceded to the EU in 2004 or 2007, opted for a structure within their ministry of finance but, tellingly, the two (Cyprus and Malta) that were most closely associated with the market economy for much longer than the rest of this cohort, chose structures within their MOF. Two preliminary conclusions flow from this table. First, at the onset of the crisis, an absolute majority of EU member states had opted for a structure within their ministry of finance. Second, despite being subject to the adaptation pressures that the prospect of EU membership creates, several new member states did not opt for a semi-autonomous body. However, if one looks beyond Greece's main referent, the trend is towards the expansion of semi-autonomous bodies.

Since the early 1990s, several countries—notably in Africa (Devas et al. 2001: 211)—have reformed their revenue administrations and have opted for a revenue authority (RA), i.e.

> a governance model for revenue administration where traditional ministry of finance departments (tax and usually customs administrations) are established as an organization or agency with a degree of autonomy from government and independence from standard public service policies. (Kidd and Crandall 2006: 5)

[43]USB: Unified semi-autonomous body; USBB: Unified semi-autonomous body with formal board or advisory group comprised of external officials; SDMOF: Single directorate in Ministry of Finance; MDMOF: Multiple directorates in MOF. The OECD has compiled this table on the basis of (a) responses to its survey and (b) research conducted by its own Secretariat (e.g. revenue body reports).

Table 1.1 Institutional arrangements for tax administration (2008)

Country	Institutional type of revenue body
OECD countries	
Australia	Unified semi-autonomous body
Austria	Single directorate in MOF
Belgium	Single directorate in MOF
Canada	Unified semi-autonomous body with board
Czech Republic	Single directorate in MOF
Denmark	Single directorate in MOF
Finland	Unified semi-autonomous body
France	Single directorate in MOF
Germany	Multiple directorates in Federal MOF and 16 State MOF
Greece	Multiple directorates in MOF
Hungary	Unified semi-autonomous body
Iceland	Unified semi-autonomous body
Ireland	Unified semi-autonomous body
Italy	Multiple directorates in MOF
Japan	Unified semi-autonomous body
Korea	Unified semi-autonomous body
Luxembourg	Multiple directorates in MOF
Mexico	Unified semi-autonomous body with board reporting to MOF
Netherlands	Single directorate in MOF
New Zealand	Unified semi-autonomous body
Norway	Unified semi-autonomous body
Poland	Multiple directorates in MOF
Portugal	Multiple directorates in MOF
Slovak Republic	Unified semi-autonomous body
Spain	Unified semi-autonomous body
Sweden	Unified semi-autonomous body
Switzerland	Single directorate in MOF
Turkey	Unified semi-autonomous body
United Kingdom	Unified semi-autonomous body with board
United States	Unified semi-autonomous body with board
Selected non-OECD countries	
Bulgaria	Unified semi-autonomous body with board
Cyprus	Multiple directorates in MOF
Estonia	Single directorate in MOF
Latvia	Unified semi-autonomous body
Malta	Multiple directorates in MOF
Romania	Unified semi-autonomous body
Slovenia	Unified semi-autonomous body

Source: Authors' adaptation of information from OECD (2009: 26)

Indeed, tax administration has been at the forefront (Crandall 2010: 4) of a broader trend towards agencification and the increasing use of independent or autonomous bodies within the New Public Management paradigm as part of the 'reinventing government' agenda (Osborne and Gaebler 1992). This was partly an ideological choice since, in that paradigm, democratic politics is often portrayed as a risk to the smooth operation of (usually benign) market forces. It was also an attempt to deal with various problems including the tax gap (i.e. lower than expected tax receipts), low compliance rates, ineffective staff, as well as corruption. Indeed, it has been argued that this model can improve accountability in terms of results, promote joined up working across revenue departments, foster skills-based management and preclude or at least reduce external influences (Kidd and Crandall 2006: 5; Taliercio 2004; see also Mann 2004).

Specifically, it has been argued that a Revenue Authority

> (i) as a single purpose agency, it can focus its efforts on a single task; (ii) as an autonomous organization, it can manage its affairs in a business-like way, free of political interference in day-to-day operations; and (iii) being outside the civil service proper, it can execute its own human resources strategy—recruiting, retaining (or dismissing) and motivating staff (Crandall 2010: 6).

The diffusion of this model is to a great extent the product of the IMF's guidance on institutional matters—issued by its Fiscal Affairs Department—that can be found in its working papers (see, e.g. Crandall 2010; Kidd 2010). As the OECD notes, the IMF's typical recommendations are very similar to those issued by the European Commission (OECD 2015: 26).

In the context of the EU's preparations for the accession of Central and Eastern European countries, the European Commission devised 'fiscal blueprints' in 1999 and updated in 2007. Their purpose was to serve as tools for the candidate countries to enhance their administrative capabilities so as to cope with the *acquis communautaire*. The commission was keen to stress the fact that the first strategic objective was to ensure that their tax administration 'is guaranteed an adequate level of autonomy' (European Commission 2007: 7, 9). References to various facets of autonomy were present in several of the corresponding strategic objectives contained in these blueprints (see Box 1.1).

Box 1.1 Overall Framework of a Tax Administration (Fiscal Blueprint 1)

Strategic objectives	Scoring (out of 100)	Key indicators
1. The tax administration is guaranteed an adequate level of autonomy	25	• Is the autonomy of the tax administration provided for by law? • Is there a statutory basis defining to whom the head of the tax administration reports? • Is the autonomy of the tax administration reflected in its organisational structure and operational responsibilities? • Is the tax administration provided with the freedom to design and implement its own operational policy? • Is there a clear description of responsibilities of bodies at the central, regional and local level?
2. The obligations of the tax administration are clearly translated into its mission, vision and objectives	15	• Are the tasks of the tax administration in line with its mission and vision? • Does the tax administration draw up strategies providing objectives, benchmarks and plans for its operations? • Is the mission of the tax administration publicised amongst taxpayers and other stakeholders, as well as amongst its personnel?
3. The tax administration has its *own structure and powers* allowing for efficient and effective operations	5	• Does the structure of the tax administration allow the fulfilment of its tasks and obligations? • Does the organisational structure of the tax administration provide for the decentralisation of responsibilities, so that decisions concerning the taxpayer are made at the most appropriate level?
4. The tax administration is provided with adequate resources to implement and manage the tax system	20	• Is the tax administration given sufficient resources and funding to ensure the efficient implementation of its policies and performance of duties?

(continued)

Box 1.1 (continued)

		• Does the tax administration stem from a budget dialogue based on performance agreements? • Does the tax administration's budget planning cycle cover several years, allowing strategic planning and the carryover of funding surpluses?
5. The tax administration is provided with a stable legal framework ensuring proper administration and enforcement of tax dues	10	• Is the tax administration responsible for the formulation of laws concerning the assessment, collection and enforcement of taxes (leaving the responsibility for the formulation of other tax laws with the ministry of finance)? • Is the tax administration provided by law with sufficient powers to efficiently undertake all its statutory responsibilities?
6. The tax administration is accountable for its operations which are subject to control and assessment	10	• Is there a system of internal audit in the tax administration? • Is there an independent external institution carrying out the tax administration's audit of operations and assessing its performance?
7. The operations of the tax administration are managed and assessed on the basis of the performance management system	15	• Is the tax administration managed in accordance with benchmarks and indicators agreed with the stakeholders while the results of its activities are constantly monitored? • Is there a proper reporting system ensuring that performance reports are delivered to the management? • Is there a quality management system allowing for the constant monitoring of quality of services rendered by the tax administration? • Are performance management models applied in the tax administration?

Source: European Commission (2007: 13–15)

The emphasis on autonomy raises the question of the precise functions to which it relates. The autonomy of revenue administrations as practised in several of the OECD's member states (and beyond) relates to several functions:

1. *Tax law interpretation*, i.e. the authority to provide authoritative interpretations of tax law provisions subject only to review by judicial bodies.
2. The authority to impose administrative *sanctions* (penalties and interest) in cases of non-compliance.

3. The power to make decisions that relate to their *organisation and management,* including the location and size of tax offices; make and carry out strategic and operational plans; allocate budgeted funds across functions to meet extant or new priorities.
4. The authority to administer their own in-house *IT systems*, or to outsource these services to private contractors.
5. The power set administrative *performance standards.*
6. *Personnel*: the ability to set qualification standards for categories of recruits, hire and fire staff, in line with relevant public sector policies and procedures, create and run staff training programmes, and negotiate staff remuneration in accordance with broader public sector-wide policies and arrangements (OECD 2007: 11–12).

Precisely how these functions are arranged in autonomous public revenue bodies can take several forms. For example, in a number of countries a management or advisory board has been placed between the revenue body and the relevant minister so as to provide independent advice on the operation of the institution and tax administration in general (OECD 2007: 12). Crandall neatly summarises the design considerations that are associated with the creation of autonomous revenue authorities (Box 1.2).

Box 1.2 Design Considerations for Autonomous Revenue Authorities

1. Degree of autonomy

The range of possibilities for the following specific areas needs to be assessed:

- *Legal form and status*—from an agency relatively close to a normal government organisation to a corporate body with considerable independence.
- *Funding*—from normal funding via parliamentary appropriations to direct retention of a percentage of collected revenues.
- *Budget flexibility*—from limited flexibility to the complete flexibility of a one-line budget.
- *Financial policies* (e.g. accounting, asset ownership and management and procurement)—from a situation where the RA is subject to standard civil service laws and regulations, or as determined by 'corporate body' status (i.e. not part of the government's accounting entity).
- *Human resources*—from being within the civil service control framework, to being outside it.
- *Operational autonomy*—from a situation where the minister has day-to-day authority to one where there is no involvement on the part of the minister in operational decisions.

2. Governance framework

- *Role of the minister of finance*—from direct supervision of the authority by the minister, to a more limited role such as appointment of the board or CEO only and limited broad strategic and tax policy directive powers.
- *Role of the board*—from no board at all to one with just advisory powers to fully empowered in legislation to take management decisions.
- *Role of commissioner general*—from a coordinating role only, to full responsibility for revenue operations with all vested powers from revenue laws.

(continued)

Box 1.2 (continued)

3. Accountability

• *Reporting to the government and parliament*—from being part of normal general government reporting, to the need to follow special requirements specified in legislation.

• *External audit*—from being a legislated responsibility of the auditor-general, to the RA or its board selecting the external auditor as it sees fit.

4. Scope

This refers to the scope of *taxes* and *taxing agencies* to be included. Usually, the RA includes the administration and enforcement of all direct and indirect taxes at the national level, and customs (and trade) administration. The RA may also include the collection of local taxes or fees and social taxes or levies, as well as the collection of social contributions

Source: Crandall (2010: 9)

In terms of autonomy, right before the onset of the crisis, the picture was one of the structured diversity (Table 1.2).

The two broad categories of public revenue administrations appear to be similar in terms of freedom to establish their organisation and office networks, determine performance standards, influence staff recruitment criteria. They appear to differ significantly in terms of budgetary autonomy, the ability to fix the levels and mix of staff, the freedom to recruit and dismiss staff and negotiate pay levels. However, it is important to note that a degree of caution is required. This is so because the information reported here is based on a table where—by necessity—the requisite degree of nuance is lacking. Rather, the report (OECD 2009: 27) presents quite

Table 1.2 Authorities held by revenue administration (2006)

	Structure of revenue administration					
	Directorate (s) within MOF	%	Semi-autonomous body	%	Total	%
Authority to establish organisation and office networks	17 of 19	89	21 of 24	88	38 of 43	88
Authority to allocate-reallocate budget	14 of 19	74	22 of 24	92	36 of 43	84
Authority to determine performance standards	19 of 19	100	24 of 24	100	43 of 43	100
Human Resources (HR)						
Fix levels/mix of staff	15 of 19	79	21 of 24	88	37 of 43	86
Influence staff recruitment criteria	19 of 19	100	24 of 24	100	43 of 43	100
Hire and dismiss	14 of 19	74	23 of 24	96	37 of 43	86
Negotiate staff pay levels	10 of 19	53	20 of 24	83	30 of 43	70

Source: Crandall (2010: 6) summarising information reported in OECD (2009)

complex institutional and legal arrangements in the form of boxes that are ticked or not thus not conveying them in a detailed enough manner.

In its 2015 report, the OECD stated that 33 (i.e. 60%) of the countries it surveyed were utilising a 'unified semi-autonomous body', with a third of them having a formal management/advisory board, 12 countries had a single and 7 multiple directorates inside the Ministry of Finance (OECD 2015: 22). The institutional landscape amongst the surveyed countries (including all OECD members) remained one of variation: the powers that are least frequently devolved relate to the internal structure of RAs (16 countries), discretion over budgetary allocations (14 countries), the power to set the levels and mix of staff within overall budgetary limits (16 countries) and power over staff remuneration levels (28 countries) but, interestingly, the OECD reported that 'there is a concentration of less autonomous forms of institutional setups among EU countries' (OECD 2015: 22). This is surprising given the importance that the European Commission attached to the autonomy-related aspects of its *Fiscal Blueprints* of 2007.

The introduction of this kind of reform can be part of the solution to known problems—such as the impact of low civil service pay rates—should not be seen as a panacea (Crandall 2010: 10) or a guarantee that political interference will vanish (Devas et al. 2001: 221). The logic of non-majoritarian institutions and RAs seems to be geared primarily towards the government in the sense that these systems regulate the relationship between the officials of these bodies and elected politicians. Yet we know that private interests too can corrupt officials directly, i.e. without the involvement of elected politicians. Moreover, these arrangements do not necessarily address the issue of the complexity of tax law, nor do they (in principle) remove the ability of government of the day to legislate in a way that is not in the public interest. While one may argue that the introduction of new legislation ensures a significant degree of transparency, in Greece's case this is not necessarily correct. Over many decades, politicians have used very opaque methods of legislating and legal drafting to achieve less than honourable objectives.[44] In addition, in Greece's case the introduction of this kind of institution is a rather recent phenomenon (1990s). Finally, it must be noted that after initially improving (in some cases quite significantly)

[44]This usually takes the form of legislative amendments, i.e. usually short legal provisions that are added to longer legislative texts with which they bear little or no relation (hence the frequently use of the term 'and other provisions' in the formal title of bills). As a result, the objective is not necessarily evident, nor do potential opponents have the ability to get to know about it and for opposition to be mobilised. Moreover, legal drafting often deliberately makes matters even more opaque. To achieve that objective it takes the form of a long list of references to already existing legal texts that the new provision modifies (e.g. by limiting or extending their scope) that only insiders will understand and goes something like this: this provision modifies section x of paragraph 2 of art. 35 of law 9999/2002 as it has been updated by paragraph 3 of art. 456 of law 0000/2006 (entitled 'ABCD and other provisions') by removing from its scope those who meet the following criteria (criteria follow). The minister is hereby granted the right to extend the period during which this provision applies. The opacity of provisions like this is further exacerbated by the non-codification of laws (i.e. their non-amalgamation into a single, clear text that could serve as a reference point for all interested parties).

effectiveness once established in African countries, performance has reached a plateau (Devas et al. 2001: 213). Indeed, the OECD points out that

> [s]tudies made to evaluate the success or otherwise of the 'revenue authority' model for tax administration *have not been able to draw any firm conclusions as to its overall impacts on revenue body efficiency and effectiveness.* (OECD 2015: 30—added emphasis)

The Puzzle, Core Argument and Structure of the Book

As indicated previously, we seek to explain the depoliticisation of Greece's public revenue administration, i.e. the switch from the previous model of direct ministerial control to an authority that operates at arm's length from the government in a country that has limited reform capacity. Reform-resistant Greece has come to adopt (in law and practice) a radically different model: a public revenue authority that is functionally independent, administratively and financially autonomous vis-à-vis the government. In other words, it has moved from one extreme of the spectrum near the other one. Our argument is that while conditionality—the essence of which is power asymmetry between Greece and its international partners—explains the choice of the direction of travel (i.e. less ministerial control), it does not account for how far the reform went; rather, the extent of the reform is the result of the priorities of the government in the final stages of the negotiations as well as, more importantly, successive Greek governments' reactions to pressure for reform that, arguably, exacerbated the problem of credibility and lack of trust in the eyes of the country's international partners.

The emphasis on power asymmetries in the first part of our argument may give the impression that this is a 'most likely case' scenario, i.e. since Greece needed the bailout funds, the enactment of this reform was inevitable. In fact, this is not the case. With Featherstone (2015: 296) who has conducted a broader study of administrative reform in Greece under the bailout programmes, we argue that—in reality—this is a least likely case scenario for four reasons. First, as indicated above, Greece has a limited reform capacity. Second, Greece has a tradition of party politicised public administration and dysfunctional central government bureaucracy. Third, the reform in question is of the kind that is likely to generate political costs in the short term, while the benefits are more likely to emerge much later. In other words, the political odds were against reform, especially in the very volatile political climate generated by the crisis. Finally, during most of the period under consideration here, Greece has been governed by multiparty governments, i.e. the kind of government under which conditionality is less likely to succeed (Ivanova et al. 2001: 29). One may also add the fact that unlike other reforms that have remained a dead letter after having been enacted (including the initial steps of the reform examined in this book—see Chap. 4), this one has actually been implemented, as we will demonstrate in Chap. 5.

The next chapter examines two central components of the reform examined in this book. The first is the logic of non-majoritarian institutions and the concomitant notion of depoliticisation. The second is conditionality. Over time conditionality has become a ubiquitous feature of both international governance and the operation of the European Union. Accession to the EU is subject to it, as is qualification for the adoption of the euro and so on. Given the unprecedented amount of money involved in Greece's three bailout agreements and the involvement of institutions such as the IMF and the EU, it is unsurprising that conditionality is the basis of Greece's adjustment programme. So, we draw on Schimmelfennig and Sedelmeier's work (Schimmelfennig and Sedelmeier 2004) to outline three hypotheses in Chap. 2. Chapters 3–5 present the empirical material that corresponds respectively to the content and implementation of the provisions of the first (2010), second (2012) and third (2015) MoUs (in relation to the reform of Greece's public revenue administration) the last of which has led to the establishment of the Independent Authority for Public Revenue (IAPR) that came into being in 2017. The purpose behind the use of this chronological order for this analysis is to demonstrate the increasing specificity of the international partners' demands and the concomitant lack of confidence in the Greek political élite's commitment to the reform package. While the reforms demanded of Greece in relation to its public revenue administration were very limited under the first bailout (2010), they became more specific in 2012 and took the form of a quasi-contract in 2015. The final chapter presents our conclusions.

Our analysis draws on a variety of documents ranging from domestic legislation, international agreements, policy and legislative documents, to press releases and the international and Greek press, as well as a total of 34 semi-structured, confidential interviews (most of which were conducted in Greek) with former and current ministers (10), officials of the Greek public revenue administration (7), staff and business representatives (3), ministerial advisers (4), secretaries general in the Greek central government (5) and international officials (5). Of those 32 were tape recorded and transcribed.

References

Afonso, Alexandre, Sotirios Zartaloudis, and Yannis Papadopoulos. 2015. "How party linkages shape austerity politics: clientelism and fiscal adjustment in Greece and Portugal during the eurozone crisis." *Journal of European Public Policy* 22 (3):315-334.

Alivizatos, Nikos K. 2010. "Unconstitutionalities: no to irresponsible outbidding." *Kathimerini*, 11 July (in Greek). Accessed 2 June 2018. http://www.kathimerini.gr/720901/opinion/epikairothta/arxeio-monimes-sthles/antisyntagmatikothtes-oxi-sthn-aney8ynh-pleiodosia.

Allison, Graham T., and Kalypso Nicolaïdis, eds. 1997. *The Greek Paradox: Promise vs. Performance*. Cambridge, MA: MIT Press.

Anastasatou, Marianthi. n.d. "Greeks don't pay taxes". In *Greek Myths and Reality*, edited by ELIAMEP, 19-24. Athens: ELIAMEP.

Anderson, Donald L. 2004. "The Textualizing Functions of Writing for Organizational Change." *Journal of Business and Technical Communication* 18 (2):141-164.

Artavanis, Nikolaos, Adair Morse, and Margarita Tsoutsoura. 2016. "Measuring Income Tax Evasion Using Bank Credit: Evidence from Greece." *The Quarterly Journal of Economics* 131 (2):739-798.

Ballas, Apostolos, and Haridimos Tsoukas. 2004. "Measuring Nothing: The Case of the Greek National Health System." *Human Relations* 57 (6):661- 690.

Bank of Greece. 2010. Interim report on monetary policy, October. Athens: Bank of Greece (in Greek).

Bermeo, Nancy. 2002. "Ministerial Elites in Southern Europe: Continuities, Changes and Comparisons." *South European Society and Politics* 7 (2):205-227.

Bertelsmann Stiftung. 2011. Policy Performance and Governance Capacities in the OECD: Sustainable Governance Indicators 2011. Gütersloh: Bertelsmann Stiftung.

Center for Social and Economic Research. 2015. Study to quantify and analyse the VAT Gap in the EU Member States - 2015 Report commissioned by the European Commission (DG TAXUD) TAXUD/2013/DE/321, FWC No. TAXUD/2010/CC/104. Warsaw/The Hague: CASE & CPB.

Christodoulakis, Nikos. 2012. "Market reforms in Greece, 1990-2008: external constraints and domestic limitations." In *From Stagnation to Forced Adjustment: Reforms in Greece, 1974-2010*, edited by Stathis Kalyvas, George Pagoulatos and Haridimos Tsoukas, 91-116. London: Hurst.

Crandall, William. 2010. Revenue Administration: Autonomy in Tax Administration and the Revenue Authority Model. edited by Fiscal Affairs Department. Washington, D.C.: IMF.

Dahlström, Carl, Victor Lapuente, and Jan Teorell. 2012. "The Merit of Meritocratization: Politics, Bureaucracy, and the Institutional Deterrents of Corruption." *Political Research Quarterly* 65 (3):656-668.

Devas, Nick, Simon Delay, and Michael Hubbard. 2001. "Revenue authorities: are they the right vehicle for improved tax administration?" *Public Administration and Development* 21 (3):211-222.

Diamandouros, Nikiforos. 1994. *Cultural dualism and political change in postauthoritarian Greece, Estudio/Working Paper 1994/50.* Madrid: Juan March Institute.

Ernst & Young. 2017. Tax evasion in Greece: causes, extent and proposals on how to combat it. Athens: DiaNEOsis (in Greek).

Ervasti, Heikki, Antti Kouvo, and Takis Venetoklis. 2018. "Social and Institutional Trust in Times of Crisis: Greece, 2002–2011." *Social Indicators Research.* https://doi.org/10.1007/s11205-018-1862-y

European Commission. 2007. Fiscal Blueprints: A path to a robust, modern and efficient tax administration. edited by Taxation and customs union. Brussels: European Commission.

European Commission. 2010. Report on Greek government deficit and debt statistics, COM(2010) 1 final. Brussels: European Commission.

Falkner, Gerda, Oliver Treib, Miriam Hartlapp, and Simone Leiber. 2005. *Complying with Europe: EU Harmonisation and Soft Law in the Member States, Themes in European Governance.* Cambridge: Cambridge University Press.

Featherstone, Kevin. 2005. "Introduction: 'Modernisation' and the Structural Constraints of Greek Politics." *West European Politics* 28 (2):223-241.

Featherstone, Kevin. 2008. *'Varieties of Capitalism' and the Greek case: explaining the constraints on domestic reform?* London: Hellenic Observatory, LSE.

Featherstone, Kevin. 2011. "The JCMS Annual Lecture: The Greek Sovereign Debt Crisis and EMU: A Failing State in a Skewed Regime." *Journal of Common Market Studies* 49 (2):193-217.

Featherstone, Kevin. 2015. "External conditionality and the debt crisis: the 'Troika' and public administration reform in Greece." *Journal of European Public Policy* 22 (3):295-314.

Featherstone, Kevin, and Dimitris Papadimitriou. 2008. *The Limits of Europeanization: Reform Capacity and Policy Conflict in Greece, Palgrave Studies in European Union Politics.* Basingstoke: Palgrave.

Featherstone, Kevin, and Dimitris Papadimitriou. 2012. "Assessing reform capacity in Greece: applying political economy perspectives." In *From Stagnation to Forced Adjustment: Reforms in Greece, 1974-2010*, edited by Stathis Kalyvas, George Pagoulatos and Haridimos Tsoukas, 31-46. London: Hurst.

Green, Mitchell. 2017. Speech Acts. In *The Stanford Encyclopedia of Philosophy*, edited by Edward N. Zalta. Stanford, CA: Stanford University.

Hadjinikolaou, Prokopis. 2011. "Refoundation of the tax collection mechanism." *Kathimerini*, 30 July (in Greek). http://www.kathimerini.gr/433309/article/oikonomia/ellhnikh-oikonomia/anasystash-foroeispraktikoy-mhxanismoy.

Handelsblatt. 2015. "Woran Griechenlands Steuerfahnder verzweifeln." 20 July. Accessed 14 May 2018. http://www.handelsblatt.com/politik/international/kampf-gegen-steuerhinterziehung-woran-griechenlands-steuerfahnder-verzweifeln-/12072776.html.

Hardouvelis, Ghikas, Theodosis Sampaniotis, and Manolis Davradakis. 2006. "State budget and deviation in its implementation." *Eurobank Research - Economy and Markets*, 18 December (in Greek).

Ioannou, Christos A. 2000. "Social Pacts in Hellenic Industrial Relations: Odysseys or Sisyphus." In *Social Pacts in Europe: new dynamics*, edited by G. Fajertag and P. Pochet, 219-236. Brussels: ETUI.

Iordanoglou, Chrissafis I. 2011. "Memorandum - a post mortem." *Athens Review of Books*, December (in Greek).

Ivanova, Anna, Wolfgang Mayer, Alex Mourmouras, and George Anayiotos. 2001. *What Determines the Success or Failure of Fund-Supported Programs?* Washington, D.C.: IMF.

Jones, Nikoleta, Chrisovaladis Malesios, Theodoros Iosifides, and Costas M. Sophoulis. 2008. "Social Capital in Greece: Measurement and Comparative Perspectives." *South European Society and Politics* 13 (2):175-193.

Kalyvas, Stathis N. 2015. *Modern Greece: What Everyone Needs to Know*. Oxford: Oxford University Press.

Kalyvas, Stathis, George Pagoulatos, and Haridimos Tsoukas, eds. 2012. *From Stagnation to Forced Adjustment: Reforms in Greece, 1974-2010*. London: C. Hurst & Co.

Kathimerini. 2012. "New head for SDOE." 10 August (in Greek). http://www.kathimerini.gr/10336/article/oikonomia/ellhnikh-oikonomia/neos-eidikos-grammateas-sto-sdoe

Khwaja, Munawer Sultan, and Indira Iyer. 2014. *Revenue Potential, Tax Space, and Tax Gap A Comparative Analysis*, *Policy Research Working Papers*. Washington, D.C.: World Bank.

Kidd, Maureen. 2010. Revenue Administration: Functionally Organized Tax Administration. Washington, DC: IMF.

Kidd, Maureen, and William Crandall. 2006. Revenue Authorities: Issues and Problems in Evaluating Their Success. edited by Fiscal Affairs Department. Washington, D.C.: IMF.

Kondylis, Panayiotis. 2011. *The causes of modern Greece's decline. The cachexia of the middle classes in modern Greek society and ideology*. 2nd ed. Athens: Themelio (in Greek).

Kopecký, Petr, Jan-Hinrik Meyer Sahling, Francisco Panizza, Gerardo Scherlis, Christian Schuster, and Maria Spirova. 2016. "Party patronage in contemporary democracies: results from an expert survey in 22 countries from five regions." *European Journal of Political Research* 55 (2):416-431.

Kornelakis, Andreas, and Horen Voskeritsian. 2014. "The Transformation of Employment Regulation in Greece: Towards a Dysfunctional Liberal Market Economy?" *Relations industrielles* 69 (2):344-365.

Kountouri, Fani. 2018. "Patterns of renewal and continuity in parliamentary elites. The Greek MPs from 1996 to 2015." *Journal of Legislative Studies* 24 (4):568-586.

Koutentakis, Fragkiskos. 2018. Financial stability is a basic condition for economic recovery. Interview with the Athens News Agency, 13 May. Athens: Athens News Agency (in Greek).

Krueger, Anne O. 1974. "The Political Economy of the Rent-Seeking Society." *The American Economic Review* 64 (3):291-303.

Ladi, Stella. 2005. "The Role of Experts in the Reform Process in Greece." *West European Politics* 28 (2):279-296.

Lakassas, Apostolos. 2018. "Unrest in dentistry schools due to...Tsakalotos." *Kathimerini*, 15 February (in Greek). http://www.kathimerini.gr/948847/article/epikairothta/ellada/anataraxh-stis-odontiatrikes-logw-tsakalwtoy.

Lavdas, Kostas A. 1997. *The Europeanization of Greece: Interest Politics and the Crises of Integration*. Basingstoke: Macmillan.

Lewis, Michael. 2011. *Boomerang: the biggest bust*. London: Penguin. Original edition, Allen Lane.
Lyberaki, Antigone, and Euclid Tsakalotos. 2002. "Reforming the Economy without Society: social and institutional constraints to reform in post-1974 Greece." *New Political Economy* 7 (1):93-114.
Mann, Arthur J. 2004. Are semi-autonomous revenue authorities the answer to tax administration problems in developing countries? A practical guide. Research paper for the project: Fiscal Reform in Support of Trade Liberalization.
Meyer-Sahling, Jan-Hinrik. 2004. "Civil service reform in post-communist Europe: the bumpy road to depoliticisation." *West European Politics* 27 (1):71-103.
Meyer-Sahling, Jan-Hinrik, and Kim Sass Mikkelsen. 2016. "Civil service laws, merit, politicization, and corruption: the perspective of public officials from five East European countries." *Public Administration* 94 (4):1105-1123.
Molina, Oscar, and Martin Rhodes. 2006. "Varieties of Capitalism and Mixed Market Economies." *APSA-EPS Newsletter of the European Politics & Society Section of the American Political Science Association*, 1 (fall-winter):11-15.
Monastiriotis, Vassilis, and Andreas Antoniades. 2009. *Reform that! Greece's failing reform technology: beyond 'vested interests' and 'political exchange', Hellenic Observatory Papers on Greece and Southeast Europe, GreeSE Paper No 28*. London: LSE/Hellenic Observatory.
Mossialos, Elias, and Sara Allin. 2005. "Interest Groups and Health System Reform in Greece." *West European Politics* 28 (2):420-444.
Mouzelis, Nicos. 1978. *Modern Greece: Facets of Underdevelopment*. London: Macmillan.
Nanopoulos, Antonis. 2010. *The organisational structure of tax administration - the Hellenic reality*. Athens: A. A. Livanis (in Greek).
OECD. 2007. Tax Administration in OECD and Selected Non-OECD Countries: Comparative Information Series (2006). In *Comparative Information Series*. Paris: OECD.
OECD. 2009. Tax Administration in OECD and Selected Non-OECD Countries. Comparative Information Series (2008). In *Comparative Information Series*. Paris: OECD.
OECD. 2011. Economic Surveys: Greece 2011. Paris: OECD.
OECD. 2015. Tax Administration 2015: Comparative Information on OECD and other Advanced Emerging Economies. Paris: OECD.
Osborne, David, and Ted Gaebler. 1992. *Reinventing Government: How the Entrepreneurial Spirit is Transforming the Public Sector*. Reading, MA: Addison-Wesley.
Pagoulatos, George. 2001. "The Enemy Within: Intragovernmental Politics and Organizational Failure in Greek Privatization." *Public Administration* 79 (1):125-46.
Pagoulatos, George. 2003. *Greece's New Political Economy: State, Finance and Growth from Postwar to EMU*. Basingstoke: Palgrave.
Papaconstantinou, George. 2016. *Game Over: The Truth about the Crisis*. Athens: Papadopoulos (in Greek). Original edition, Game Over: Η Αλήθεια για την Κρίση.
Pappas, Takis S., and Zina Assimakopoulou. 2012. "Party patronage in Greece: political entrepreneurship in a party patronage democracy." In *Party patronage and party government in European democracies*, edited by Petr Kopecký, Peter Mair and Maria Spirova, 145-162. Oxford: Oxford University Press.
Perry, Victoria, Graham Holland, Allan Jensen, and Janet Dowling. 2005. Greece: A Plan for Improving Tax Compliance. edited by Fiscal Affairs Department. Washington, DC: IMF.
Peters, B. Guy, and Jon Pierre. 2004. "Politicization of the civil service. Concepts, causes, consequences." In *Politicization of the civil service in comparative perspective*, edited by B. Guy Peters and Jon Pierre, 1-13. London/N.Y.: Routledge.
POE-DOY. 2012. Press release, 20 March: They must, at last take responsibility for the public revenue administration's condition. Athens: POE-DOY (in Greek).
Putnam, Linda L., and François Cooren. 2004. "Alternative Perspectives on the Role of Text and Agency in Constituting Organizations." *Organization* 11 (3):323-333.

Putnam, Robert D. 1993. *Making democracy work: civic traditions in modern Italy*. Edited by Robert Leonardi and Raffaella Nanetti. Princeton, N.J: Princeton University Press.

Rapanos, Vassilis Th. 2007. *The drafting and implementation of the state budget: European experience and Greek reality*. Athens: IOBE/Foundation for Economic and Industrial Research (in Greek).

Rapanos, Vassilis Th., and Georgia Kaplanoglou. 2014. "Governance, growth and the recent economic crisis. The case of Greece and Cyprus." *Cyprus Economic Policy Review* 8 (1):3–34.

Rothstein, Bo. 2013. "Corruption and Social Trust: Why the Fish Rots from the Head Down." *Social Research* 80 (4):1009-1032.

Schimmelfennig, Frank, and Ulrich Sedelmeier. 2004. "Governance by conditionality: EU rule transfer to the candidate countries of Central and Eastern Europe." *Journal of European Public Policy* 11 (4):661-679.

Skouras, Spyros, and Nicos Christodoulakis. 2014. "Electoral misgovernance cycles: evidence from wildfires and tax evasion in Greece." *Public Choice* 159 (3):533-559.

Smith, Barry. 1990. "Towards a History of Speech Act Theory." In *Speech Acts, Meanings and Intentions. Critical Approaches to the Philosophy of John R. Searle*, edited by A. Burkhardt, 29-61. Berlin/New York: de Gruyter.

Sotiropoulos, Dimitri A. 2012. "The paradox of non-reform in a reform-ripe environment: lessons from post-authoritarian Greece." In *From Stagnation to Forced Adjustment: Reforms in Greece, 1974-2010*, edited by Stathis Kalyvas, George Pagoulatos and Haridimos Tsoukas, 9-30. London: Hurst.

Sotiropoulos, Dimitri A., and Dimitris Bourikos. 2002. "Ministerial Elites in Greece, 1843-2001: A Synthesis of Old Sources and New Data." *South European Society and Politics* 7 (2):153-204.

Sotiropoulos, Dimitris A. 2001. *The Top Levels of the Clientelist State. Organization, Staffing and Politicization of the Higher Grades of the Central Administration in Greece*. Athens: Potamos (in Greek).

Sotiropoulos, Dimitris A., and Leonidas Christopoulos. 2016. *Polynomy, bad law-making, and red tape in Greece*: διαNEOσις (in Greek).

Spanou, Calliope. 1996. "Penelope's Suitors: Administrative Modernisation and Party Competition in Greece." *West European Politics* 19 (1):97-124.

Spanou, Calliope. 2008. "State reform in Greece: responding to old and new challenges." *International Journal of Public Sector Management* 21 (2):150-173.

Spanou, Calliope. 2012. "The quandary of administrative reform: institutional and performance modernization." In *From Stagnation to Forced Adjustment: Reforms in Greece, 1974-2010*, edited by Stathis Kalyvas, George Pagoulatos and Haridimos Tsoukas, 171-193. London: Hurst.

Spanou, Calliope, and Dimitri A. Sotiropoulos. 2011. "The Odyssey of administrative reforms in Greece, 1981-2009: a tale of two reform paths." *Public Administration* 89 (3):723-737.

Spourdalakis, Michalis, ed. 1998. *PASOK: Party - State - Society*. Athens: Patakis (in Greek).

Steinbrück, Peer. 2010. *Unterm Strich*. Hamburg: Hoffmann und Campe.

Story, T., T. Byrd, W. Crandall, J. Leamy, J. Nagy, I. Petrova, B. Russell, E. Empl, F. Van Driessche, P. Weinzierl, S. Weinzierl, and C. Wendling. 2013. Greece - fourth joint assessment by the IMF and the European Commission: revenue management and institutional reforms. IMF/European Commission.

Ta Nea. 2012a. "All heads of tax office, SDOE and customs heads to be replaced." 19 October (in Greek). Accessed 17 May 2018. http://www.tanea.gr/news/economy/article/4761548/?iid=2.

Ta Nea. 2012b. "Who is Stelios Stasinopoulos." 3 October (in Greek). Accessed 14 May 2018. http://www.tanea.gr/news/greece/article/4756657/?iid=2.

Taliercio, Robert. 2004. *Designing Performance: The Semi-Autonomous Revenue Authority Model in Africa and Latin America*. Washington D.C.: World Bank.

Telloglou, Tassos. 2012. "The 'unknown war' inside SDOE." *Kathimerini*, 14 October (in Greek). Accessed 14 May 2018. http://www.kathimerini.gr/470818/article/epikairothta/ellada/o-agnwstos-polemos-sto-eswteriko-toy-sdoe.

Theocharis, Yannis, and Jan W. van Deth. 2015. "A modern tragedy? Institutional causes and democratic consequences of the Greek crisis." *Representation* 51 (1):63-79.

Thomadakis, Stavros B. 1997. "The Greek economy: performance, expectations and paradoxes." In *The Greek paradox: promise vs. performance*, edited by Graham T. Allison and Kalypso Nicolaidis, 39-60. Cambridge, MA: MIT Press.

Tinios, Platon. 2012. "The pensions merry-go-round: the end of a cycle?" In *From Stagnation to Forced Adjustment: Reforms in Greece, 1974-2010*, edited by Stathis Kalyvas, George Pagoulatos and Haridimos Tsoukas, 117-131. London: Hurst.

Tsakalotos, Euclid. 2010. Contesting Greek exceptionalism: The political economy of the current crisis. edited by Unpublished mimeo. Athens.

Tsoukalas, Constantine. 1969. *The Greek Tragedy*. London: Penguin.

Tsoukalas, Constantine. 1993. "Free-riders in wonderland: on Greeks in Greece." *Hellenic Political Science Review* (1):9-52 (in Greek).

Tsoukalis, Loukas. 1997. "Beyond the Greek Paradox. In The Greek Paradox: Promise vs. Performance." In *The Greek Paradox: Promise vs. Performance*, edited by Graham T. Allison and Kalypso Nicolaidis. Cambridge, MA/London: MIT Press.

Tsoukas, Charidimos K. 2012. "Close friends are always preferable." *Kathimerini*, 2 September (in Greek). Accessed 22 March 2017. http://www.kathimerini.gr/731682/opinion/epikairothta/arxeio-monimes-sthles/oi-kollhtoi-einai-panta-protimoteroi.

Wildavsky, Aaron. 1975. *Budgeting: A Comparative Theory of Budgetary Processes*. Boston, MA: Little, Brown & Co.

World Bank Group. 2016. "Doing Business - Measuring Business Regulations: Ease of Doing Business in Greece." World Bank, accessed 30 August. http://www.doingbusiness.org/data/exploreeconomies/greece - close.

Zambarloukou, Stella. 2006. "Collective Bargaining and Social Pacts: Greece in Comparative Perspective." *European Journal of Industrial Relations* 12 (2):211-229.

Chapter 2
Non-majoritarian Institutions, Conditionality and Domestic Reform

The purpose of this chapter is twofold. First, it places this reform in its broader context, i.e. the increasing (indeed, now, prevalent) use of non-majoritarian institutions and executive agencies that operate at arm's length from the government in advanced liberal democracies (and beyond). This reform exemplifies this trend. The key element of this reform—and the idea that lies at the heart of this trend—is the notion of depoliticisation. Indeed, the first section of this chapter explores this notion. The second section discusses the logic that underpins the increasing use of these institutions, and then highlights their limitations, especially in terms of design, accountability and effectiveness. As we will see, depoliticisation does not necessarily entail the absence of political accountability but achieving the latter in relation to non-majoritarian institutions (NMIs) and various executive agencies is not an easy task. The chapter's second purpose is to set out the logic of the key tool (conditionality) used for the purpose of bringing about this domestic reform in Greece. The final section discusses the logic of conditionality, sets out its main characteristics in the European context and then presents the three hypotheses that will be examined empirically in the remainder of this book.

The Concept of Depoliticisation

Depoliticisation is the concept that permeates the reform that is analysed in this book. It is a controversial concept which essentially relates to 'the denial of political contingency and the transfer of functions away from elected politicians' (Flinders and Wood 2014: 135; see also Flinders and Buller 2006). It has been defined as 'a process whereby public officials prefer to disavow or devolve responsibility for more and more areas of public policy away from the state' (Buller et al. 2019: 2). The term

D. Dimitrakopoulos, A. Passas, *The Depoliticisation of Greece's Public Revenue Administration*, https://doi.org/10.1007/978-3-030-23213-9_2

'depoliticisation' has been used to denote essentially two sets of partially overlapping ideas.[1]

The first is what one can call 'the retreat of the political', i.e. a *systemic state of affairs* characterised by the shrinking of space and opportunities for contestation, deliberation and participation in political life in liberal democracies. In this line of reasoning which is directly linked to discussions—such as Colin Hay's (Hay 2007)—of the public's disaffection and disengagement from political life, depoliticisation entails a growing attachment to a powerful mode of neoliberal governmentality, consensual decision making focused on output rather than input legitimacy, an emphasis on 'what works' (i.e. how objectives are achieved is of, at best, secondary importance), the use of non-partisan experts, the confinement of policy ambitions to what managers and experts present as feasible, the lack of clarity in terms of lines of accountability, particularly if things go wrong (Buller et al. 2019: 4–6). In this 'post-political' arrangement, while the formalities of liberal democracy are observed, in reality citizens play a passive and limited role, real power is actually exercised through interactions between elected governments on the one hand and elites representing mainly business interests in what Colin Crouch appositely called 'post-democracy' (Crouch 2004).[2] The post-democratic/post-political order 'has replaced debate, disagreement and dissensus with a series of technologies of governing that fuse around consensus, agreement, accountancy metrics and techno-cratic [. . .] management' (Swyngedouw 2009: 601). But this has systemic implications: since elected politicians go out of their way to give the impression that they do not have the power or the intention to govern, the public's disengagement from politics comes as no surprise (Flinders and Wood 2014: 137; Hay 2007; Chaps. 3 and 4). This understanding of depoliticisation appears to overlap with what Wood and Flinders call 'societal' and 'discursive' depoliticisation (Wood and Flinders 2014: 158–164).

The second ensemble of ideas on depoliticisation has been usefully described not as a systemic state of affairs in advanced liberal democracies, but as a *governing strategy* (Buller et al. 2019: 10; Burnham 2001). Writing in that vein, Burnham has defined depoliticisation 'as the process of placing at one remove the political character of decision making' (Burnham 2001: 127). Crucially, though, this is not tantamount to the devolution of power. Rather, politicians do it so as to benefit from the image or impression of irresponsibility while, in reality, they retain a degree of control behind the scenes. Unlike its first usage which amounts to a retreat of the political, in its second usage, depoliticisation 'remains highly political' since 'In many respects, state managers retain arm's-length control over crucial economic processes whilst benefiting from the distancing effect of depoliticisation' (Burnham

[1]For a useful overview, see Buller et al. (2019).

[2]This 'post-politics' argument has been challenged empirically (Dean 2013; Hay 2007) and an array of scholars—including Mouffe, Žižek and Rancière—discuss ways out of it although, as Buller et al. note (2019: 8) the systemic nature of depoliticisation seen in this vein, means that change appears to require a revolution.

2001: 136). The intended benefits—at least in terms of economic management, a key policy area where this practice has been extensively utilised—relate both to (a) market expectations with regard to the effectiveness and credibility of policy making and (b) shielding politicians from the political consequences of unpopular but apparently necessary policies (Burnham 2001: 129). In that line of reasoning, non-majoritarian institutions (NMIs) are one of the tools used by politicians seeking to implement this governing strategy. This is akin to what Flinders and Buller call 'institutional depoliticisation',[3] i.e.

> [a] formalised principal–agent relationship [. . .] in which the former (elected politician) sets broad policy parameters while the latter (appointed administrator or governing board) enjoys day-to-day managerial and specialist freedom within the broad framework set by ministers (Flinders and Buller 2006: 298).

Depoliticisation is the central component of non-majoritarian institutions such as independent revenue administrations. In the next section, we examine the logic of these institutions in greater detail.

The Purpose of Non-majoritarian Institutions

The generic term 'non-majoritarian institutions' relates to a whole array of diverse institutional constructs (Everson 1995: 186). The ideas that underpin NMIs stem from the presidential system of the USA,[4] which is based on a strict understanding of the separation of powers doctrine although the model of executive agencies that operate at arm's length from the government of the day has been present in Europe too, well before the advent of New Public Management (see below).

Proponents of NMIs argue that in democracies government *pro tempore*—in essence *party* government (Castles 1982; Schmidt 1996)—is associated with three problems to which NMIs are an appropriate response (Majone 1996). The first of these problems is *temporal (in)consistency*. This means that, even though some problems require long-term solutions,[5] a policy considered to be optimal at one point in time may be reversed later in line with the exigencies of the electoral cycle, i.e. policy may change (1) ahead of an election so that incumbents win votes or (2) after an election so as to honour electoral pledges. *Credibility of commitments* is the second important problem to which NMIs are portrayed as a solution (Majone 1994). It means that all cases of alleged breaches ought to be dealt with in the same, fair and transparent way in line with applicable rules irrespective of who is involved

---

[3]It is also akin to what Wood and Flinders call 'governmental depoliticisation' (Flinders and Wood 2014: 145).

[4]For a discussion of their emergence in Europe (see Thatcher 2002: 126ff.). As regards the motivation for delegation in parliamentary democracies, see Strøm (2003).

[5]In the area of monetary policy, this relates to the fixed rules versus discretion dilemma (Kydland and Prescott 1977).

in them. Finally, there is a third, cognitive problem that appears in democratic polities: in light of the increasingly technical nature of public policy issues, democratically elected politicians may well lack the *expertise* that is required to make or adapt policy to changing conditions.[6] As a consequence, non-majoritarian institutions staffed by experts are a necessary element of modern policy making in democratic polities. More broadly, the advent of institutions that enjoy a considerable degree of autonomy from elected politicians is also associated with the effort to deal with a whole range of issues including organisational inefficiencies, relating, inter alia, to inadequate systems for human resources, expenditure management and general administration (Crandall 2010: 3).

Non-majoritarian institutions, i.e.

> governmental entities that (a) possess and exercise some grant of specialised public authority, separate from that of other institutions, but (b) are neither directly elected by the people, nor directly managed by elected officials (Thatcher and Stone Sweet 2002: 2),

are a response to the aforementioned three problems of democratic (party) government. As specialised agencies staffed with neutral experts, they possess the technocratic expertise that is needed for the implementation of public policy with the requisite efficiency and effectiveness that politicians or generalist civil servants do not possess. As regards the issue of credibility of commitments, the delegation of power is 'best understood as a means whereby governments can commit themselves to regulatory strategies that would not be credible in the absence of such delegation' (Gatsios and Seabright 1989: 46). Electoral or other kinds of expediency might tempt government ministers to interfere in administrative decisions so as to favour one outcome over another without changing the law and thus avoiding the publicity, transparency and scrutiny that such a change would normally entail. This risk is greater in a country such as Greece where politicisation, clientelism and corruption are known significant problems in the public sector (Spanou 1996; Tsekos 2013; Sotiropoulos 2001). Placing such institutions at arm's length from direct ministerial interference and keeping operational decisions shielded from such interventions is a response to the issue of credibility of commitments. In a given sector of public policy where an NMI has received some grant of specialised authority, government ministers are explicitly forbidden from interfering in or, indeed, dictating operational decisions, i.e. the application of abstract rules in specific cases. Rather, this task is entrusted in NMI officials, so as to ensure that a major cause of lack of credibility of commitments is (at least in theory) addressed. This is done on the basis of legal provisions that also seek to circumscribe the government's influence via (a) budgetary arrangements and (b) the strategic appointment of partisan heads, i.e. the means typically used to cope with the problem of bureaucratic drift (Huber 2000; Dahlström and Niklasson 2013; Peters and Pierre 2004; Ennser-Jedenastik 2016).

---

[6]One could also mention two additional rationales, namely the need for efficiency (with politicians dealing with the broad terms of policy while NMIs deal with narrow, specific issues and problems) and blame avoidance when it comes to unpopular policies (Thatcher and Stone Sweet 2002: 4) but they are arguably more specific forms of the need for expertise and policy credibility, respectively.

The professionalism of the relevant experts is another instrument that promotes this type of credibility, as does the collective ethos of the organisation for which they work. Individual officials and organisations do not want their reputation to suffer. So, officials endeavour to comply with norms of appropriate behaviour that are shared by the members of the corresponding community of experts. That is the essence of professionalism. In case of conflict with other potential influences, such as politicians' preferences, professional norms are expected to prevail. As Terry Moe notes, professionalism lies at the heart of bureaucratic autonomy because

> [p]rofessionals are oriented by goals, standards of conduct, and career opportunities that derive from their professional community, giving them strong reasons for resisting interference and direction by political outsiders; and their specialized information and expertise give them formidable resources for resisting with some measure of success (Moe 1987: 291).

Keeping potential sources of political interference at arm's length, and relying on technocratic expertise as well as professionalism are also bulwarks against the problem of inconsistency that may result from 'incomplete contracting'. This problem has two facets. First, legislators cannot foresee all circumstances or cases in which legislation will need to be applied. Matching a particular case to existing laws is a key (and inevitable) reason why implementing agencies (irrespective of their form) have a degree of discretion. Second, the issue becomes more acute once a non-majoritarian institution is up and running (see below).

Finally, it is important to note that formal independence enshrined in law does not necessarily preclude the appointment of ruling parties' political allies to independent agencies' leadership positions. Recent research covering approximately 700 top-level appointments to more than 100 regulatory agencies in 16 West European countries between 1996 and 2013 demonstrates that 'politicians respond to high levels of formal agency independence with greater efforts at appointing political allies to the agency leadership' (Ennser-Jedenastik 2016: 515–516). Moreover, the analysis of biographical information of more than 300 CEOs in 100 West European regulatory agencies between 2000 and 2013 shows that a third had discernible party links and most (73 out of 105) partisan appointees were appointed when their party was in government (Ennser-Jedenastik 2014: 834). There is variation between countries but also between types of agencies: 'when looking at government and opposition affiliates combined, there seems to be a slight tendency toward partisan appointees in more independent agencies' (Ennser-Jedenastik 2014: 836).

NMIs, Executive Agencies and the Issue of Accountability

In terms of intellectual heritage, NMIs and executive agencies that operate at arm's length from the government of the day are associated with New Public Management (Hood 1991; Osborne and Gaebler 1992). The core idea that underpins them relates to (a) democratic politics and the limits that its operation may create for the functioning of the market and (b) the need to inject to the public sector elements of business management. Although executive agencies of this kind have operated for many years in Europe—notably in Sweden—the dramatic expansion of NMIs and these agencies is a product of the political and intellectual hegemony of the New Right, especially since Margaret Thatcher and Ronald Reagan took office in the UK and the USA in 1979 and 1981, respectively. It appears to sit rather uneasily next to an increase in the politicisation of senior civil service posts in the West[7] over the past two to three decades (Peters and Pierre 2004; Dahlström 2009). Nevertheless, it is important to note that the idea had been on the table in the UK at least since the Fulton Report (which cited the Swedish example admiringly) published in 1968 (Rhodes 1996: 7; Gay 1997). Since—in this line of reasoning—the operation of the market ought to remain as unfettered as possible, NMIs are needed so as to increase the distance between the market and the decisions of democratically elected politicians. There is little to object to in this line of reasoning to the extent that this growing distance is meant to ensure equality of treatment in similar cases. Indeed, that is the whole point behind key tenets of liberal democracy such as an independent judiciary. However, this is not the only, nor is it (arguably) the most significant facet of the logic that underpins these institutions. In the case of executive agencies that operate at arm's length from the government of the day, the injection of business ethos ['cutting waste', introducing 'business-like management practices', etc. (Panchamia and Thomas n.d.: 4–5)] in the public sector was a key motive but the idea of privatisation was not far away from it. This is clearly indicated in the four tests that are associated with agencification under the 'Next Steps' programme of the Conservative administrations of the 1980s and 1990s in the UK.[8]

The existence and operation of these institutions raises significant issues in terms of democratic legitimacy and accountability (Moe 1990; Everson 1995; Maggetti 2010). As regards democratic legitimacy, placing policy decisions outside the realm of democratic politics by virtue of removing the power to make them from the arsenal of elected politicians contributes to the hollowing out of democratic politics. In a nutshell, if citizens cannot opt for alternative policies, what is the point of holding elections in a democracy? Part of the answer to this criticism relies on the distinction between input legitimacy and output legitimacy (Scharpf 1999). The former relates to process while the latter focuses on outcomes. Supporters of NMIs also point out that the decisions to grant these powers to such agencies are actually made by *elected* politicians who also retain the power to take them back or amend them, most notably via the ordinary legislative route, i.e. by amending the relevant laws. This is particularly important given the fact that 'agencies can acquire political power over time and eventually subvert the logic of delegation' (Maggetti and

[7]In Central and Eastern Europe, the enactment of laws that sought to insulate the civil service from political interference did not stop such interference (Meyer-Sahling 2004: 72).

[8]These were as follows: 'does the job need to be done at all (e.g. cuts)? Does the government have to be responsible for it (e.g. privatisation)? Does the government have to carry out the task itself (e.g. market testing)? Is the organisation properly structured and focused on the job to be done (e.g. agencification)?' (Rhodes 1996: 7–8).

Papadopoulos 2018: 172) as empirical studies have demonstrated (see, e.g. Maggetti 2009; Bach 2012).

As regards, the key issue of *credibility of commitments*, supporters of this model point out that keeping these institutions at arm's length from elected politicians is the best available means of ensuring that all cases of alleged breaches are dealt with in the same, fair way in line with applicable rules, irrespective of who is involved in them. Elected politicians should not have the right to interfere with the day-to-day decisions that relate to policy implementation, just like they should not tell the police whether to arrest someone or what kind of evidence to collect. Democracy, in other words, should not undermine the rule of law. Finally, the cognitive reason behind NMIs relates to a particular kind of legitimacy: *expertise* is not distributed evenly amongst the population and holding office as a result of a democratic election is not tantamount to having the expertise that modern policy making requires. On the contrary, recruitment based on expertise, i.e. merit rather than political allegiance, is one of the checks and balances that are needed in contemporary democracies.

As indicated previously, the ideas that underpin NMIs stem from the presidential system of the USA. The relationship between elected legislators who are members of Congress and regulatory agencies is complex. However, two initial schools of thought have been identified as to the terms of this relationship, namely (a) 'Congress dominance' (indicating the power of elected principals) and (b) 'runaway bureaucracy' (highlighting the agents' autonomy). Both schools of thought are associated with the principal-agent model (for reviews, see Bendor et al. 2001; Pollack 2002). That model rests on two key assumptions as to the relationship between principals and agents, namely (a) differing preferences and (b) the asymmetrical distribution of information between elected principals and their unelected agents. Taken together these assumptions generate the need for oversight and control mechanisms, i.e. ways that the principals need to use so as to ensure that their agents achieve the tasks assigned to them without producing unwanted consequences.

The supporters of NMIs argue that lack of accountability does not necessarily flow from the non-majoritarian nature of these institutions. Several mechanisms can be used to ensure that these agencies remain accountable for their actions. At the individual level, reputation is a powerful mechanism for the experts who work for these agencies. If they make mistakes, their reputation amongst their peers will suffer and so will their career prospects. This is important since these agencies deal with highly technical issues (varying from monetary policy to the regulation of telecommunications) and technocratic expertise is the common language amongst their officials. At the institutional level, accountability can be promoted through legislation, including the laws that create these agencies (Majone 1996: 12). This involves clearly defined objectives that they must strive to meet, judicial review, transparent decision making and judicialisation.[9] Crucially, one can add important procedural requirements (such as regular reporting including to elected officials such as

[9]See Majone (1996: 12–13) on the one that occurred in the USA since the passage of the Administrative Procedures Act (APA) in 1946.

parliamentarians) as part and parcel of relational contracting which is a response to the inevitable issue of incomplete contracting. This means that politicians and officials

> do not agree on detailed plans of actions but on goals and objectives, on general provisions that are broadly applicable, on the criteria to be used in deciding what to do when unforeseen contingencies arise, on who has what power to act and the bounds limiting the range of actions that can be taken, and on dispute resolution mechanisms to be used if disagreements do occur (Milgrom and Roberts 1992: 131 quoted by Majone 1996: 9).

Keeping agencies under control (i.e. accountable) while also ensuring that no one controls them (Moe 1987: 291) is likely to require a combination of several of these tools.

Conditionality

The Logic of Conditionality

The adjustment programmes that have been put in place as part of Greece's three bailout agreements of 2010, 2012 and 2015 are couched in the logic of conditionality. Conditionality is believed to serve a purpose at least in three types of situation: (a) the two sides have different views on the appropriateness of policy; (b) the target government agrees with the policy and is committed to it (as is the other side to supporting it) but there is domestic resistance; (c) the target government needs a signalling device vis-à-vis potential private investors (World Bank 2005b: 3). The first part of this section draws on the literature on conditionality and sketches out key lessons from it, thus paving the way for the presentation (in the second sub-section) of the three hypotheses that inform this study.

The literature on conditionality is vast (see, e.g., World Bank 2005b; Spanou 2016) and this reflects the controversy (for a summary of critiques see Koeberle 2003: 251–256) that surrounds this concept,[10] the evolution of its content (Koeberle et al. 2005), the extent of its use—especially by the IMF and, later on, the World Bank (IMF 2012b; World Bank 2005a) but also individual countries acting on a bilateral basis (Dijkstra 2002)—as well as the diversity of the contexts in which it has been utilised, i.e. countries that range from the developing world to emerging powers, countries of the former Soviet bloc and, recently, members of the Eurozone.[11]

[10]This has to do with a myriad of factors including conditionality's relationship with justice (European Network on Debt and Development 2006) and democracy (Montinola 2007).

[11]Here we are referring to the provision of international aid. The use of conditionality within the EU is not new (see the next sub-section).

The literature on conditionality[12] highlights several key lessons that relate to domestic institutional reform induced by conditionality-based programmes. Despite the technocratic element that it entails, conditionality is political for it is built on *power asymmetry* (Spanou 2016: 7; Hughes et al. 2005: 2; Morrissey 2005) in the sense that the lender/donor possesses a resource that the crisis-hit country desperately needs. As a consequence, coercion is a key mechanism in the operation of conditionality-based adjustment programmes. This asymmetry is demonstrated by the use of memoranda of understanding (MoU), roadmaps, deadlines, control mechanisms, penalties, rewards as well as the attendant terminology of 'prior actions', 'deliverables', etc. (Spanou 2016: 8). In principal-agent terms, the aforementioned institutional machinery that is associated with conditionality indicates (a) the power asymmetry between the two sides but—equally importantly—the *lack of trust* that underpins their relationship (for if trust underpinned that relationship, there would be less need for that machinery) and (b) the centrality of information. The institutional and procedural armoury that is associated with conditionality is also the flipside of what critics say is the very large number and detailed nature of the conditions that are associated with adjustment programmes (Koeberle 2003: 252).

Conditionality's effectiveness is *contested* and international financial institutions (IFI) including the IMF are aware of it (Milanovic 2003: 7–9; IMF 2012a: 7; Easterly 2005; World Bank 2005b; Spraos 1986). As a consequence, conditionality—construed as a process—has become more *interactive* over time (IMF 2012b: 19–21; World Bank 2005b: 6) than is commonly acknowledged and this is demonstrated by (a) 'tailoring' programmes to country-specific conditions (Koeberle et al. 2005) and (b) offering targeted technical assistance (World Bank 2005a: 22; Morrissey 2004). The days when implementation-related considerations were ignored (Thomas and Grindle 1990) appear to be gone.

Neither tailoring nor the interactive nature of the conditionality process negates the asymmetry of power that underpins it. Indeed, when governments do not completely fulfil their obligations, conditionality becomes *stricter* (Buira 2003), thus reconfirming the power asymmetry between the two sides although some evidence suggests that there is a Laffer conditionality curve, i.e. as a programme's severity[13] increases, compliance is reduced (see the sources mentioned in Bird 2001). On the other hand, the mere need to make conditionality stricter may also be taken as an indication that strictness alone is not a sufficient response to an adjustment programme's implementation problems.

As Checkel notes,

> conditionality, particularly in its stronger versions, creates an ownership problem domestically. Reforms are seen to be the result of external imposition; the incentive to comply is lower given foreign domination of the reform process. Support for policy change thus lacks a strong political base and compliance becomes problematic (Checkel 2000: 3).

[12]For a useful overview, see Spanou (2016).

[13]Koeberle notes (2003: 255–256) that more conditions 'tend to be negatively correlated with ratings for adjustment loan outcomes'.

Programme ownership—a term that cannot conceal the importance of power asymmetries—is of central importance. It is defined as the

> willing assumption of responsibility for an agreed program of policies, by officials in a borrowing country who have the responsibility to formulate and carry out these policies, based on an understanding that the programme is achievable and is in the country's own interests (IMF 2001: 6)

It relates to beliefs as well as capacity (Thomas and Grindle 1990; Boughton and Mourmouras 2002; Nelson 1996; Drazen 2002; Killick 1997; Güven 2012; World Bank 2005a: 4). This means that when the domestic actors whose task is to carry it out do not agree with it, or do not have the means to carry it out, programme success becomes less likely. Conversely, domestic support increases the likelihood of programme success. Programme ownership is a managerial way of referring to the willingness and ability of domestic actors to spend political capital (and other resources) in support of the implementation process. The flipside is this conditionality has the advantage of blame shifting (Pagoulatos 2012: 251) since the target government can seek to reduce the political costs of unpopular reforms by blaming the relevant external actors. Programme ownership is also key because it relates directly to the political and institutional conditions in which conditionality-based adjustment programmes are carried out. Indeed, the likelihood of programme success is lower in polities where vested interests are strong, political polarisation is high, or in the case of multi-party governments (Ivanova et al. 2001: 25, 27), while political instability too is detrimental (Dollar and Svensson 2001: 901).

The choice of *rhythm* [i.e. speed and sequence (Spanou 2016: 16)] of reform is controversial. Some favour gradualism, others prefer the dominant 'big bang' approach (Rodrik 2016; Tommasi and Velasco 1995). The virtues of one are weaknesses of the other. For example, in a key area such as tax collection, opting for a speedy and radical type of reform may well make sense in political terms for any reformer who seeks to capitalise on the opportunities that a crisis creates since it demonstrates the ineffectiveness of established practices. On the other hand, radical and swift reform in that area entails a big risk for public finances because, for example, during a crisis-induced recession, incomes take a hit, credit becomes scarce or unavailable, economic activity shifts from the formal to the informal sector etc. (Brondolo 2009: 5–6). An issue that is linked to conditionality's rhythm is the *time horizon* that is associated with different types of conditionality-based reform programmes.[14] As Spanou rightly points out, while economic stabilisation and fiscal adjustment programmes are associated with measures (such as spending cuts) aiming to deliver an immediate impact, institutional reforms have a longer time frame and (often) much less public visibility (Spanou 2016: 14–15). The time frame relates both to the period needed for the introduction of these reforms and their

[14]Differences in time horizons also characterize the two central organisations with which the Greek authorities had to deal in the context of the crisis. While the IMF is used to acting in an aid-receiving country over a short period of 2–3 years, for the EU 'Greece is part of the family', as a senior official put in at a meeting held in London in January 2018 under the Chatham House rule.

sustainability (Rodrik 1990). In other words, there are good reasons why conditionality is better approached as a process (Hughes et al. 2004: 548).

Conditionality as practised at least by the IMF is associated with a panoply of measures devised, promoted and monitored by IMF technocrats and is decidedly couched in technocratic language implying technical superiority, despite the highly contested record of adjustment programmes. However, the policy solutions that it embodies are not devoid of clear *normative content* (see Babb 2013). In terms of the institutional architecture of public revenue administrations, clear evidence is offered by the emphasis that is often placed by the IMF on functional independence, i.e. independence from the influence of democratically elected politicians (Crandall 2010). This implies not only that this influence is necessarily detrimental to the effectiveness of tax collection but also that it is more important than other potential sources of ineffectiveness such as corruption by private interests. The value-laden nature of conditionality-based programmes may also account for the fact that these programmes do not necessarily include objectively superior solutions to extant policy problems, given the conditions that a crisis-hit country faces. Indeed, as Koeberle notes, critics have argued that (in the earlier version of conditionality) conditions often reflect best practice and theoretical fixes but 'with no objective investigation of their actual economic effectiveness and no consideration of political, social, cultural, and environmental features and limitations' (Koeberle 2003: 252). Moreover, in the case of the IMF it has been found that conditionality's content is the result of bargaining and compromise between IMF staff and between the IMF and the borrowing states (Stiles 1990).

Finally, since conditionality applies very often in conditions of acute crisis (i.e. periods when time is of the essence), it transforms the domestic policymaking apparatus into a compliance mechanism but it also alters the balance of power between domestic institutions for it leads to 'the reassertion of the executive vis-à-vis the legislature', involving the bypassing of ordinary institutional procedures, and (crucially) undermines opportunities for debate and deliberation while also raising important issues such as transparency and the quality of legislation (Spanou 2016: 3, 13).

As a consequence—and in line with historical institutionalist thinking on institutional change—we would expect institutional change to be a conflict-ridden and inefficient process; while it is often incremental and piecemeal, in critical junctures it can also be radical and dramatic; while it is often affected by prevailing norms and ideas, it is also couched in power differentials between the supporters and opponents of change.

Institutional change, i.e. a change in 'formal structure, organizational culture and goals, programme or mission' (DiMaggio and Powell 1991: 81), is a key feature of conditionality-based adjustment programmes. These programmes are the key instrument used by international financial institutions and the European Union (EU) in their dealings with, inter alia, crisis-hit member states. These countries receive much-needed funds in exchange for reforming (inter alia) their institutional infrastructure.

Conditionality and the European Union

The European Union is an enduring user of conditionality. The uses it has historically made of conditionality relate both to its internal operation and its external relations. These uses range from setting criteria for the accession of third countries that apply for membership, to various aspects of its internal operation including spending programmes (Vita 2017) and, most prominently, the adoption of the Euro (see, e.g. Blavoukos and Pagoulatos 2008).

In the context of the study of the European Union, enlargement to Central and Eastern Europe (predominantly the 'big bang' of 2004) has been the main focus of attention in the study of conditionality whereby accession to the EU is conditional on and a reward for compliance with the Copenhagen criteria and the *acquis communautaire* (Schimmelfennig and Sedelmeier 2005a; Hughes et al. 2005; Haughton 2007; Kahn-Nisser 2013; Schimmelfennig et al. 2003; Dimitrova 2002). One common point between the use of conditionality for the adoption of the Euro and accession to the EU is that—until the onset of the crisis in the Eurozone—the influence of the criteria had been found to wane after the cut-off point which is the actual adoption of the Euro and accession to the EU, respectively, although outcomes are not uniform across time and space (Blavoukos and Pagoulatos 2008; Falkner et al. 2008; Falkner 2010; Hughes et al. 2005). Awareness about this fact and the vast sums of money required for the bailouts were conducive to the intrusive and particularly intensive form that the conditionality regime took in the case of Greece, with regular and highly mediatised visits of IMF and EU staff to Greece and the very tight association of compliance with commitments undertaken with the provision of vital funding.

In their influential analysis of this process Schimmelfenning and Sedelmaier posit three models for the adoption of EU rules (Schimmelfennig and Sedelmeier 2005b: 10–25). While the first is couched in the logic of consequences, the other two follow the logic of appropriateness (March and Olsen 1989). The first is the *external incentive model.* In this rationalist bargaining model, which reflects the logic of consequences, domestic actors operate as strategic utility maximisers who are keen to preserve or enhance their welfare. In general, the relative bargaining power of the two sides determines the outcome of bargaining. This power reflects the uneven distribution of (a) information and (b) the benefits that are expected to derive from a specific agreement (Schimmelfennig and Sedelmeier 2005b: 10). The more and better information one side has, the more able it is to shape the outcome of bargaining and the less need one side has to reach a specific agreement, the more power it has to achieve its objective by threatening to withhold cooperation.[15] In the context of EU enlargement, the adoption of its rules by third countries is a condition that the EU sets to third countries that seek rewards from it. These rewards range

[15]This is the standard model in the study of World Bank- or IMF-related programmes (see, e.g. Haggard and Webb 1994) and it is also a key feature of the literature on Europeanisation (Hix and Goetz 2000).

from assistance to full membership. In that context, the EU provides the reward if the conditions are met and withholds it if they are not (reactive reinforcement or reinforcement by reward).[16]

In this model bargaining starts in the presence of a mismatch between the domestic status quo, on the one hand, and EU rules on the other. Conditionality is used to alter the incentives that support the domestic status quo. This can be done through intergovernmental bargaining, i.e. by directly impacting the domestic government's calculation of the costs and benefits of the status quo in comparison to the adoption of EU rules (top-down). It may also work in a less direct (and more bottom-up) manner, i.e. through the differential empowerment of some domestic actors. In the latter case, conditionality changes the domestic opportunity structure in favour of the domestic actors (in government or society) that wanted but were hitherto unable to bring about change 'to the extent that [their] opponents share the goal of EU membership and expect to benefit from the EU's rewards' (Schimmelfennig and Sedelmeier 2005b: 12). This leads to the first hypothesis:

> *a government adopts EU rules if the benefits of EU rewards exceed the domestic adoption costs* (Schimmelfennig and Sedelmeier 2005b: 12).

In turn, this cost–benefit balance depends on (1) the determinacy of conditions, (2) the size and speed of rewards, (3) the credibility of threats and promises, and (4) the size of adoption costs (Schimmelfennig and Sedelmeier 2005b: 12–17). Determinacy refers to the clarity as well as the formality of a rule. It is important because it (a) enables governments to know precisely what they need to do so as to obtain the reward (informational value) and (b) it relates to conditionality's credibility since it makes it difficult for either party to claim unjustly that the rule in question has or has not been fulfilled. Determinacy is higher when a rule is legalised and binding, and its behavioural implications are clear. The size and speed of rewards are also consequential. While the former determines what is at stake, the latter can affect the speed of the domestic response to the conditions set. The credibility of threats and promises is a key element of the operation of conditionality. It means that the actor that sets the conditions must be (a) able to withhold the reward (if the conditions are not met) at little or no cost and (b) less interested in granting the reward than the target government is in receiving it. Credibility is also a matter of consistency in the sense that the actor setting the conditions must not be perceived to subject its decisions to other considerations that would make it appear either lenient or unfair. Credibility also means that the actor who sets the conditions must have the capability to obtain the requisite information, e.g. through regular monitoring. Finally, this model highlights the relevance of domestic adaptation costs. As Schimmelfennig and Sedelmaier note, these costs may (a) be opportunity costs resulting from foregoing rewards for adopting other courses of action (including maintaining the status quo), (b) relate to the redistribution of power and/or welfare

[16]As Schimmelfenning and Sedelmaier (2005a, b: 11) note other alternative strategies include reinforcement by punishment (which entails inflicting costs for non-compliance) and reinforcement by support (through the provision of additional benefits).

amongst public and private actors but in any case ought to be weighed in relation to the rewards expected from the EU (Schimmelfennig and Sedelmeier 2005b: 16). Given that conditionality focuses on the action of domestic governments—for they are the ones that must implement the requisite reforms—their preferences and the views held by other domestic veto players are key determinants of conditionality's success or failure. Both veto player theory and the broader literature on conditionality indicate that significant changes to the status quo become less likely as the number of veto points and the distance between them goes up (Tsebelis 1995; Ivanova et al. 2001).

The logic of appropriateness is the basis of two alternative models. The *social learning model* relies on internalised identities and shared norms (Schimmelfennig and Sedelmeier 2005b: 18–20) and has been used in the study of international socialisation (Checkel 2001), the analysis of conditionality (Checkel 2000) and Europeanisation (Börzel and Risse 2003). From that perspective, the EU is a formal organisation of a European international community that is defined by a specific underlying common identity and is underpinned by a concrete ensemble of common values and norms. As a consequence, the adoption of EU rules by non-members depends on whether they regard EU rules as appropriate, i.e. corresponding to a collective set of values, norms and identity (Schimmelfennig 2003: 83–90). This leads to the second hypothesis:

> *a state adopts EU rules if it is persuaded of the appropriateness of EU rules* (Schimmelfennig and Sedelmeier 2005b: 18).

This process may—just like in the previous model—affect either the target government directly or indirectly (i.e. via other domestic social actors that are empowered by the EU through the conferral of its legitimacy). Unlike the previous model which relies on bargaining about conditions and rewards, coercion and mere behavioural adaptation, here adaptation depends on the legitimacy and the appropriateness of rules, persuasion and complex learning. Assuming such rules exist and are determinate (i.e. clear and specific) their legitimacy is a key determinant of the likelihood of their adoption. In the context of the EU's enlargement, applicant countries do not have a formal say in the content of EU legislation and this generates the risk that the adoption of these rules will be perceived to be the result of foreign imposition. This runs counter to the lessons drawn about the overwhelming significance of programme ownership in international conditionality-based adjustment programmes (Killick 1997; Drazen 2002; Thomas and Grindle 1990). The antidote to this is engagement of target governments in a deliberative process and the association of reforms with more abstract, legitimate principles and norms that underpin the community to which applicant states aspire to belong. The legitimacy of EU rules is also boosted when they are seen to be equitable and do not conflict with the rules of other bodies such as international organisations. Finally, social learning is also affected by resonance. If domestic rules do not exist or have lost their legitimacy or have failed, it is more likely that new rules will be adopted (Checkel 2001: 562–563). The same applies if the norms (including procedural ones) on which EU rules are based are accepted domestically and when they resonate with existing domestic ones that enjoy legitimacy (Cortell and Davis 1996). While, in this model, adaptation is likely to start from the level of discourse, if change is sincere it will be followed through in formal and behavioural terms (Schimmelfennig and Sedelmeier 2005b: 20).

The final model (*lesson-drawing*) builds on the broader literature on lesson-drawing in public policy (Dolowitz and Marsh 2000; Gilardi 2010; May 1992; Sabatier 1987; Simmons et al. 2007; Rose 1991). Lesson-drawing is couched in domestic dissatisfaction with extant policy and/or institutions and it is this dissatisfaction which generates a search for arrangements that operate elsewhere. This also includes a prospective assessment of their transferability to the domestic context (Rose 1991: 10, 23). Schimmelfennig and Sedelmaier highlight the existence of a rationalist and a sociological variant of learning. While the former involves simple learning (i.e. a change in means but not ends, as a result of new information), the latter takes the form of complex learning and involves a change of goals but in both cases this model differs from the other two[17] in that it does not ascribe to the EU the decisive role in bringing about domestic change (Schimmelfennig and Sedelmeier 2005b: 21). Membership of the EU has created a space where member states look for solutions (often in the context of the EU's formal policy process) when faced with domestic policy or institutional failure. Under this model, EU conditionality can shape domestic change by setting boundaries to the range of options that domestic actors consider or by offering a menu of acceptable models. Adaptation in the former case is a domestic decision that results—not from a calculus of the adjustment costs—but from the perceived utility of imported solutions while in the latter case the external incentives model may explain change and lesson-drawing the specific form that has been chosen. So, the third hypothesis is as follows:

> *a state adopts EU rules if it expects these rules to solve domestic policy problems effectively* (Schimmelfennig and Sedelmeier 2005b: 22).

Dissatisfaction with domestic arrangements is the most basic condition of this model. The intensity and regularity of interactions with other EU member states—coupled with geographical proximity—facilitates a search for solutions that is geared towards the EU and the political systems of its individual member states but the transferability of rules is key. This, in turn, is affected by the similarity of the conditions that operate in the two relevant countries/systems, i.e. the resources required for putting these rules into effect, the political acceptability of these rules (Hall 1989), and their compatibility with the prevailing domestic political discourse. A major difference between this and the external incentives model is this:

> while the latter assumes a domestic equilibrium that is upset by the incentives that the EU provides, the lesson-drawing model takes as its starting point a domestic disequilibrium in which the balance of domestic pressures favours a departure from the status quo (Schimmelfennig and Sedelmeier 2005b: 24).

[17]On the contrary, the first model highlights the important of rewards offered by the EU while the second underlines the role of its efforts at persuading domestic actors.

Our use of theoretical models initially developed for the study of enlargement requires an explanation. After all, enlargement is about *non*-members, whereas Greece has been a member since 1981, i.e. for nearly three decades before the crisis hit it. In practical terms, this means that enlargement differs from the handling of the crisis in two key ways. First, non-members do not have a say in the making of the *acquis communautaire* with which they need to comply as a condition for accession. Second, the decision as to whether a non-member is to enter the EU is taken by institutions that are external to the state in question. On the contrary, Greece was one of the member states that had a direct say in both the making of Economic and Monetary Union and the EU's crisis management. Both points are correct but their importance must not be over-estimated for several reasons for, in the opposite case, one runs the risk of missing the key similarity between enlargement and the handling of the crisis, namely *power asymmetry* between Greece and the EU/IMF side.

When the crisis hit Greece, it was widely acknowledged that the EU collectively and the Eurozone in particular did not have the tools that were required to respond to it. This is not a matter of opinion, nor is this limited to the famous no bailout clause of the Treaty. The EU's unpreparedness is demonstrated by the whole set of institutions that were subsequently put in place, involving—most prominently—the establishment of the European Stability Mechanism as well as its forerunners, the development of the banking union, the enhancement of the surveillance mechanisms inside the Eurozone and beyond [notably via the so-called 'two-pack' (European Parliament and Council of the EU 2013a, b) and 'six-pack' (Council of the EU 2011a, b; European Parliament and Council of the EU 2011a–d)] and, above all, the funds that were desperately needed not only by Greece but also the European banking system that was facing a meltdown. None of these key tools were in place when the crisis hit Greece. Greece's involvement in their making (as a member of the Eurozone) did not happen while Greece was on an equal footing with the other member states; rather Greece was a *démandeuse*, a country whose credibility was virtually non-existent in the eyes of its key partners on whose assistance it was desperately dependent. The IMF too has had to change its own rules (Schadler 2017: 35) so as to be able to provide the financial assistance that Greece needed in 2010. In other words, just like a non-member country must comply with rules made by the EU, Greece has had to comply with rules made via a process where its own weight was, at best, negligible.

During this process which unfolded in conditions of acute financial, economic and leadership crisis, on the EU's side of the so-called Troika, the role of the Eurogroup became not only much more visible, but it took a turn that further underlines Greece's role as a *démandeuse*. The Eurogroup normally seeks to build consensus amongst its members, as do the normal formations of the full Council (of Ministers). However, unlike the latter, this consensus-seeking in the Eurogroup did not operate (until the establishment of the European Stability Mechanism) in the shadow of the qualified majority (QMV) rule. This institutional characteristic, coupled with the absence of EU funds that could be used—at least initially, which is when the tone was set for the entire process—meant that the EU's response took a decidedly intergovernmental turn. However, in intergovernmental settings member states are *not* equal (Moravcsik 1998). This was perfectly demonstrated in the EU's response to the crisis. The Eurogroup very quickly turned into a decision-making forum that was dominated by the wealthiest member of the Eurozone: Germany, supported by its EMU allies, i.e. mainly Austria, Finland and the Netherlands—a group of countries that were reluctant, to put it mildly, to make the necessary (national) funds available. Germany's role was always significant in the running of EMU but grew exponentially during the crisis. This is clearly demonstrated by the ESM's architecture. Only Germany has effective veto power for decisions that need the support of a qualified majority (either by the Board of Governors or the Board of Directors). This is so because those decisions require the support of 80% of the votes cast (Art. 4 para. 5 of the Treaty establishing the ESM) and the distribution of voting power is based on the number of shares in the authorised capital stock of the ESM to which Germany's contribution is the largest and amounts to 27.1%. The depth of the intergovernmental nature of the arrangement is worth noting. Due to their own internal constitutional arrangements, the poisonous rhetoric that dominated political discourse both in the debtor countries and the lender states, and—certainly in the case of Greece—the deep and justified sense of distrust vis-à-vis the Greek political *élite*, the response to the crisis took a form that was far more strict than the process that applied in the 2004 enlargement. While funds have been made available, the disbursal of individual tranches was made subject to not only conditions but also the political judgment of national parliamentarians in other member states, most notably Germany, and repeatedly so. All this paints a picture of overwhelming asymmetry rather similar to the one that characterises the enlargement process. Three other similarities are worth noting. First, in addition to funds, Greece's bailouts also included the provision of technical assistance. This is a major similarity between conditionality as practised by the EU and (at least in the recent past) IFIs. The details of the technical assistance that Greece received in relation to the reform of its public revenue administration will be presented in the next chapter but two of its implications are worth highlighting here. Unlike the IMF, the EU and its member states did not charge Greece for the assistance that they provided to the debt-stricken country. In theoretical terms, the provision of technical assistance may well contribute to the operation of the third theoretical model outlined above (lesson-drawing). While the external incentives model may be the best explanation of rule adoption, lesson-drawing may account for the choice of specific rules from a larger universe of conforming rules (Schimmelfennig and Sedelmeier 2005b: 21–22). Taken together, these two considerations mean that the provision of technical assistance may well be a key factor in the choice of rules. Second, the management of the bailout programmes involved regular monitoring and reporting exercises including rather intrusive inspections. Finally, both involved a clear and concrete stake. While that stake took a different form (the provision of funds, rather than accession to the EU), the scale of its significance was comparable.

All three models are focused on domestic actors and their behaviour. However, their *prima facie* relevance is not identical. The aforementioned overwhelming asymmetry is the reason why we expect the first model to explain at least why the reform process commenced. The reform examined here was couched in power asymmetry and actively managed by the stronger party in this asymmetrical relationship. So, it is reasonable to expect the external incentives model to be applicable. However, in the past, major reforms have been introduced in Greece in the absence of a specific external constraint—as the introduction in 1993 of written exams for entry into the civil service rather emblematically demonstrates. This was due partly to dissatisfaction with domestic policies. This dissatisfaction is a key part of both the second and third models. Previous studies have also found evidence of learning as a cause of change (see, e.g., Dimitrakopoulos 2001; Zahariadis 2014; Paraskevopoulos 2001). Crises can open up a window of opportunity for the introduction of reforms. In addition, the IMF as well as the EU and individual European countries provided a lot of technical assistance to Greece in relation to the implementation of the requirements of the MoUs (and beyond). Clearly, an argument can be made that is assistance was, *prima facie*, a potential channel for learning. Nevertheless, (a) the intensity of the social unrest and political polarisation unleashed by the crisis and its handling, the adversarial rhetoric that went with it, undermine learning by drowning out reformist voices or concealing the desirability of some reforms and (b) as Featherstone rightly notes, at the political level, clientelism and rent-seeking heavily limit the will to reform, a trend that finds further support in trade union and party circles (Featherstone 2015: 299) while legalism, centralism and relentless emphasis on process—as opposed to outcomes or innovation—are key features of the Greek administrative tradition.

The next chapter is the first of three that examine the empirical material upon which this book is based. Specifically, it examines the process of reform that commenced in late 2009 before and during the implementation of the first Memorandum of Understanding up until the end of 2011.

References

Babb, Sarah. 2013. "The Washington Consensus as transnational policy paradigm: Its origins, trajectory and likely successor." *Review of International Political Economy* 20 (2):268-297.

Bach, Tobias. 2012. "The involvement of agencies in policy formulation: explaining variation in policy autonomy of federal agencies in Germany." *Policy and Society* 31 (3):211-222.

Bendor, J., A. Glazer, and T. Hammond. 2001. "Theories of delegation." *Annual Review of Political Science* 4 (1):235-269.

Bird, Graham. 2001. "IMF Programs: Do They Work? Can They be Made to Work Better?" *World Development* 29 (11):1849-1865.

Blavoukos, Spyros, and George Pagoulatos. 2008. "The Limits of EMU Conditionality: Fiscal Adjustment in Southern Europe." *Journal of Public Policy* 28 (2):229-253.

Börzel, Tanja A., and Thomas Risse. 2003. "Conceptualising the domestic impact of Europe." In *The Politics of Europeanization*, edited by Kevin Featherstone and Claudio Radaelli, 55-78. Oxford: Oxford University Press.

Boughton, James A., and Alex Mourmouras. 2002. Is policy ownership an operational concept? Washington, D.C.: IMF.

Brondolo, John. 2009. Collecting Taxes During an Economic Crisis: Challenges and Policy Options. Fiscal Affairs Department/IMF. Washington, D.C.: IMF.

Buira, Ariel. 2003. An analysis of IMF conditionality. Paper prepared for the XVI Technical group meeting of the Intergovernmental Group of 24. Port of Spain, Trinidad and Tobago, February 13-14.

Buller, Jim, Pınar E. Dönmez, Adam Standring, and Matthew Wood. 2019. "Depoliticisation, Post-politics and the Problem of Change." In *Comparing Strategies of (De)Politicisation in Europe: Governance, Resistance and Anti-politics*, edited by Jim Buller, Pınar E. Dönmez, Adam Standring and Matthew Wood, 1-24. Basingstoke: Palgrave.

Burnham, Peter. 2001. "New Labour and the politics of depoliticisation." *The British Journal of Politics & International Relations* 3 (2):127-149.

Castles, Francis G., ed. 1982. *The Impact of Parties: Politics and Policies in Democratic Capitalist States*. London: Sage.

Checkel, Jeffrey T. 2000. *Compliance and Conditionality*. Oslo: ARENA.

Checkel, Jeffrey T. 2001. "Why comply? Social learning and European identity change." *International Organization* 55 (3):553-88.

Cortell, Andrew P., and James W. Davis Jr. 1996. "How do international institutions matter? The domestic impact of international rules and norms." *International Studies Quarterly* 40 (4):451-78.

Council of the EU. 2011a. Council Directive 2011/85/EU of 8 November 2011 on requirements for budgetary frameworks of the Member States. Official Journal of the European Union L 306, 23 November.

Council of the EU. 2011b. Council Regulation (EU) No 1177/2011 of 8 November 2011 amending Regulation (EC) No 1467/97 on speeding up and clarifying the implementation of the excessive deficit procedure. Official Journal of the European Union, L306, 23 November.

Crandall, William. 2010. Revenue Administration: Autonomy in Tax Administration and the Revenue Authority Model. Fiscal Affairs Department. Washington, D.C.: IMF.

Crouch, Colin. 2004. *Post-Democracy, Themes for the 21st Century*. Cambridge: Polity.

Dahlström, Carl. 2009. *Political appointments in 18 democracies, 1975–2007*. Gothenburg: University of Gothenburg/The Quality of Government Institute.

Dahlström, Carl, and Birgitta Niklasson. 2013. "The politics of politicization in Sweden." *Public Administration* 91 (4):891-907.

Dean, Jonathan. 2013. "Tales of the Apolitical." *Political Studies* 62 (2):452-467.

Dijkstra, A. Geske. 2002. "The effectiveness of policy conditionality: eight country experiences." *Development and Change* 33 (2):307-334.

DiMaggio, Paul J., and Walter W. Powell. 1991. "The Iron Cage Revisited: Institutional Isomorphism and Collective Rationality in Organization Fields." In *The New Institutionalism in Organizational Analysis*, edited by Walter W. Powell and Paul J. DiMaggio, 63-82. Chicago, IL: Chicago University Press.

Dimitrakopoulos, Dionyssis G. 2001. "Learning and steering: changing implementation patterns and the Greek central government." *Journal of European Public Policy* 8 (4):604-22.

Dimitrova, A. 2002. "Enlargement, Institution-Building and the EUs Administrative Capacity Requirement." *West European Politics* 25 (4):171-190.

Dollar, David, and Jakob Svensson. 2001. "What Explains the Success or Failure of Structural Adjustment Programmes?" *The Economic Journal* 110 (466):894-917.

Dolowitz, David P., and David Marsh. 2000. "Learning from Abroad: The Role of Policy Transfer in Contemporary Policy Making." *Governance* 13 (1):5-24.

Drazen, Allan. 2002. *Conditionality and Ownership in IMF Lending: A Political Economy Approach, IMF Staff Papers*. Washington, D.C.: IMF.

Easterly, William. 2005. "What did structural adjustment adjust? The association of policies and growth with repeated IMF and World Bank adjustment loans." *Journal of Development Economics* 76 (1):1-22.

Ennser-Jedenastik, Laurenz. 2014. "Credibility Versus Control: Agency Independence and Partisan Influence in the Regulatory State." *Comparative Political Studies* 48 (7):823-853.

Ennser-Jedenastik, Laurenz. 2016. "The Politicization of Regulatory Agencies: Between Partisan Influence and Formal Independence." *Journal of Public Administration Research and Theory* 26 (3):507-518.

European Network on Debt and Development. 2006. World Bank and IMF conditionality: a development injustice. Brussels: EURODAD.

European Parliament, and Council of the EU. 2011. Regulation (EU) No 1176/2011 of the European Parliament and of the Council of 16 November 2011 on the prevention and correction of macroeconomic imbalances. Official Journal of the European Union, L306, 23 November.

European Parliament, and Council of the EU. 2013a. Regulation (EU) No 472/2013 of the European Parliament and of the Council of 21 May 2013 on the strengthening of economic and budgetary surveillance of Member States in the euro area experiencing or threatened with serious difficulties with respect to their financial stability. Official Journal of the European Union L140, 27 May.

European Parliament, and Council of the EU. 2013b. Regulation (EU) No 473/2013 of the European Parliament and of the Council of 21 May 2013 on common provisions for monitoring and assessing draft budgetary plans and ensuring the correction of excessive deficit of the Member States in the euro area. Official Journal of the European Union L140, 27 May.

Everson, Michelle. 1995. "Independent agencies: Hierarchy beaters?" *European Law Journal* 1 (2):180-204.

Falkner, Gerda. 2010. "Institutional Performance and Compliance with EU Law: Czech Republic, Hungary, Slovakia and Slovenia." *Journal of Public Policy* 30 (1):101-116.

Falkner, Gerda, Oliver Treib, Elisabeth Holzleithner with Emannuelle Causse, Petra Furthlehner, Marianne Schulze, and Clemens Wiedermann. 2008. *Compliance in the Enlarged European Union: Living Rights or Dead Letters?* Aldershot: Ashgate.

Featherstone, Kevin. 2015. "External conditionality and the debt crisis: the 'Troika' and public administration reform in Greece." *Journal of European Public Policy* 22 (3):295-314.

Flinders, Matthew, and Jim Buller. 2006. "Depoliticisation: Principles, Tactics and Tools." *British Politics* 1 (3):293-318.

Flinders, Matthew, and Matt Wood. 2014. "Depoliticisation, governance and the state." *Policy & Politics* 42 (2):135-149.

Gatsios, Konstantine, and Paul Seabright. 1989. "Regulation in the European Community." *Oxford Review of Economic Policy* 5 (2):37-60.

Gay, Oonagh. 1997. *The Accountability Debate: Next Steps Agencies*. London: House of Commons Library.

Gilardi, Fabrizio. 2010. "Who Learns from What in Policy Diffusion Processes?" *American Journal of Political Science* 54 (3):650-666.

Güven, Ali Burak. 2012. "The Feasibility of IFI-Led Institutional Reform: Four Turkish Experiments Compared." *Development Policy Review* 30 (4):425-449.

Haggard, Stepaen, and Stephen B. Webb. 1994. "Introduction." In *Voting for Reform: Democracy, Political Liberalization and Economic Adjustment*, edited by Stephan Haggard and Stephen B. Webb, 1-36. Oxford: Oxford University Press for the World Bank.

Hall, Peter A. 1989. "Conclusion: the politics of Keynesian ideas." In *The Political Power of Economic Ideas: Keynesianism across Nations*, edited by Peter A. Hall, 361-92. Princeton, N.J.: Princeton University Press.

Haughton, Tim. 2007. "When does the EU make a difference? Conditionality and the accession process in Central and Eastern Europe." *Political Studies Review* 5 (2):233–246.

Hay, Colin. 2007. *Why we hate politics*. Cambridge: Polity.

Hix, Simon, and Klaus H. Goetz. 2000. "Introduction: European integration and national political systems." *West European Politics* 23 (4):1-26.

Hood, Christopher. 1991. "A public management for all seasons?" *Public Administration* 69 (1):3-19.

Huber, John D. 2000. "Delegation to civil servants in parliamentary democracies." *European Journal of Political Research* 37 (3):397-413.

Hughes, James, Gwendolyn Sasse, and Claire Gordon. 2004. "Conditionality and Compliance in the EU's Eastward Enlargement: Regional Policy and the Reform of Sub-national Government." *Journal of Common Market Studies* 42 (3):523-551.

Hughes, James, Gwendolyn Sasse, and Claire Gordon. 2005. *Europeanization and Regionalization in the EU's Enlargement to Central and Eastern Europe: The Myth of Conditionality, One Europe or Several?* Basingstoke: Palgrave.

IMF. 2001. Strengthening Country Ownership of Fund Supported Programs, Prepared by the Policy Development and Review Department. Washington, D.C.: IMF.

IMF. 2012a. 2011 Review of Conditionality - Background Paper 1: Content and Application of Conditionality. Prepared by the Strategy, Policy and Review Department. Washington, D.C.: IMF.

IMF. 2012b. 2011 Review of Conditionality: Overview Paper Prepared by the Strategy, Policy, and Review Department in consultation with other Departments. Washington, D.C.: IMF.

Ivanova, Anna, Wolfgang Mayer, Alex Mourmouras, and George Anayiotos. 2001. *What Determines the Success or Failure of Fund-Supported Programs?* Washington, D.C.: IMF.

Kahn-Nisser, Sara. 2013. "Conditionality, Communication and Compliance: The Effect of Monitoring on Collective Labour Rights in Candidate Countries." *Journal of Common Market Studies* 51 (6):1040-1056.

Killick, Tony. 1997. "Principals, agents and the failings of conditionality." *Journal of International Development* 9 (4):483-495.

Koeberle, Stefan, Harold Bedoya, Peter Silarsky, and Gero Verheyen, eds. 2005. *Conditionality revisited: concepts, experiences, and lessons*. Washington, D.C.: World Bank.

Koeberle, Stefan G. 2003. "Should policy-based lending still involve conditionality?" *World Bank Research Observer* 18 (2):249-273.

Kydland, Finn E., and Edward C. Prescott. 1977. "Rules rather than discretion: the inconsistency of optimal plans." *Journal of Political Economy* 85 (3):473-92.

Maggetti, Martino. 2009. "The role of independent regulatory agencies in policy-making: a comparative analysis." *Journal of European Public Policy* 16 (3):450-470.

Maggetti, Martino. 2010. Legitimacy and Accountability of Independent Regulatory Agencies: A Critical Review. *Living Reviews in Democracy* 2. Accessed 12 February 2018.

Maggetti, Martino, and Yannis Papadopoulos. 2018. "The Principal–Agent Framework and Independent Regulatory Agencies." *Political Studies Review* 16 (3):172-183.

Majone, Giandomenico. 1994. "The rise of the regulatory state in Europe." *West European Politics* 17 (3):77-101.

Majone, Giandomenico. 1996. *Temporal consistency and policy credibility: Why democracies need non-majoritarian institutions*. Florence: European University Institute.

March, James G., and Johan P. Olsen. 1989. *Rediscovering Institutions: The Organizational Basis of Politics*. New York: Free Press.

May, Peter J. 1992. "Policy Learning and Failure." *Journal of Public Policy* 12 (4):331-54.

Meyer-Sahling, Jan-Hinrik. 2004. "Civil service reform in post-communist Europe: the bumpy road to depoliticisation." *West European Politics* 27 (1):71-103.

Milanovic, Branko. 2003. "The Two Faces of Globalization: Against Globalization as We Know It." *World Development* 31 (4):667-683.

Moe, Terry M. 1987. "Interests, Institutions, and Positive Theory: The Politics of the NLRB." *Studies in American Political Development* 2:236-299.

Moe, Terry M. 1990. "Political Institutions: The Neglected Side of the Story." *Journal of Law, Economics, & Organization* 6 (special issue: papers from the Organization of Political Institutions Conference):213-253.

Montinola, Gabriella R. 2007. When Does Aid Conditionality Work? Davis, CA.

Moravcsik, Andrew. 1998. *The Choice for Europe: Social Purpose and State Power from Messina to Maastricht*. Ithaca, NY: Cornell University Press.

Morrissey, Oliver. 2004. "Conditionality and aid effectiveness re-evaluated." *World Economy* 27 (2):153-171.

Morrissey, Oliver. 2005. "Alternatives to conditionality in policy-based lending." In *Conditionality revisited: concepts, experiences, and lessons*, edited by Stefan Koeberle, Harold Bedoya, Peter Silarsky and Gero Verheyen, 237-247. Washington, D.C.: World Bank.

Nelson, Joan M. 1996. "Promoting policy reforms: The twilight of conditionality?" *World Development* 24 (9):1551-1559.

Osborne, David, and Ted Gaebler. 1992. *Reinventing Government: How the Entrepreneurial Spirit is Transforming the Public Sector*. Reading, MA: Addison-Wesley.

Pagoulatos, George. 2012. "The political economy of forced reform and the 2010 Greek economic adjustment programme." In *From stagnation to forced adjustment: reforms in Greece 1974-2010*, edited by Stathis Kalyvas, George Pagoulatos and Haridimos Tsoukas, 247-274. London: Hurst & Co.

Panchamia, Nehal, and Peter Thomas. n.d. *The Next Steps Initiative*. London: Institute for Government.

Paraskevopoulos, Christos J. 2001. *Interpreting Convergence in the European Union: Patterns of Collective Action, Social Learning and Europeanization*. Basingstoke: Palgrave.

Peters, B. Guy, and Jon Pierre, eds. 2004. *Politicization of the Civil Service in Comparative Perspective. The Quest for Control*. London: Routledge.

Pollack, Mark A. 2002. "Learning from the Americanists (again): theory and method in the study of delegation." *West European Politics* 25 (1):200-19.

Rhodes, Rod A. W. 1996. *The New European Agencies - Agencies in British Government: Revolution or Evolution?* Florence: European University Institute.

Rodrik, Dani. 1990. "How should structural adjustment programs be designed?" *World Development* 18 (7):933-947.

Rodrik, Dani. 2016. "The Elusive Promise of Structural Reform." *The Milken Institute Review*, 2nd quarter.

Rose, Richard. 1991. "What is Lesson-Drawing?" *Journal of Public Policy* 11 (1):3-30.

Sabatier, Paul A. 1987. "Knowledge, Policy-Oriented Learning, and Policy Change. An Advocacy Coalition Framework." *Knowledge* 8 (4):649-92.

Schadler, Susan. 2017. "Living with Rules: The IMF's Exceptional Access Framework and the 2010 Stand-By Arrangement with Greece." In *Background Papers for the IMF and the Crises in Greece, Ireland, and Portugal*, edited by Moisés J. Schwartz and Shinji Takagi, 35-61. Washington, D.C.: Independent Evaluation Office of the International Monetary Fund.

Scharpf, Fritz W. 1999. *Governing in Europe: Effective and Democratic?* Oxford: Oxford University Press.

Schimmelfennig, Frank. 2003. *The EU, NATO and the Integration of Europe*. Cambridge: Cambridge University Press.

Schimmelfennig, Frank, Stefan Engert, and Heiko Knobel. 2003. "Costs, Commitment and Compliance: The Impact of EU Democratic Conditionality on Latvia, Slovakia and Turkey." *Journal of Common Market Studies* 41 (3):495-518.

Schimmelfennig, Frank, and Ulrich Sedelmeier, eds. 2005a. *The Europeanization of Central and Eastern Europe. Cornell Studies in Political Economy Series*. Ithaca, NY: Cornell University Press.

Schimmelfennig, Frank, and Ulrich Sedelmeier. 2005b. "Introduction: conceptualizing the Europeanization of Central and Eastern Europe." In *The Europeanization of Central and Eastern Europe*, edited by Frank Schimmelfennig and Ulrich Sedelmeier, 1-28. Ithaca, N.Y.: Cornell University Press.

Schmidt, Manfred G. 1996. "When parties matter: a review of the possibilities and limits of partisan influence on public policy." *European Journal of Political Research* 30 (2):155-83.

Simmons, Beth A., Dobbin, Frank and Garrett, Geoffrey. 2007. "The Global Diffusion of Public Policies: Social Construction, Coercion, Competition or Learning?" *Annual Review of Sociology* 33:449-472.

Sotiropoulos, Dimitris A. 2001. *The Top Levels of the Clientelist State. Organization, Staffing and Politicization of the Higher Grades of the Central Administration in Greece*. Athens: Potamos (in Greek).

Spanou, Calliope. 1996. "Penelope's Suitors: Administrative Modernisation and Party Competition in Greece." *West European Politics* 19 (1):97-124.

Spanou, Calliope. 2016. *Policy conditionality, structural adjustment and the domestic policy system. Conceptual framework and research agenda*. Badia Fiesolana: European University Institute/Robert Schuman Centre for Advanced Studies.

Spraos, John. 1986. *IMF Conditionality: Ineffectual, inefficient, mistargeted, Essays in International Finance no. 166*. Princeton, N.J.: Department of Economics, Princeton University.

Stiles, Kendall W. 1990. "IMF conditionality: coercion or compromise?" *World Development* 18 (7):959-974.

Strøm, Kaare. 2003. "Parliamentary Democracy and Delegation." In *Delegation and Accountability in Parliamentary Democracies*, edited by Kaare Strøm, Wolfgang C. Müller and Torbjörn Bergman. Oxford: Oxford University Press.

Swyngedouw, Erik. 2009. "The Antinomies of the Postpolitical City: In Search of a Democratic Politics of Environmental Production." *International Journal of Urban and Regional Research* 33 (3):601-620.

Thatcher, Mark. 2002. "Delegation to independent regulatory agencies: pressures, functions and contextual mediation." *West European Politics* 25 (1):125-47.

Thatcher, Mark, and Alec Stone Sweet. 2002. "Theory and practice of delegation to non-majoritarian institutions." *West European Politics* 25 (1):1-22.

Thomas, John W., and Merilee S. Grindle. 1990. "After the decision: Implementing policy reforms in developing countries." *World Development* 18 (8):1163-1181.

Tommasi, Mariano, and Andrés Velasco. 1995. Where Are We in the Political Economy of Reform? Los Angeles, CA: UCLA.

Tsebelis, George. 1995. "Decision making in political systems: veto players in presidentialism, parliamentarism, multicameralism and multipartyism." *British Journal of Political Science* 25 (3):289-325.

Tsekos, Theodore N. 2013. "Structural, Functional, and Cultural Aspects of the Greek Public Administration and Their Effects on Public Employees' Collective Action." *Comparative Labor Law & Policy Journal* 34 (2):457-477.

Vita, Viorica. 2017. "Revisiting the Dominant Discourse on Conditionality in the EU: The Case of EU Spending Conditionality." *Cambridge Yearbook of European Legal Studies* 19 (116–143).

Wood, Matt, and Matthew Flinders. 2014. "Rethinking depoliticisation: beyond the governmental." *Policy & Politics* 42 (2):151-170.

World Bank. 2005a. Review of World Bank conditionality. Washington, D.C.: World Bank.

World Bank. 2005b. Review of World Bank conditionality - the theory and practice of conditionality: a literature review. Washington, D.C.: World Bank.

Zahariadis, Nikolaos. 2014. "Powering over Puzzling? Downsizing the Public Sector during the Greek Sovereign Debt Crisis." *Journal of Comparative Policy Analysis: Research and Practice*:1-15. doi: https://doi.org/10.1080/13876988.2013.861971.

Chapter 3
The First MoU: Piecemeal Change and External Assistance in Conditions of Crisis

The Onset of the Crisis

The global economic crisis that started in 2008 was always likely to affect a small country like Greece not only because of the size of the country's debt, but also because its political *élite* was—with some notable exceptions—unwilling to tell voters the truth, let alone take drastic action to address the causes of these problems. The reforms introduced between 1993 and the country's adoption of the euro in 2001 had given way initially to reform fatigue followed, from 2004 onwards, by a return to unsustainable policies such as the vast expansion of public sector employment financed by debt which at that point in time was relatively cheap. Unwillingness and inability to collect public revenues were part and parcel of the problem (see the Introduction). Between 2004 and 2009, 'while output increased in nominal terms by 40%, central government primary expenditures increased by 87% against an increase of only 31% in tax revenues' (Ministry of Finance 2010: 14). After the onset of the global financial crisis in 2008 but nearly a year before the national elections of 2009, the centre-right government of ND had been publicly warned—by no lesser figure than Costas Simitis, the respected former prime minister who led the country into the Eurozone[1]—about the prospect of having to resort to the IMF in the absence of drastic action to redress the country's public finances (Simitis 2008). No meaningful action followed on the part of the government though the country was at least 3 years away from the next general election. Around about the same time, George

[1]In an incident that clearly highlights key traits of Greece's adversarial political culture, upon taking office in spring 2004, the centre-right administration of ND stated to EU institutions that the previous administration had achieved this hugely significant objective by 'cooking the books'. This was not true and hinged on a retrospective change in the way in which the cost of defence procurement is accounted for in public financial accounts (Simitis and Stournaras 2012; Simitis 2014: 3–5). EU institutions accepted both the original and the revised method. The Karamanlis-led administration did this in an attempt to discredit its political opponents and extricate itself from ND's own pre-electoral pledges.

D. Dimitrakopoulos, A. Passas, *The Depoliticisation of Greece's Public Revenue Administration*, https://doi.org/10.1007/978-3-030-23213-9_3

Papandreou, then leader of the main opposition party (PASOK) was warned by Peer Steinbrück, then Finance Minister of Germany and a fellow social democrat, about the magnitude of the task lying ahead (Steinbrück 2010: 121–122). Yet, when Prime Minister Kostas Karamanlis called an early election, Papandreou led a campaign arguing that 'the money is there' and won a robust majority on 4 October 2009. Almost immediately after this election victory, the new government informed European Union (EU) institutions of the real size of Greece's budget deficit which at that point in time was approaching 10% (and rising), far higher than what the previous government had falsely stated to the very same EU institutions (European Commission 2010c). This was a necessary action but also a devastating blow to the Greek political *élite's* credibility in the eyes of the country's EU partners. Greece was quickly frozen out of the global financial markets—including the French and German banks—that had been lending it money irresponsibly. Greece was facing bankruptcy and the Eurozone was on the verge of a major banking and broader economic crisis for which it was institutionally, economically and politically unprepared. As a result, and in the absence of a Eurozone-specific mechanism for crisis management, Greece has had to ask the IMF and the Eurozone's member states to bail it out in spring 2010. In return for an unprecedented credit facility of 110 billion euros aimed at avoiding Greece's sovereign debt default and the attendant Eurozone-wide banking crisis, the Greek government agreed to introduce a series of policy and institutional changes. That was in line with the conditionality model that prevails in IFIs as was the decision to spread payments over time so as to retain control of the programme's implementation. This is demonstrated in Table 3.1.

This was the first of three bailout agreements and was couched in the corresponding (first) Memorandum of Understanding (MoU) (2010a, b).

Table 3.1 Disbursement or authorisation of payments under the first programme (in billion Euros)

Disbursement or authorisation	Date	Euro area member states	IMF	
1	9 May 2010		5.5	
2	18 May 2010	14.5		
3	10 September 2010		2.57	
4	13 September 2010	6.5		
5	17 December 2010		2.5	
6	19 January 2011	6.5		
7	14 March 2011		4.1	
8	16 March 2011	10.9		
9	2 July 2011	12		
10	8 July 2011		3.2	
11	21 October 2011 and 29 November	5.8		
12	5 December 2011		2.2	
	Totals	56.2	20.07	76.27

Source: Compiled by the authors on the basis of information from Bundesministerium der Finanzen (n.d.) supplemented by information from European Commission (2011c), Karkagiannis (2011)

The First MoU and the Reform of the Greek Public Revenue Administration: Timid Ad Hocery in Conditions of Crisis

The first MoU reflected a clear understanding of the direct link[2] between the programme's cornerstone (frontloaded fiscal consolidation) and the government's declared commitment to 'strengthening the fiscal policy framework and fiscal institutions' in a country where efficiency in tax collection 'is low' and the revenue administration is 'weak' (2010a: 3, 6, 1, respectively). Specifically, the prevailing view was that higher taxes and/or deeper spending cuts would be required in the absence of major improvements in tax collection; yet these extra measures risked generating unsustainable macroeconomic and political tensions (IMF 2010b: 17). However, the first MoU did not reflect a clear, system-wide and detailed plan for the reform of Greece's public revenue administration, despite references to the government's determination 'to implement an ambitious program of reforms to modernize the public sector' (2010a: 3). In particular, it did not refer to a reform plan involving increased independence or autonomy vis-à-vis the minister of finance (2010a, b). On the contrary, the prevailing sense is one of ad hoc changes—such as the establishment of a unit that would deal with large taxpayers,[3] the use of quantitative performance indicators, etc. (European Commission 2013: 25)—in a system that was apparently meant to remain part of the hierarchy of the Ministry of Finance.

Specifically, in relation to the public revenue administration, the MoU's authors distinguished between short-term measures and a medium-term strategy. The former entailed a focus on

> safeguarding revenue from the largest taxpayers, stronger enforcement and auditing of high-wealth individuals and self-employed (where risk of evasion is largest) and prosecuting the worst offenders, strengthening enforcement of VAT filing and payment, and collecting on the large stock of tax arrears (2010a: 7).

On the other hand, the medium-term strategy entailed a programme of structural reforms in key areas of tax compliance and administration that included

> developing and maintaining a comprehensive compliance risk management framework (notably preparing a compliance strategy for 2012); developing taxpayer service capacity to support compliance improvement efforts; substantially improving enforcement operations, particularly in audit, using risk-based approaches; and building headquarters strategic management and planning capabilities in tax and customs administration (2010a: 7).

---

[2]Improved tax collection would reduce the macroeconomic and political tensions that would otherwise result from the need for higher tax rates and/or deeper spending cuts.

[3]The IMF had recommended this back in 2005 (in line with a broader international trend) because of the complexity of these taxpayers' tax affairs, their use of services and professionals aiming to minimise their tax bills and the concomitant risks that these affairs entail in terms of tax compliance (with enormous potential for tax revenue losses, as the IMF put it). As a result, it makes sense to establish dedicated organisations aiming 'to optimize the tax authority's ability to closely monitor and control *all* the tax affairs of such taxpayers' (see Perry et al. 2005).

Given the provision (by party political appointees) of false budget figures to EU institutions by the previous administration, but also broader awareness of the Greek state's limited capacities,[4] it is unsurprising that the first MoU also made reference to the creation of institutional capacity—with the provision of technical assistance by the EU and the IMF—in the form of an 'independent fiscal agency attached to parliament' so as to better handle the challenges of making and implementing the state's budget (2010a: 7). This reference was part of an emerging view of at least the EU that Greece's problems directly related to the entire *ensemble* of institutions that manage the country's public finances, namely

(a) the General Accounting Office (GAO - *Γενικό Λογιστήριο του Κράτους*) which is formally responsible (as part of the Ministry of Finance) for drafting and monitoring the budget;
(b) the public revenue administration;
(c) the National Statistical Service (*Εθνική Στατιστική Υπηρεσία*) which was responsible for compiling statistical information that was subsequently submitted to EU institutions, e.g. under EMU's Excessive Deficit Procedure (EDP).

At that point in time, i.e. early on in the handling of the crisis, all three were under the direct control of the minister of finance. Historically, all three were headed by party political appointees but by the beginning of 2010 the latter of the three had been found to have fiddled the figures as a result of 'political interference' (see below).

What accounts for the first MoU's timid and ad hoc strategy? It cannot have been the result of the existence of alternative domestic plans because no[5] such plan existed at the time (interviews, Athens, 2 June 2017 and 9 November 2018). This is so despite the fact that newly elected Prime Minister George Papandreou was a veteran[6] of frontline Greek politics who had campaigned on a platform emphasizing the need to end waste and tax evasion. Timing and the very acute crisis that had engulfed the country by the time of the conclusion of the first MoU help explain this strategy (interviews, Athens, 1 August 2016 and 9 November 2018). As an international official pointed out (interview, Athens, 30 March 2017), the first MoU was drafted in conditions of crisis:

> In that kind of situation I think you cannot come up with a fully-fledged plan except if you have one plan on the shelf which you use for any country, which is not the case. So, the teams come in, they discover a series of issues and then say here is how you can improve by this and that and this is how it went in the first programme. When you come during a crisis, you go for quick wins; you cannot write a long thing. You have to be short and efficient.

[4]For example, at that point in time nobody knew the precise number of Greece's civil servants.

[5]The then ruling PASOK's programme on taxation did not actually propose any structural reforms of the public revenue administration except the establishment of regional centres that would be assessed on the basis of their performance and would be incentivised accordingly (PASOK n.d.).

[6]An iconic example of what Greeks call οικογενειοκρατία (which loosely translates as family rule, i.e. the tradition whereby a handful of very powerful families effectively rule the country) he is the son and grandson of two Prime Ministers. Prior to becoming PM in 2009, he had served as MP uninterruptedly since 1981 and had been a member of every PASOK government since 1985.

However, at least the IMF's team did not start from scratch. It had at its disposal the previous recommendations (Perry et al. 2005) made by the IMF mission to Greece in the mid-2000s. Although these did not relate to the issue of political interference in operational decisions of the public revenue administration, they did include some of the aforementioned actions such as a strategic plan to improve tax compliance, ameliorating enforcement through the use of risk analysis and, of course, building the corresponding capacity at the revenue administration's headquarters.[7]

The fact that—unlike the second and third MoUs (see Chaps. 4 and 5)—the first did not include a great amount of detail on the reform of the public revenue administration and certainly nothing on the issue of depoliticisation means that—in theory—domestic reformers had a degree of leeway. In other words, there was some policy space that domestic reformers could attempt to fill. Indeed, partial reforms were in the making even before the conclusion of the first MoU.

This important work, which was in line with and informed by (Papaconstantinou 2016: 103) the IMF's recommendations of 2005 (Perry et al. 2005), demonstrates the presence of at least some domestic support for reform, including an attempt to consider the idea of an independent revenue administration (see below). Reality, however, was much more complicated, as a series of contradictions demonstrates. Despite the aforementioned pledge to fight waste and tax evasion, Papandreou appointed as Finance Minister and junior Finance Minister two reform-minded politicians who had impeccable technocratic credentials[8] but no frontline ministerial experience.[9] More strikingly, he did not appoint a junior minister in charge of tax collection.[10] Tellingly, despite the prime minister's rhetorical emphasis on ending

[7]There was also some common ground between these proposals and those put forward by the Georgakopoulos commission in 2002 that, unlike the IMF's report of 2005, did highlight the need for 'complete independence of tax inspectors' while they are carrying out their duties (Commission for the reform of the Greek tax system ('Georgakopoulos commission') 2002: e.g. 30–31, 197, 200 and esp. 203).

[8]Minister George Papaconstantinou has a Ph.D. in economics from the LSE and has worked for many years at the OECD. Junior Minister Philippos Sachinids has a Ph.D. in economics from the University of Manchester. Both had served as advisers in former Prime Minister Costas Simitis' office.

[9]In a further contradiction, Papandreou chose as Secretary General for Tax and Customs Dimitris Georgakopoulos, a former MP who (a) had served as junior Finance Minister in the mid-1980s and between 1993 and 1996 but (b) did not see eye to eye with the new Finance Minister (interviews, Athens, 20 July 2016 and 2 June 2017). When Georgakopoulos resigned in March 2011, he was replaced by Ioannis Kapeleris who had hitherto headed the Financial Crime Squad (SDOE), was a member of the then ruling PASOK and had been its candidate in the legislative elections of 2007 (Naftemporiki 2007). Georgakopoulos was not the first top public revenue official to enjoy the confidence of the PM but not the Finance Minister. Spyros Kladas was another example under the Karamanlis-led ND administration of the mid-2000s (Kathimerini 2008).

[10]This may be linked to his willingness to lead a small government, unlike most of his predecessors. However, this did not prevent him from appointing two junior ministers in ministries that did not necessarily need them such as the Ministry of Education and the Ministry of Transport. This means that the then Finance Minister may have missed an opportunity to lobby harder so as to obtain an additional junior post (interview, Athens, 2 June 2017).

waste and tax evasion, and in the absence of a clearly articulated domestic plan for the reform of the public revenue administration (or at least ending political interference in its operational decisions), Papandreou's first Minister of Finance felt he had to follow a much more cautious approach. Indeed, George Papaconstantinou, then Finance Minister, opted for a step-wise process of reform and avoided the path of radical reform involving the creation of a fully fledged independent revenue authority based on the Internal Revenue Service (IRS) of the US federal government. Though he later regretted it, his decision was at least partly influenced by the IMF's warning that such a radical step could dramatically reduce tax revenues in the short term in a country that was at risk of bankruptcy (Papaconstantinou 2016: 102–103). Indeed, IMF staff providing technical assistance before the first MoU warned about the risk of the country's public revenues taking a 2-year hit if the route of immediate depoliticisation were taken (interview, Athens, 2 June 2017). This disruption was certainly not an option at the time of acute crisis for the establishment of a fully fledged independent revenue authority in these conditions was tantamount to rebuilding (instead of repairing) a ship at sea during a storm (interviews, Athens, 1 August 2016 and 9 November 2018).

However, the other relevant point here is that—as he notes—he was not certain that he could convince the rest of the Cabinet about the need for this type of radical reform (Papaconstantinou 2016: 103; also interviews, Athens 2 June 2017 and 5 November 2018). The same applies to two other ideas, namely (a) that staff within the public revenue administration ought to be offered incentives so as to become more effective and (b) heads of tax offices ought to be appointed on the basis of a special procedure that would differ from those applicable elsewhere in the public sector. Both were opposed within the Cabinet because they conflicted with other government objectives[11] or for fear of setting a precedent that other ministers would subsequently seek to use[12] (interviews, Athens, 2 June 2017 and 5 November 2018). As a former senior official noted, the idea of autonomy or independence appeared 'quite alien as a concept' and since ongoing discussions were also touching upon the status of the General Accounting Office (GAO) as well, some officials thought that if both the GAO and the public revenue administration were split from the ministry,

> you might as well abolish the ministry of finance as a whole so that we are the first country without a finance ministry for what will be left for it to do? (interview, Athens, 5 November 2018).

[11]The corresponding minister was trying to close loopholes that had hitherto allowed ministers to bypass ASEP's meritocratic procedures for recruitment and promotion.

[12]The fear of not setting a precedent is understandable given (a) the prevailing political culture that treats the law as a problem that one ought to overcome (see Chap. 1) and (b) the routine expansion of exceptions to serve popularity rather than effectiveness. When it comes to offering monetary incentives to the revenue administration's staff, opponents of this idea could legitimately argue that such incentives existed in the past (officials of the Ministry of Finance were the best paid within government) but this did not prevent the onset of corruption.

This shows that—at that point in time—the second model (social learning) did not apply specifically in relation to the core issue of the status of the public revenue administration because of the absence of genuine programme ownership *across* the government. The same can be argued in relation to the third model (lesson-drawing) since only the Finance Minister appeared to link the status of the public revenue administration with Greece's problems with tax collection.

The fact that no progress was made in relation to the institutional status of the country's public revenue administration, does not mean that (a) there was no need for reform or, indeed, (b) the depoliticisation of key segments of the public sector more broadly was not on the table—two points that are intimately linked to each other. Although he knew there was no political support for his view within the government, Finance Minister George Papaconstantinou placed the issue of semi-autonomy on the table even before the conclusion of the first bailout agreement and attendant MoU partly because of frustration caused by the administration's inability to provide reliable information necessary for effective policy making,[13] the well-known issue of corruption and other major problems (interview, 2 June 2017, Athens). This stance was consistent with (a) his own status (as he was not a member of parliament); (b) awareness of what was likely to be lying ahead for the entire country, i.e. an adjustment programme that was bound to involve tax rises in a country with low tax compliance; and (c) the view that crises can open up a window of opportunity for reform. Placing the public revenue administration at arm's length from the government of the day could, in theory, protect tax collection from political interference just at the time when pressure for such interference was likely to rise significantly alongside the need for more effective tax collection. By the same token having a Minister of Finance who did not have to defend a parliamentary seat was also likely to be an advantage during the implementation of the adjustment programme that was bound to entail unpopular measures such as tax rises and cuts in public expenditure. Indeed, all of Papaconstantinou's successors (bar one) who served in elected governments between the 2009 and January 2015 general elections

[13]One measure that was popular with officials in the public revenue administration's HQ is the nominal value of fines imposed for alleged breaches of tax law. The figure was often impressive and made the headlines but reality was quite different since only a tiny percentage of these sums were subsequently collected. Indeed, these sums were often not collectable since they were imposed shortly before the deadline imposed by the statute of limitations and often very long after the corresponding firm had ceased trading. This was one reason why past administrations had made very extensive use of tax amnesties (see the Introduction) which allowed tax payers facing fines to pay a fraction of the fine which was often much more attractive (for those who wanted to remain in this side of legality) than the other option which was to fight the case through Greece's very slow justice system. The trouble was that many of these figures were hard to calculate with the degree of reasonable accuracy that rational policy making requires.

were exactly in the same position.[14] Having unelected individuals in key parts of the state apparatus could be beneficial for the government of the day by distancing it from unpopular decisions, especially in a country where ministers rarely resign (interview, Athens, 3 April 2017).

The point about information and the administration's inability to provide it to ministers goes a lot deeper in terms of relevance for the management of Greece's public finances. Upon taking office, Papaconstantinou discovered that the senior officials who had a direct role in making and implementing the annual budget (i.e. officials of the General Accounting Office, the public revenue administration and the Bank of Greece) had never actually sat around the same table for a meeting. Indeed, as he pointedly indicates, the Ministry of Finance had no institutionalised procedure in place that would require them to do so in the process of making the annual budget (Papaconstantinou 2016: 34). This reflects the pre-crisis pattern of highly problematic public budgeting (for detailed accounts of its problems see Rapanos 2007; Hawkesworth et al. 2008) and lax public management more broadly (see the Introduction) and has directly informed the first MoU which stipulated that the government would carry out a reform of the GAO, including the following elements:

- [p]rovision of safeguards for GAO staff against political interference, and personal accountability in the provision of reliable data
- [s]trengthen the institutional mechanisms for providing reliable and plausible official budgetary forecasts that take into account available recent execution developments and trends; to this end, the official macroeconomic forecasts should be reviewed by external experts (2010a: 6)

So, due to weak domestic support the issue of depoliticisation was not on the formal reform agenda at that point in direct relation to the public revenue administration. On the contrary, it did appear on the formal reform agenda in relation to the country's formal statistics and in particular Greece's National Statistical Service. Even prior to the conclusion of the first MoU acting in an effort to restore some credibility and in light of (a) the aforementioned provision of false information to EU institutions under the previous administration and (b) pressure from the very same EU institutions, the Papandreou administration enacted a law that turned the country's statistics agency into a fully fledged independent statistical authority (ELSTAT) operating at arm's length from the government of the day (2010). This happened in March 2010, i.e. 2 months prior to the conclusion of the first MoU. In August 2010 Andreas Georgiou—an economist and career IMF official—took over

[14]This point refers to 'normal' governments stemming from legislative elections, not the one that was headed by the former ECB Vice President Loukas Papademos. Professors Yiannis Stournaras and Ghikas Hardouvelis are the most emblematic examples. Both served under Prime Minister Antonis Samaras in ND-PASOK governments during the crisis. Evangelos Venizelos is the exception for he was a member of parliament while he was also the country's Minister of Finance in the last administration that was led by George Papandreou.

as head of ELSTAT after an open competition.[15] Within a year, he found himself under investigation by public prosecutors after being accused [by both former officials of the national statistics agency and their allies in the country's political *élite*, such as the then leader of the opposition (Eleftherotypia 2010; Samaras 2010)] of artificially inflating the country's deficit figures thus effectively facilitating the imposition of austerity measures, although (a) he took over 5 months *after* the conclusion of the first bailout agreement and (b) EUROSTAT formally endorsed Greece's formal public finance statistics by lifting in November 2010 all reservations it had hitherto placed on them.[16] This was just the beginning of a lengthy saga (for a complete chronology, see International Statistical Institute 2018) that has had an enduring impact on the process of depoliticisation under the first, second and third MoUs (interviews, Athens, 2 June and 3 April 2017; see also Chaps. 4 and 5) but at that point in time it amplified the lack of trust and highlighted both the need to place the issue of depoliticisation far higher in the formal reform agenda, as well as the strength of domestic opposition to reform.

Despite this broader resistance to radical change, at that point in time a credible and well-thought out reform plan instigated by the Greek government could, in principle, have at least been tolerated by the country's partners as long as it served the common objective—clearly spelled out in the bailout agreement—which was to drastically improve tax collection and combat tax evasion. The existence of this scope for domestic initiatives (and the presence of the corresponding political will on the part of the then leadership of the Ministry of Finance) is demonstrated by three important decisions of the government of the day. The first was the creation of the country's first ever medium-term action plan aiming to combat tax evasion. This is linked to the fact that the initial anti-tax evasion measures implemented in the course of 2010 (i.e. *prior* to the creation of the aforementioned medium-term plan) were not sufficiently successful 'and need[ed] considerable strengthening' (European Commission 2011b: 19). Although many governments had tried to make political capital by denouncing tax evasion or promising to fight against it, the first actual operational plan was adopted as late as March 2011, i.e. 3 years into the crisis (2011a). The same piece of legislation created an Internal Affairs Department inside the Ministry of Finance, reporting directly to the minister. The anti-evasion operational plan covered

---

[15]Until then the heads of that agency were party political appointees, usually hand-picked by the Finance Minister. During that period the country's public finances were under-reported to the EU, as a European Commission report of January 2010 found (Schmidt 2016; Harford 2013). As the Commission pointed out, '[t]hese most recent revisions are an illustration of the lack of quality of the Greek fiscal statistics (and of macroeconomic statistics in general) and show that the progress in the compilation of fiscal statistics in Greece, and the intense scrutiny of the Greek fiscal data by Eurostat since 2004 (including 10 EDP visits and 5 reservations on the notified data), have not sufficed to bring the quality of Greek fiscal data to the level reached by other EU Member States' (European Commission 2010c: 3).

[16]For an analysis as to how he is—according to those who accuse him—supposed to have inflated the figures so as to justify Greece's recourse to external aid and why these accusations are wrong see (Vatikiotis 2018; Walker 2017, respectively). The international community of statisticians has vehemently defended Georgiou (Bodin 2018: 25; Lemoine 2018: 10) as has he (Georgiou 2019).

the 3 years through to 2013 and included quantitative performance indicators aiming to improve transparency and accountability. In addition to the commitments undertaken by the Greek government under the first MoU, it involved the creation of a ministerial committee for the fight against tax evasion.[17] The third and final point which demonstrates that there was scope for domestic initiatives (and reform-minded politicians at the helm of the Ministry of Finance) prior to the conclusion of the first MoU was the use of modern technology and cross-checking methods to uncover pockets of tax evasion. One example[18] is the use of satellite images by tax inspectors to ascertain whether the number of declared private swimming pools was accurate. They discovered that only 324 such pools out of a total of 16,974 had actually been declared (Daley 2010).

Under the impulse of the IMF, the EU and the reform-minded leadership of the Ministry of Finance, five working groups were established to deal with specific sets of issues [on the basis of expert technical assistance (IMF 2010a: 7)] with the aim to increase the effectiveness of the public revenue administration, namely speeding up the implementation of new tax legislation; increasing the collection of tax arrears; reorganising the public revenue administration's unit dedicated to large taxpayers; strengthening the tax audit of high-wealth and high-income individuals and, finally, improving taxpayer services and strengthening filing and payment controls.[19] In the eyes of the IMF this was meant to be the basis of a medium-term anti-tax evasion and compliance agenda (IMF 2010a: 7) but at that point in time it was not system-wide and did not touch upon the issue of depoliticisation.

In a further sign of the centrality of tax collection for the adjustment programme and the priority attached to it, the government committed to cross-checking tax information with data on actual wealth and spending habits (Ministry of Finance and Bank of Greece 2010, para. 7). The five working groups were placed under the leadership of a Bank of Greece official who had been seconded to the Finance Minister's office (interview, Athens, 2 June 2017). The progress that followed was acknowledged by the European Commission in its first review—and subsequent reports (European Commission 2010b: 68)—of the programme although these reforms had not yet produced tangible results in terms of revenue (European Commission 2010a: 7, 45). However, by the end of 2011 they were deemed to have successfully completed their tasks and this is why they were integrated in the structure of the Ministry of Finance (interview, Athens, 9 November 2018).

---

[17]Since tax evasion relates to various parts of the government apparatus (e.g. justice and civil service), the plan's implementation was going to be monitored on a monthly basis by a separate committee (inside the Ministry of Finance) composed of senior officials from the relevant ministerial departments.

[18]Another example is the use of clients' lists from luxury car dealerships to identify the real owners of luxury cars who declare them to be company cars (Daley 2010).

[19]For example, as late as the end of 2010 the Greek public revenue administration was collecting information on taxpayers (such as payments and declarations) but data gathering was ad hoc without a central unit with dedicated staff for monitoring and compliance (IMF 2010b, Table 13).

The ad hoc nature of the measures that were gradually being put in place was noted by the European Commission in the same report that also underlined the need for a medium-term structural reform programme to modernise the Greek public revenue administration (see also European Commission 2011b, Table 2). The programme would include, inter alia, the introduction 'of proven strategic and operational management practices and streamlining of the organisational structure' (European Commission 2010a: 29). A key reason why ad hocery was beginning to show its limitations was the gradual realisation of the multifaceted nature of the Greek revenue administration's problems. For example, as early as December 2010 IMF staff were reporting that core revenue administration functions were stifled by various barriers (e.g. the lack of access to key information needed for tax audits) while the management of human resources was not sufficiently flexible and that included 'rarely used and lengthy dismissal procedures' (IMF 2010b: 10–11).

As time went by, revisions of the first MoU added further details to it as a result of the realisation on the part of the IMF and the EU that setting targets—after the initial period where the overwhelming emphasis was on deficit reduction—was not producing the desired results; they consequently had to deal with institutional mechanisms too (interviews, Athens, 2 June 2017 and 5 November 2018). The fourth revision of the first MoU (July 2011) added further details in relation to the reform of the public revenue administration by touching upon the thorny issue of personnel. The government undertook to reassess tax auditors' qualifications and hire new ones by the end of September 2011 (Ministry of Finance and Bank of Greece 2011b: 6). This was linked to a broader (as opposed to a public revenue-specific) attempt to begin to address some of the entire public administration's significant weaknesses in a country where at the onset of the crisis even ministers did not know how many individuals were on the government's payroll. Moreover, agreement was reached to merge or close 200 (of the nearly 300[20]) tax offices (DOYs—*Δημόσια Οικονομική Υπηρεσία*) around the country for they had been identified as 'uneconomic and inefficient' (Ministry of Finance and Bank of Greece 2011b: 7). Doing so within 6 months (i.e. by the end of 2011), which was the revised MoU's objective, was unrealistic not only because domestic reformers would need to spend considerable political capital,[21] but also because—as the country's partners quickly realised—the requisite IT infrastructure was not put in place quickly enough (see below). Nevertheless, this reform was worth pursuing considering that—according to an

[20]Australia has a total of 60 such offices.

[21]This is so because all local MPs in constituencies that stood to lose 'their' tax office would protest against such closures even though, as was the case throughout Greece, this closure would not lead to job losses for tax officials. The protests were mainly based on the fact that these branches' well-paid staff also supported the local economy (e.g. by renting or buying property, spending cash locally, etc.) but the most prominently used argument would be the need for local taxpayers to have to travel further afield to manage their tax affairs. There is some value to the latter argument in a country with literally thousands of small islands and villages. On the other hand, during the pre-crisis period when the head of the local tax office could exercise her discretion, chances were that this would also happen in cases involving members of their own family (interview, Athens, 9 November 2018).

independent study commissioned when George Papaconstantinou was Minister of Finance—less than 20 tax offices yielded approximately 90% of the country's public revenue (interview, Athens, 2 June 2017). Reducing the number of tax offices without reducing the total number of staff also spoke to two other parts of the emerging reform agenda, namely the fight against corruption and the more rational deployment of existing human resources. Reducing the number of tax offices coupled with the increasing use of IT means that fewer taxpayers would need or be able to come into direct contact with tax inspectors and this would (a) reduce opportunities for corruption and (b) free up tax inspectors so that they could then be deployed elsewhere, e.g. checking the content of tax returns as opposed to inputting data from them into the IT system. The scale of this task is demonstrated by the fact that only 10–15% of each DOY's staff was assigned to inspection duties (interview, Athens, 3 April 2017) though this is not only a matter of allocation of resources but also one that relates to the revenue administration's poor skills base.[22] The aforementioned reform also went against established practice which staff union officials ascribed to ministerial decisions.[23] Nevertheless, the process of merging tax offices commenced in September 2011 with the closure of the first 11 provincial offices (Minister of Finance 2011b). This was part of an effort to rationalise the deployment of staff and to concentrate work on areas that were likely to yield better results as demonstrated also by the establishment of a new unit dealing with large companies, in line with the MoU's provisions (Minister of Finance 2011a).

The fifth and final revision of the first MoU further expanded the reform agenda in relation to Greece's public revenue administration (Ministry of Finance and Bank of Greece 2011a: 8–9). The Greek government undertook to introduce performance-based contracts for auditors,[24] replace those who do not meet their targets, recruit new ones and reassess existing auditors' qualifications. It also reaffirmed its commitment to the anti-tax evasion targets of the operational plan enacted a year earlier. This became a 'structural benchmark' for the programme.[25] Predictably, only 30 (instead of 200) tax offices were closed or merged and their key functions consolidated in larger offices within 6 months due to the fact that the requisite IT support could not be

[22]This problem appears in other parts of the Ministry of Finance. For example, at the onset of the crisis the main task of the vast majority of staff at its Secretariat General for IT (GGPS) was to manually input information from taxpayers' tax returns into the ministry's IT system (interview, Athens, 5 November 2018). This is why the closure and merger of tax offices and the concomitant use of IT can help increase effectiveness by reducing the need or opportunity for person-to-person contact between the revenue administration's officials and the taxpayer.

[23]As one of them said on record, 'The orders from above were to do everyday tax processing [. . .]. We were busy going over forms, checking on those who pay taxes, not those who didn't'. (Daley 2010).

[24]This idea was mentioned in the then ruling party's electoral programme in relation to how the heads of the (proposed) regional offices should be incentivized and held to account by the ministry's HQ (PASOK n.d.).

[25]In the IMF's terminology this denotes '(often non-quantifiable) reform measures that are critical to achieve program goals and are intended as markers to assess program implementation during a review' (IMF 2018).

put in place and, as a result, the target was rolled over to the following year (Ministry of Finance and Bank of Greece 2011a: 9, 45; IMF 2011a: 18).

Nevertheless, a year later the IMF noted that there was still considerable work that needed to be done to improve the country's revenue administration and public financial management. IMF staff were 'concerned about the shallow support shown for elements of these reforms during parliamentary debate'. As if they were determined to prove this point, a month later the government changed the system for the appointment of heads of units, deputy directors and directors in the Ministry of Finance to one that required only the minister's decision by derogation from hitherto applicable procedures (Hellenic Parliament 2011, art. 55, para. 21). The staff union denounced this development (interview, Athens, 13 February 2017; see also POE-DOY 2011) but the key point was that—as this was one of the first decisions made by the new Minister of Finance Evangelos Venizelos (Hadjinikolaou 2011)—it highlighted the prevailing intention to retain direct control over the operation of the public revenue administration and demonstrated that Venizelos—a seasoned MP and government minister[26]—could not be counted amongst the most ardent supporters of domestic reform. Indeed, his appointment was the result of the fact that as domestic opposition to the adjustment programme was growing stronger and louder by the day, Greece's single-party (PASOK) government was rapidly losing support, even from within the ruling party's ranks. As a consequence, Prime Minister George Papandreou felt the need to replace reform-minded George Papaconstantinou in the summer of 2011.

The aforementioned report by the IMF also pointedly noted that 'It is imperative for the government to develop broader support for these key reforms, not least through careful public explanation of their necessity' (IMF 2011b: 32). This task was rendered much more difficult—even if such explanation were on offer—in the febrile atmosphere generated by the onset of the crisis and the implementation of the adjustment programme. It was even more difficult in a country where what passes for a debate between politicians is mainly the exchange of slogans and insults, rather than the reasoned discussion of alternative proposals (see the Introduction). If it is acceptable to govern without having fully worked-out reform plans for the country's major problems—as is the norm in Greece—one cannot expect the quality of the public debate to be better than that. In essence, the aforementioned argument made by IMF staff relates to programme ownership, which is at the heart of the second model (social learning). A key minister's support was never going to be sufficient, nor does it amount to genuine programme ownership, especially if one takes into account the passivity of or even active resistance emanating from the civil service (Weinzierl 2015: 451). In a similar way, we argue that the third model (lesson-drawing) did not apply at that point in time because its starting point is a domestic disequilibrium where the domestic balance of forces prefers a departure from the status quo. No wonder then that in his annual report the governor of Greece's central bank noted that, in spite of the major reforms announced in relation to the operation

[26]He is also a lawyer, like a plurality of his colleagues in Parliament (Kountouri 2018: 570).

of the public sector, no real progress had materialised in the segments that generated the deficit—such as the public administration, local administration and the plethora of institutions and bodies that are controlled by the state, including the public revenue administration (Bank of Greece 2011: 23). The following year's report indicated that improving the public revenue administration and combating tax evasion remained key targets of the programme, pointedly noting that (after 2 years of severe austerity measures) the enhancement of the country's public finance institutions was a condition for the sustainable improvements in tax collection (Bank of Greece 2012: 131–132). By the end of 2011, the reforms were beginning to show some signs of success (e.g. tax debt collection targets had been exceeded) though the revenue administration was not meeting other targets (such as those that related to audits of large taxpayers and high-wealth individuals) (IMF 2011a: 8) and the VAT gap was estimated to be the second highest in the EU in 2012 (CASE and IEB 2018: 80). Moreover, Professor Diomidis Spinellis' resignation from a very sensitive top post in the Ministry of Finance in October 2011 demonstrated that the country's ruling *élite* was still finding it difficult to act entirely as if improving tax collection were of the utmost importance, or at least there were pockets of resistance in its midst.[27]

The whole issue was not only down to the absence of a domestic coalition supportive of reforms. It was also linked to the country's 'significant administrative capacity constraints' (IMF 2011b: 29). This is a key reason—alongside the increasing complexity of the adjustment programmes over time (see Chaps. 4 and 5) and the extremely intrusive nature of the IMF and the EU's inspection missions to Athens which is part and parcel of the conditionality model—why alongside the 'stick' (i.e. linking prior actions to the disbursement of funds), a significant programme of technical assistance was also put in place by each of the aforementioned organisations. While this is a routine feature of the IMF's practice of conditionality and—as

[27]Professor Diomidis Spinellis, a computer scientist and a non-party political appointee was head of the ministry's Secretariat General for Information Systems (GGPS) since late 2009. His appointment is perhaps the most emblematic example of the transparency-promoting initiative undertaken by George Papandreou's administration whereby top public posts were advertised (and in some cases filled) openly, as opposed to being reserved for party members. He resigned in October 2011 officially citing personal reasons but press reports on subsequent judicial inquiries linked his resignation to the fight against tax evasion and the illicit trade in fuel. Specifically, after having introduced a series of IT systems aiming to boost tax collection—including the means to cross-check information that was hitherto available in IT systems that did not communicate with each other—he resigned after Ioannis Kapeleris (the then head of the public revenue administration) decided to postpone the collection of taxes worth approximately 15 million euros due on fuel trade, pending a reform that was expected to make the applicable legislation less stringent. Kapeleris effectively told public prosecutors that all he did was to postpone (rather than forego) the collection of this sum partly so as to avoid having to close down 3500 petrol stations across the country which is what the hitherto applicable legislation would entail (Karamanoli 2011a, b, c; Nikas 2011). This case brings together several of the key features of the Greek public revenue system and the broader public sector including strict legislation entailing severe penalties, the involvement of party political appointees in (non-)implementation, the retrospective change of the law once implementation has commenced, etc.

indicated above—started even before the conclusion of the first bailout agreement, in the case of the European Commission a whole new structure (Task Force for Greece) was established specifically for Greece in July 2011.[28] Indeed, by the end of the first MoU's implementation period, European Commission officials were aware that the magnitude of the reforms that needed to be prepared, implemented and followed up 'was continuously testing the capacity limits of the Greek administration' (European Commission 2011a: 4). Given that the adjustment programme covered several policy sectors, the European Commission created the Task Force for Greece (headed by Horst Reichenbach and Georgette Lalis, respectively a German seasoned Commission official and one of the most distinguished Greek officials of the same institution) in an effort to co-ordinate the technical assistance that the EU provided to the crisis-hit country. This assistance covered projects relating to statistics (led by EUROSTAT), the absorption of structural funds (led by the Commission and the European Investment Bank) as well as the management of public finances. The next section presents the technical assistance programme in relation to the reform of Greece's public revenue administration.

The Provision of Technical Assistance

The major limitations of Greece's central administration, especially in conditions of acute crisis, were laid bare in the course of the initial stages of crisis management. The very intrusive nature of the conditionality apparatus—especially the regular visits by IMF and EU staff to Athens but also the myriad of legislative initiatives (e.g. to give a legal grounding to pension cuts and tax increases) and other requisite measures meant that there was very little else that central government officials could do during the initial stages of the crisis management process. The problem was further exacerbated by the gradual broadening of the first MoU's scope.[29] At the same time though, many of the reforms and especially those that related to the Athenian bureaucracy, needed not only time but also training and support so as to bed in and become part and parcel of the administration's daily routines. The Ministry of Finance had already been receiving technical assistance from the IMF on issues of budgeting, tax policy and revenue administration where the IMF's expertise and experience was considered to be superior but the European

[28]It reported directly to the President of the Commission and the Commissioner for Economic and Monetary Affairs. Unlike the rather costly technical assistance offered by the IMF, EU-provided technical assistance was free of charge to the Greek government (interview, Athens, 3 April 2017). In 2015 it was replaced by the Commission's Structural Reform Support Service (SRSS) that is available to several other EU member states. The cost of the assistance provided by individual European states at the initial stage was covered by these countries (Weinzierl 2015: 450).

[29]The gradual expansion of the scope of the first MoU was not limited to issues that related to the public revenue administration. As Spanou notes, its third and fourth reviews extended it to education, the judiciary and governance issues too (Spanou 2018: 7).

Commission too became active in the latter two aspects of the programme. The Task Force was also empowered to recommend measures not only based on internal expertise but also drawing on the resources and expertise of several other European states (including non-members of the EU)[30] and international organisations (such as the OECD, ILO, UNECE) with a view to rapidly deploying projects that could help boost growth and enhance the country's administrative capacity so as to then be better able to implement the adjustment programme—with tax collection and administrative reform being amongst the priorities of the Task Force (European Commission 2011a: 43). This assistance was furnished upon request from the Greek authorities. The Task Force comprised about 30 staff and co-ordinated its work with the IMF, including in relation to the public revenue administration and public budgeting (IMF 2011a: 30). This work involved a major programme of training tax inspectors and other actions [such as attending crash courses at Harvard (interview, Athens, 2 August 2017)] that for the 2011–2013 period absorbed approximately 5 million euros (European Court of Auditors 2015, chart 4).

To conclude, at the end of 2011, one could speak of a reform programme (for one emerged incrementally during the process of implementing the first MoU). It involved some far-reaching reforms (such as focusing the organisation of the revenue administration more along functional as opposed to tax-specific lines[31]) though it (a) did not seek to address the issue of political interference in operational decisions nor (b) was it purely or mainly based on domestic reform-minded politicians. Indeed, they remained in a minority. As a consequence, this indicates the absence of programme ownership across government—a point also noted by the IMF in its ex-post review of the programme (IMF 2013: 40)—and this means that the second model (social learning) was not applicable at that point in time. The same can be said about the third model (lesson-drawing) since the domestic balance of forces did not favour a radical departure from the status quo. However, the programme of technical assistance can in theory be said to have opened the possibility of generating the expectation that these two models could apply in the next stages of the adjustment programme.

References

2010a. Memorandum of Economic and Financial Policies, 3 May.
2010b. Memorandum of Understanding on Specific Economic Policy Conditionality, 3 May.

[30]Within a year, these were 19 in number (European Commission 2012). For example, France took the lead in relation to the country's central government and Germany in relation to local government (Spanou 2018: 19).

[31]The former places its main emphasis on the function that ought to be performed (e.g. monitoring the filing of tax returns or the payment of taxes due or providing information to taxpayers) while the latter focuses on specific taxes (such as capital tax and income tax). Greece's pre-crisis public revenue administration was based on a combination of the two but with the balance tilting towards the latter model (Nanopoulos 2010: 23).

Bank of Greece. 2011. The Governor's report for 2010. Athens: Bank of Greece (in Greek).
Bank of Greece. 2012. The Governor's report for 2011. Athens: Bank of Greece (in Greek).
Bodin, Jean-Louis. 2018. "Andreas Georgiou, un feuilleton juridique sans précédent." *Statistique et société* 6 (2):21-25.
Bundesministerium der Finanzen. n.d. "Chronologie der Stabilisierung der Wirtschafts- und Währungsunion." accessed 15 February 2019. http://tinyurl.com/y6duuy3u.
CASE and IEB. 2018. Study and Reports on the VAT Gap in the EU-28 Member States: 2018 Final Report, TAXUD/2015/CC/131. Warsaw.
Commission for the reform of the Greek tax system ('Georgakopoulos commission'). 2002. Report. Athens (in Greek).
Daley, Suzanne. 2010. "Greek Wealth Is Everywhere but Tax Forms." *The New York Times*, 1 May, Europe. Accessed 1 November 2018. http://www.nytimes.com/2010/05/02/world/europe/02evasion.html?pagewanted=all.
Eleftherotypia. 2010. "Ant. Samaras: PASOK has 'inflated' the deficit." 1 February (in Greek). Accessed 26 December 2018. http://www.enet.gr/?i=news.el.politikh&id=127601.
European Commission. 2010a. The Economic Adjustment Programme for Greece. First review – summer 2010. Directorate-General for Economic and Financial Affairs. Brussels.
European Commission. 2010b. The Economic Adjustment Programme for Greece. Second review – autumn. Directorate-General for Economic and Financial Affairs. Brussels.
European Commission. 2010c. Report on Greek government deficit and debt statistics, COM(2010) 1 final. Brussels: European Commission.
European Commission. 2011a. The Economic Adjustment Programme for Greece. Fifth review. Directorate-General for Economic and Financial Affairs. Brussels.
European Commission. 2011b. The Economic Adjustment Programme for Greece. Third review. Directorate-General for Economic and Financial Affairs. Brussels.
European Commission. 2011c. Statement by the European Commission, the ECB and IMF on the Fifth Review Mission to Greece, MEMO/11/684. Brussels.
European Commission. 2012. One year of Task Force for Greece. Press release, 15 October. Brussels: European Commission.
European Commission. 2013. The Second Economic Adjustment Programme for Greece. Second Review – May 2013. Directorate-General for Economic and Financial Affairs. Brussels.
European Court of Auditors. 2015. More attention to results needed to improve the delivery of technical assistance to Greece. Special report no.19/2015. Luxembourg: European Court of Auditors.
Georgiou, Andreas. 2019. Sisyphus retold by Kafka. Interview to Rand Richards Cooper. *Amherst Magazine*, Winter, 5 December 2018.
Hadjinikolaou, Prokopis. 2011. "Refoundation of the tax collection mechanism." *Kathimerini*, 30 July (in Greek). http://www.kathimerini.gr/433309/article/oikonomia/ellhnikh-oikonomia/anasystash-foroeispraktikoy-mhxanismoy.
Harford, Tim. 2013. "Lies, damned lies and Greek statistics." *Financial Times*, 25 January. Accessed 26 January. https://www.ft.com/content/fc5e295a-663b-11e2-b967-00144feab49a.
Hawkesworth, Ian, Daniel Bergvall, Richard Emery, and Joachim Wehner. 2008. "Budgeting in Greece." *OECD Journal on Budgeting* 8 (3):1-50.
Hellenic Parliament. 2011. Law 4002/2011: amendment of the public pension legislation; provisions on growth and public finances; issues that relate to the ministries of Finance, Culture and Tourism, Employment and Social Security. Government Gazette A180, 22 August (in Greek).
IMF. 2010a. Greece: First Review Under the Stand-By Arrangement. IMF Country Report No. 10/286. September. Washington, D.C.: IMF.
IMF. 2010b. Greece: Second Review Under the Stand-By Arrangement. IMF Country Report No. 10/372. December. Washington, D.C.: IMF.
IMF. 2011a. Greece: Fifth Review Under the Stand-By Arrangement. IMF Country Report No. 11/351. January. Washington, D.C.: IMF.

IMF. 2011b. Greece: Fourth Review Under the Stand-By Arrangement and Request for Modification and Waiver of Applicability of Performance Criteria. IMF Country Report No. 11/175. July. Washington, D.C.: IMF.

IMF. 2013. Greece: Ex Post Evaluation of Exceptional Access under the 2010 Stand-By Arrangement Washington, D.C.: IMF.

IMF. 2018. IMF conditionality factsheet. Washington D.C.: IMF.

International Statistical Institute. 2018. Court proceedings against Andreas Georgiou, former President of ELSTAT (the Hellenic Statistical Authority).

Karamanoli, Eva. 2011a. "I. Kapaleris to face financial crime prosecutors." *Kathimerini*, 23 November (in Greek). Accessed 25 November 2016. http://www.kathimerini.gr/443586/article/epikairothta/ellada/ston-oikonomiko-eisaggelea-o-iw-kapelerhs.

Karamanoli, Eva. 2011b. "Spinellis' resignation due to other reasons." *Kathimerini*, 4 November (in Greek). Accessed 5 November 2016. http://www.kathimerini.gr/441610/article/epikairothta/ellada/alloi-oi-logoi-paraithshs-spinellh.

Karamanoli, Eva. 2011c. "What Kapeleris told prosecutors in relation to the fines and Spinellis' resignation." *Kathimerini*, 27 November (in Greek). Accessed 25 November 2016. http://www.kathimerini.gr/444049/article/oikonomia/ellhnikh-oikonomia/ti-kate8ese-o-kapelerhs-gia-ta-prostima-kai-thn-paraithsh-spinellh.

Karkagiannis, Kostas. 2011. "Disbursement of the fifth tranche approved." *Kathimerini*, 5 July (in Greek). http://www.kathimerini.gr/430979/article/oikonomia/ellhnikh-oikonomia/egkri8hke-h-5h-dosh-met-empodiwn-to-neo-paketo-xrhmatodothshs.

Kathimerini. 2008. "Maximou signals support for Kladas." 17 April (in Greek), Politics. http://www.kathimerini.gr/319652/article/epikairothta/politikh/mhnyma-sthri3hs-klada-apo-to-ma3imoy.

Kountouri, Fani. 2018. "Patterns of renewal and continuity in parliamentary elites. The Greek MPs from 1996 to 2015." *Journal of Legislative Studies* 24 (4):568-586.

Lemoine, Benjamin. 2018. "Démocratie des "faits" ou démocratie défaite? Politique et statistique pendant la crise grecque." *Statistique et société* 6 (2):9-19.

Minister of Finance. 2011a. Ministerial decision on the commencement of operation of the Tax Revenue Office for Large Companies, Δ6Α 1133675 ΕΞ2011, 23 September. Athens (in Greek).

Minister of Finance. 2011b. Ministerial decision on the suspension of operation of some tax offices, Δ6Α 1131253 ΕΞ2011, 20 September. Athens (in Greek).

Ministry of Finance. 2010. Update of the Hellenic Stability and Growth Programme including an updated Reform Programme. Ref. Ares(2010)23198 - 15/01/2010. Athens: Ministry of Finance.

Ministry of Finance and Bank of Greece. 2010. First update of the Memorandum of Understanding, 6 August. Athens.

Ministry of Finance and Bank of Greece. 2011a. Fifth update of the Memorandum of Understanding, 30 November.

Ministry of Finance and Bank of Greece. 2011b. Fourth update of the Memorandum of Understanding, 2 July. Athens.

Naftemporiki. 2007. "PASOK's list of candidates for the general election of 16 September 2007." 19 August (in Greek). https://www.naftemporiki.gr/story/165129/ta-psifodeltia-tou-pasok-gia-tis-ethnikes-ekloges-tis-16is-septembriou-2007.

Nanopoulos, Antonis. 2010. *The organisational structure of tax administration - the Hellenic reality*. Athens: A. A. Livanis (in Greek).

Nikas, Sotiris. 2011. "Fuel smugglers to see fines frozen." *Kathimerini*, 18 October, Greece. http://www.kathimerini.gr/440321/article/epikairothta/ellada/pagwnoyn-ta-prostima-se-la8remporoys-kaysimwn.

Papaconstantinou, George. 2016. *Game Over: The Truth about the Crisis*. Athens: Papadopoulos (in Greek). Original edition, Game Over: Η Αλήθεια για την Κρίση.

PASOK. n.d. Redistribution measures in relation to income tax. Unpublished mimeo (in Greek).

Perry, Victoria, Graham Holland, Allan Jensen, and Janet Dowling. 2005. Greece: A Plan for Improving Tax Compliance. edited by Fiscal Affairs Department. Washington, DC: IMF.

POE-DOY. 2011. Resolutions of POE-DOY's congress, 5–7 December. Athens: POE-DOY (in Greek).

Rapanos, Vassilis Th. 2007. *The drafting and implementation of the state budget: European experience and Greek reality*. Athens: IOBE/Foundation for Economic and Industrial Research (in Greek).

Samaras, Antonis. 2010. Speech by the President of Nea Demokratia on the occasion of the presentation of ND's economic programme 'Strategy of hope for exit from the crisis', Zappeio, Athens, 7 July (in Greek).

Schmidt, Robert. 2016. "Greece's Least Wanted Man Lives in Maryland." Bloomberg, 30 September, accessed 20 April 2017. https://www.bloomberg.com/news/articles/2016-09-30/greece-s-least-wanted-man-lives-in-maryland.

Simitis, Costas. 2008. Speech delivered during the parliamentary debate on the budget. Original edition, Ομιλία κατά την συζήτηση στη Βουλή για τον Προϋπολογισμό.

Simitis, Costas. 2014. *The European debt crisis: the Greek case*, *European Policy Research Unit Series*. Manchester: Manchester University Press.

Simitis, Costas, and Yannis Stournaras. 2012. "Greece did not cause the euro crisis." *The Guardian*, 27 April. http://www.guardian.co.uk/global/2012/apr/26/greece-europe-north-south-divide.

Spanou, Calliope. 2018. "External influence on structural reform: Did policy conditionality strengthen reform capacity in Greece?" *Public Policy and Administration*:1-23. doi: https://doi.org/10.1177/0952076718772008.

Steinbrück, Peer. 2010. *Unterm Strich*. Hamburg: Hoffmann und Campe.

Vatikiotis, Leonidas. 2018. "Pour l'indépendance des statistiques grecques contre l'intervention de la main "invisible" des créanciers." *Statistique et société* 6 (2):27-37.

Walker, Marcus. 2017. "Was Greece's Deficit Inflated?", WSJ, Real Time Brussels blog, posted on 6 February, accessed 1 March. https://blogs.wsj.com/brussels/2017/02/06/was-greeces-deficit-inflated/.

Weinzierl, Sebastian. 2015. "Die EU-Task-Force für Griehcenland: internationale Beratung am Beispiel der griechischen Steuerverwaltung." In *Die Krise in Griechenland: Ursprünge, Verlauf, Folgen*, edited by Ulf-Dieter Klemm and Wolfgang Schultheiß, 448-460. Frankfurt/New York: Campus.

Chapter 4
The Second MoU: Externally Imposed Change Despite Domestic Opposition

The Introduction of Semi-Autonomy

The recession that followed the onset of the crisis and the conclusion of the first bailout agreement and concomitant Memorandum of Understanding (MoU) was far deeper than initially expected (European Commission 2012b: 11) and Greece's wide-ranging problems took a turn for the worse in the course of 2011. Compliance with some aspects of the adjustment programme too suffered, including in relation to the fight against tax evasion, despite an increase in the number of conducted audits (European Commission 2012b: 21 and 34, respectively). Several academic economists and policy makers had maintained quite early on that Greece's mountain of debt was unsustainable and—as a consequence—debt restructuring (haircut) was a necessary part of the broader requisite response but this idea was initially (and vehemently) rejected by several European governments for political reasons and the European Central Bank (ECB) due to fears of Lehman Brothers-like consequences on Europe's very fragile banking system (Thomas and Castle 2011). Things came to a head during the second half of that year, after the crisis had been allowed to spread to other countries of the Eurozone's periphery and Greece was in the midst of a severe recession. Despite the huge reduction of the budget deficit,[1] Greece needed another bailout which its EU partners and the IMF made conditional on the implementation of additional austerity measures and domestic reforms under a new, second adjustment programme. The alternative was Greece's exit from the Eurozone with all the suffering that it would entail for ordinary Greeks (Dimitrakopoulos 2011), despite the assistance package that German Finance Minister Wolfgang Schäuble—who offered this route to the Papandreou administration—attached to it (Papaconstantinou 2016: 293). Prime Minister George Papandreou surprised the country's EU partners by announcing a referendum on the new bailout plan which was expected to be worth an unprecedented 130 billion euros and would include a

[1]From 15.8% in 2009 to 6.5% in 2011 (Süddeutsche Zeitung 2012).

D. Dimitrakopoulos, A. Passas, *The Depoliticisation of Greece's Public Revenue Administration*, https://doi.org/10.1007/978-3-030-23213-9_4

significant restructuring (i.e. reduction) of Greek public debt. Papandreou subsequently backed down in relation to the referendum—largely due to the negative reaction of EU leaders—but faced with huge domestic pressure and social unrest in Greece,[2] resigned on 10 November, 2011, thus paving the way for a new 'special purpose' government to be sworn in. As if it were meant to demonstrate the Greek political elite's commitment to depoliticisation, the new government was led by a non-MP, namely Professor Lucas Papademos, the respected former Vice President of the European Central Bank and former Governor of the Bank of Greece, and was bound to be short lived since it was meant to give way to legislative elections expected to be held a few months later, in spring 2012. The Papademos-led government had much broader support in parliament than its predecessor, combining support from the centre-Left PASOK, conservative ND (under new leader Antonis Samaras, who came from the nationalist wing of the party) and the small far-Right LAOS (Popular Orthodox Rally) party, i.e. the explicit support of 255 of a total of 300 MPs.[3] The new government's core task was to enact and commence the implementation of a series of measures in accordance with

(a) [t]he requirements of the first MoU so that the country could obtain the sixth instalment of the original loan agreed in 2010 as well as
(b) [t]he new agreement reached by Greece, its EU partners, the IMF and, remarkably, private investors who agreed to a 50% nominal write-down of Greek debt with the aim to make it sustainable by reducing it to 120% of Greece's GDP by 2020 (Heads of state or government of the members of the Eurozone 2011).

In his maiden speech Prime Minister Papademos became the first political officeholder to clearly spell out in Parliament what the policy of internal devaluation actually entailed while also highlighting economic sectors where Greece could seek to foster growth and sustainable job creation. The new PM's personal credibility, technocratic credentials, commitment to the adjustment programme as well as the country's membership of the Eurozone were beyond reproach in the eyes of the country's partners, but the same could not be said of Greece's political establishment. This is why the European Commission and the ECB demanded and obtained letters from the leaders of the three ruling parties indicating their commitment to the pluriannual adjustment programme (Eleftherotypia 2011; Kathimerini 2011a, b). Understandably, given the domestic political elite's credibility problem and knowledge of the social and political turmoil that was also engulfing the country, Greece's partners indicated clearly (European Commission and European Council 2011) that they did not want any domestic, party political games to be played on the back of their own and their respective national parliaments' commitment to the adjustment

[2]As former Minister of Finance Papaconstantinou noted, the atmosphere was more akin to a Latin American country in the run up to a *coup d'état* than a European country (Papaconstantinou 2016: 299).

[3]Only populist Left SYRIZA, the unreconstructed Communist Party and the small Eurocommunist party DIMAR (Democratic Left) voted against the new government.

programme and concomitant, unprecedented loan. Indeed, when newly appointed PM Papademos visited Brussels shortly after taking office, the European Commission's President was keen to publicly stress two points. The first was the need for 'national consensus' that the crisis demanded (European Commission 2011). This meant greater emphasis on 'implementation—less politics and more commitment. This is not a speed race but a marathon' (Karkagiannis 2011), a point that explains the request for the three political party leaders' letters of enduring commitment to the adjustment programme. The second was that 'tax administration and administrative reform' were priority areas for the provision of technical assistance on the European Commission's part (European Commission 2011).

The second conditionality-based MoU that was subsequently concluded (February 2012) was far more detailed than the first one[4] and wide-ranging in relation to the reform of the Greek public revenue administration (see below). This applies to several other policy areas as well (Spanou 2018: 7). This denotes growing awareness on the part of Greece's partners of the magnitude of the problems that the country faced and the weaknesses of its state apparatus but also underlines two other relevant points. The first is the enduring issue of the trust deficit in the eyes of the country's partners. Delays and inefficiencies encountered in various policy areas during the implementation of the first MoU (which was a shorter and much less detailed text) made the EU and the IMF go for a different approach involving a more detailed, quasi-contract-like text in relation to the reform of the revenue administration, because although the country had made progress in terms of fiscal consolidation and was spending about as much as other Eurozone countries (in GDP terms), the key problem of the imbalance between the size of the state and its capacity to collect revenue remained in place (IMF 2012: 8).

> Where they used to write a paragraph or three bullet points, they switched to writing three pages and being entirely prescriptive and the reason why they became prescriptive is that when they wrote a paragraph what they had in mind did not materialise. So, there is a loss of trust since 2010 [. . .]—a loss of trust that does not always relate to ministers, this varies over time and across ministers—which is often to do with the ability and the intent of the administration to implement. [. . .] In tax administration, they started being far more detailed and everything took the form of prior actions (interview, Athens, 2 June 2017).

Secondly, as time went by and IMF and EU officials worked more closely with Greek civil servants, they obtained feedback from the more effective amongst the latter who told them that 'I want to do X but if it does not appear in the MoU it will never happen' (interview, Athens, 2 June 2017). There is also no doubt about the fact that after nearly two years, EU and IMF staff were much more aware of Greece's need for technical assistance in terms of strengthening its institutional capacity. As a

[4]Another difference was the source of funding. While the first programme was funded (on the EU side) via direct bilateral loans provided by Eurozone member states, the second was funded by the EFSF, which had, in the meantime, been created and funded by the same countries. The IMF contributed to both programmes but the instrument changed from a stand-by arrangement (SBA) to an extended fund facility (EFF) that allowed for a longer repayment period (European Commission 2012b: 5).

consequence, the Eurogroup called on the European Commission to enhance and render permanent its presence on the ground in Greece so as to improve its capacity to provide and coordinate the technical assistance offered by the EU and Eurozone member states whose experts would be integrated into the Task Force for Greece (Eurogroup 2012).

The second MoU acknowledged Greece's 'ongoing problems with tax compliance' and underlined the centrality of that area by projecting that the achievement of the agreed primary surplus target of 4.5% GDP by 2014 would require additional measures (inter alia) to the tune of 1.5% GDP 'in tax administration improvements' in 2013–2014 (European Commission and Hellenic Republic 2012, para. 6). The Greek government acknowledged that the revenue administration and the broader public financial management system needed 'deep restructuring', that 'gains can only be achieved over time with resolute efforts' and declared its determination to 'undertake the needed reforms with urgency'. In particular, it noted that the revenue administration 'will need to be overhauled completely' (European Commission and Hellenic Republic 2012, paras. 11 and 12). Planned reforms included short-term priorities aiming to strengthen the revenue administration's operation.[5]

But beyond these statements, the second MoU was not only more detailed but it also introduced *two key innovations* in comparison to the first MoU. First, it raised the issue of the depoliticisation (albeit without using this term) of Greece's public revenue administration. Second, it did so in a way that appears to favour a particular model, namely a semi-autonomous public revenue system involving a limited degree of administrative and financial autonomy vis-à-vis the Ministry of Finance (European Commission and Hellenic Republic 2012, paras. 11 and 12). This point was stressed by IMF and EU staff in a joint mission in Greece in January 2012, i.e. shortly before the conclusion of the second bailout agreement (European Commission 2012b: 35). In order to create 'an independent but accountable tax administration, with a functional organization centered in a strong headquarters',

[5]Some—like the dispute resolution system or obtaining and making better and quicker use of information from the banking system—were technical in nature but others were much more likely to face overt or covert opposition. The former included completing the reassessment and recruitment of 1000 tax auditors with the aim of increasing their total number to 2000, establishing within four months a formal performance review framework involving specific targets against which existing managers' performance would be assessed, with the specific commitment to 'replace managers that have underperformed their targets'. Among the latter were personnel-related actions and anti-corruption measures. These included actually setting up the internal affairs department that the previous government had established (see Chap. 3), improving the protection of whistleblowers reporting corruption within the public revenue administration, introducing procedures for the rotation of managers, setting targets for the audit of asset declarations submitted by the revenue administration's own officials and preparing (by September 2012) a fully fledged anti-corruption plan (European Commission and Hellenic Republic 2012, para. 12).

Table 4.1 Disbursements under the second programme (in billion euros)

Disbursement	Date	EFSF	IMF	Total
1 (7 tranches)	March–June 2012	7.4	1.8	9.2
2.1	December 2012	34.3	–	34.3
2.2	January 2013	7.2	–	7.2
2.3	January 2013	2.0	3.24	5.24
2.4	February 2013	2.8	–	2.8
2.5	May 2013	2.8	–	2.8
3.1	May 2013	4.2	1.74	5.94
3.2	June 2013	3.3	–	3.3
4.1	July 2013	2.5	1.8	4.3
4.2	December 2013	0.5	–	0.5
5.1	April 2014	6.3	3.6	9.9
5.2	July 2014	1.0	–	1.0
5.3	August 2014	1.0	–	1.0
			Grand total	87.48

Source: Adapted from European Commission (n.d.-a)

several measures would be taken,[6] emblematic amongst which was the appointment (within a month) as Secretary General[7] (i.e. head) of the revenue administration of 'an individual with an impeccable track record of tax compliance and with significant expertise in tax matters. Equally important is the commitment to (a) supporting the revenue administration's independent decision making by delegating from the ministerial to the administrative level "the control of core business activities and human resource management" and (b) ensuring that the activities of the revenue administration's HQ are externally audited' (European Commission and Hellenic Republic 2012, para. 12). Many of these measures (including the aforementioned delegation of powers from the ministerial to the administrative level) were designated as *prior* actions (European Commission and Hellenic Republic 2012, Table 2). This means that these measures ought to be taken *before* the IMF could approve the disbursal of funds or complete a review (IMF 2018). Table 4.1 lists the disbursements (19 in total) made under the second MoU which covered the period from March 2012 until August 2014 and thus demonstrates the tight control that the EU and the IMF had over the development of the programme.

[6]These included (in the course of 2012) allocating more staff to the debt collection directorate, doubling the audit capacity of the large taxpayer unit created under the first MoU, closing around 200 underutilised tax offices (a process that had commenced but stalled under the previous administration) and securing the revenue administration HQ's greater (and more target-orientated) control over the remaining tax offices. This was in response to the problem of extreme fragmentation that technical assistance teams diagnosed early on (Weinzierl 2015: 453).

[7]A secretariat general is the largest unit (equivalent to a division in a British ministerial department) in the internal organisation of a Greek ministerial department and usually covers a broad area of policy or set of tasks.

As if to underline a much more complete knowledge of the institutional and political landscape and the country's formal loss of sovereignty, the MoU also included the government's undertaking to completely forego any tax amnesties, i.e. one of the traditional practices that prevented the creation of a culture of tax compliance within the country. Although, technically, this is a tax policy issue, its ramifications relate to the operation of the revenue administration as well. This is so because (a) abolishing tax amnesties would boost the incentives for the public revenue administration to make greater use of risk-based techniques so as to increase tax compliance in a sustainable way and (b) the Minister of Finance would no longer be able to use their discretion to achieve a temporary but unsustainable increase in revenues. If one includes additional measures aiming to rationalise the use of human resources—such as stopping payments in cash and cheques in tax offices so that staff time can be used on more value-added operations such as audits, collection enforcement or advising taxpayers—and modernising infrastructure, e.g. by putting in place within a year a new IT system [which the organisation desperately needed (interviews, Athens, 30 March 2017 and 9 November 2018)] that interconnects all tax offices, one can argue that the second MoU was far closer than the first one to constituting a wide-ranging reform plan of Greece's public revenue administration.

The enactment of the second MoU was followed swiftly by not one but two legislative elections on 6 May and 17 June 2012. The second electoral contest became necessary because no clear majority emerged from the first one. Indeed, in May the two parties that alternated in power since 1974 (and were rhetorically committed to the second MoU) were decimated in electoral terms in comparison to 2009: ND dropped from 33.5% to 18.85% and PASOK from 43.9% to 13.18%. The party system was changing very rapidly with the rise of three parties that had campaigned against the bailouts and the austerity they entailed.[8] Of the seven parties that were represented in Parliament at that point in time four were opposed to the bailouts and MoUs.[9] After the elections of June 2012 that took place in the midst of a major economic, social and political crisis and under the fear of the country's potential default and exit from the Eurozone, a coalition government was formed mainly[10] with the support of ND and PASOK,[11] i.e. the two parties that had alternated in government since the end of the military junta in 1974.

[8]SYRIZA came second by increasing its score from 4.6% to 16.78%. This score could have been higher in the absence of the newly established DIMAR, which got 6.11% and 19 seats. DIMAR split from SYRIZA after the internal battle for the latter's leadership. On the right of the party system, although ND had in the meantime elected nationalist Antonis Samaras as its leader, the newly established nationalist, populist ANEL (Independent Greeks, a break-away party from ND) got 10.6% of the votes (and 22 seats in the 300-strong Parliament) and the neo-Nazi Golden Dawn rose from 0.29% to 6.97% and 21 seats in Parliament.

[9]Between them they had obtained 42.83% of the vote and 132 out of 300 seats.

[10]DIMAR too participated in it, prior to withdrawing from it a year later.

[11]The parties that opposed the MoUs and were represented in Parliament had obtained 45.83% of the vote and 121 out of 300 seats in Parliament.

Despite the broad parliamentary base of the new government, two factors did not bode well for the subsequent implementation of the adjustment programme, including its depoliticisation agenda. First, the main opposition party (SYRIZA) was ambivalent about the country's membership of the Eurozone. Secondly (and more importantly), new Prime Minister Antonis Samaras had voted against the first bailout and MoU (also 'whipping' his party's MPs to do the same) in Parliament and had repeatedly (and inaccurately) stated in public that the 2009 deficit figures had been artificially inflated by George Papandreou's administration (see e.g. Samaras 2010; Eleftherotypia 2010). In that sense, he could not be counted as one of the adjustment programme's domestic supporters, even though only a few months earlier he had signed a letter of (political) commitment to the programme (see *supra*).

Upon taking office Samaras made two important appointments that reflected both a degree of commitment to the adjustment programme—in line with the aforementioned letter—and his own willingness to depart from it, if he could, in relation to the depoliticisation of Greece's public revenue administration. Indeed, on the one hand he chose the Oxford-educated University of Athens economics Professor Yannis Stournaras as his Minister of Finance. In addition to his technocratic credentials, Stournaras was intimately associated with the country's successful effort to enter the Eurozone in the late 1990s and early 2000s under Prime Minister Costas Simitis and was well known in the corresponding Eurozone circles. The appointment of this reform-minded technocrat signalled the new government's determination to keep the country inside the Eurozone. Fittingly for a government aware of the need to take painful and unpopular domestic measures, the new Minister of Finance was not a member of Parliament. This made the new Finance Minister politically expendable in terms of the domestic front.[12] If the logic that dictated the need to distance the government (or at least the main ruling party) from unpopular decisions was at play at that point in time, this did not extend beyond the choice of Finance Minister. Indeed, the second appointment was that of the head of SDOE, the country's Financial Crime Squad. In line with virtually all of his predecessors, Samaras chose a former tax inspector who was, reportedly, also a boyhood friend and a close confidant of his (Ta Nea 2012; Kathimerini 2012). There is no doubt that this appointment indicated resistance to the MoU's depoliticisation agenda given that, at that point in time, SDOE had some powers that related to the collection of public revenues (see below). The inclusion of a greater amount of detail in the revised version of the second MoU came as no surprise and was the direct product of domestic opposition (or at least reticence) towards reform. In line with the literature on conditionality, the greater the perceived domestic resistance to reform, the greater

[12]This was part of PM Samaras' strategy. This is why he chose the Berkeley- and Harvard-educated Ghikas Hardouvelis as Stournaras' replacement when the latter was appointed head of the Bank of Greece, the country's central bank. Like Stournaras, Hardouvelis is a professor of economics who has worked in banking and has never been a member of Parliament. Hardouvelis has worked as a head of the economics desk in the PM's office when Costas Simitis was prime minister immediately before and right after Greece's adoption of the euro.

the external pressure for reform in this relationship that is based on fundamental inequality between the two parties involved in it (see Chap. 2).

This revision of the second MoU was agreed in December 2012 (i.e. only 10 months after the first one was enacted) after the procedures had been completed for the implementation of the agreed debt restructuring[13] and six months after the Samaras administration had taken office. The revised second MoU spells out the logic as well as the pace of the reform that it introduces in relation to the country's public revenue administration:

> The Government will reform the current institutional framework in line with that in many other OECD and EU economies to ensure more autonomy for the tax administration department, especially for day-to-day operations, while leaving policy matters in the hands of the Government. The reform can be undertaken in a gradual way after assessing carefully the impact of each step undertaken (2012b: 8).

It reiterates the government's commitment to markedly reducing tax evasion by means of 'an independent revenue administration with a modern operating structure and methods' and the specific measures that the reform programme entails indicating clearly that implementing key reforms from this programme 'will be a prior action for the [programme's] review', i.e. a requirement for the disbursement of funds (2012a, para. 35). Key amongst these individual measures are:

- The appointment of 'a new Secretary General of the tax administration' in line with legislation enacted in the run-up to the revision of the second MoU (see below) that requires (in addition to what was mentioned in the first version of the second MoU) senior management experience
- The stipulation (i.e. beyond the generic statement of the first version of the same MoU) that the decision-making powers that the Minister of Finance must delegate to the Secretary General for tax administration will include 'the competence to make operational decisions, direct and control local offices, manage human resources, replace underperforming senior managers, manage the budget of the tax administration, and manage all information with due confidentiality'
- Finally, the Greek government's commitment to the 'establishment of independence'—while in February 2012 the same MoU referred to 'steps towards independence'—by means of a new law that would establish 'the new semi-autonomous tax agency' by the end of February 2013, that the MoU explicitly designates as a structural benchmark, i.e. a formal condition for the provision of funding (IMF 2018). Going way beyond the first version of the second MoU, the second version states that the new law will stipulate the new organisation's degree of autonomy and governance framework (including its accountability arrangements), the legal powers of its head, its relationship with other agencies, the framework for its management of information (including controls against sharing confidential operational information with the Minister of Finance) and its initial staffing, the aim being to make 'the agency' fully operational in March 2014

[13]This amounted to a debt reduction of about 107 billion euros (European Commission n.d.-b).

(2012a, para. 35). Overall, the new legislation will 'establish a significantly more autonomous tax administration' (2012b: 10), which was also highlighted as a necessary reform in the quarterly report of the European Commission's Task Force for Greece (Weinzierl 2015: 454, fn. 13).

Aware of the existence of not only a political audience (i.e. the government of the day) but an intra-institutional one too (i.e. the public revenue administration's own staff), the second MoU spells out the flipside of autonomy in terms of institutional accountability: for key frontline staff (such as auditors dealing with high-wealth individuals) the line of accountability now ends at the door of the Secretary General, not the Minister of Finance (2012b: 9).

The prescriptive nature of the second MoU's revised version reflects a clear lack of trust in the Greek government and was not confined to the key issue of the public revenue administration's institutional status. Rather, it extended to organisational and HR-related issues too such as (a) the establishment of specialist debt management units in larger tax offices[14] and (b) the allocation of 'at least 10% of local staff to this function' by the end of 2012. The lack of trust in the government is also demonstrated by the inclusion of details bordering on micromanagement such as the reference to the deployment of a specific number (100) of 'experienced tax auditors' to the large taxpayer unit (2012b: 9).

There is also evidence that Greece's partners were also learning the lessons of recent experience. For example, in February 2012 they mandated the Greek government to close 200 underused tax offices by the end of the year but in December 2012 they scaled back this target to 150 and gave the Greek government till March 2013[15] to achieve that objective.[16]

The tight deadlines and the fact that several of the aforementioned reforms were designated as prior actions in the second MoU (see 2012a, Table 4 and Annex VI respectively, 2012b: 10–11) demonstrate the priority attached to these reforms, the lack of trust vis-à-vis the Greek government, as well as awareness of the delays that had occurred during that year. This view was shared by another independent institution, namely the Bank of Greece. In its annual report for 2012 it noted the need to increase the effort to reform the revenue administration, fight harder against tax evasion and thus overcome the delays of 2012 (Bank of Greece 2013: 144, 24 and 169 respectively).

[14]Another example is the decision to centralize and focus audit functions, filing enforcement and debt management in a smaller number of larger tax offices, with the remainder of the network of tax offices switching to customer service provision without audit and enforcement roles.

[15]The same applied to the aforementioned target of increasing the number of auditors to 2000.

[16]Another example indicating that ineffective tax compliance was also linked to the arcane nature of Greece's tax law is the revised second MoU's stipulation that, in addition to the simplification of income tax legislation, a new Tax Procedures Code would be enacted by May 2013 (as a structural benchmark) so as to remove ambiguities and excessive cross-references and make it more accessible to taxpayers.

Another remarkable point is the terminological confusion involving references to both independence and semi-autonomy even in the same paragraph (see above). A key example is the reference to 'a new agency' whereas in reality the second MoU's authors were referring to a new Secretariat General *within* the Greek Ministry of Finance. It is true that the new head of the public revenue administration would not be handpicked by the minister on the basis of party or personal loyalty—unlike all other secretaries general who, as the most senior executives of a department's political leadership, (a) are routinely recruited from outside the civil service and usually leave after a ministerial reshuffle and (b) enjoy the minister's confidence partly on the basis of party allegiance, the new arrangement was much closer to semi-autonomy[17] than independence. This is demonstrated by the fact that, while the revised version of the second MoU indicated that the new Secretary General would set performance targets for the formal grading of all staff, including tax auditors, and introduce twice yearly performance assessment, a ministerial decision would still be required to set appointment and end-of-tenure procedures for department heads, quarterly performance targets as well as reporting and assessment procedures. Finally, Greece's international partners did not see semi-autonomy necessarily as the end of the depoliticisation process. In fact, as the second MoU indicated, the reform of the public administration would be kept under review and if its assessment indicated that further steps were necessary, they would be taken. This applied in particular to semi-autonomy, as agreed by the Minister of Finance too. This reform would not have been introduced at that point in time in the absence of this external pressure (interviews, Athens, 4 April 2017, 2 June 2017 and 9 November 2018). The next section deals with its implementation and its aftermath.

The Implementation and Limits of Semi-Autonomy

In response to these demands and in the context of the very tight operation of conditionality, Law 4093 of November 2012[18] contains a series of provisions that, while not amounting to wholesale paradigm change, provide clear indications as to the direction of travel of the reform process through a limited increase in the administrative and financial autonomy of the newly established Secretariat General for Public Revenue (SGPR), i.e. the part of the finance ministry in charge of collecting public revenues (Hellenic Parliament 2012). The law was drafted under

[17]That is the term used by the European Commission too (see, e.g. European Commission 2014: 3).

[18]It is also known as 'omnibus law' because it incorporates into Greek law a series of policy and other commitments that the then government made so as to obtain the second bailout's funds. It also involved debt restructuring for the part of government debt that was in private hands (PSI).

the supervision of IMF and EU officials and had to meet the criteria indicated in a checklist that they compiled.[19]

In essence, the new law is based on the distinction between the making of tax policy (for which the formal responsibility remains with the Minister of Finance) and its implementation, the responsibility for which is handed to the SGPR. For that purpose, the law tasked the head of the SGPR to develop the institution's strategy, define and internally allocate qualitative and quantitative targets, assessment criteria of its own units and personnel and keep the finance minister accordingly informed. Another indication of the head's increased administrative autonomy is the (new) power to make key decisions (such as the selection and termination of tenure of heads of units) on the basis of performance (Koutnatzis 2016: 231) and ensure that the SGPR's plans and operation reflect existing policy goals. Another indication of increased administrative autonomy is the SGPR head's power to (a) grant (or revoke from) unit chiefs the formal authority they need to carry out their tasks, (b) transfer 'resources' between the SGPR's units and (c) partly reshape the internal structure of the organisation but only up to the directorate level (Koutnatzis 2016: 232). The new law also contained a generic clause stipulating the transfer to the SGPR's head of powers to organise and manage tax administration matters, enforce tax law that relates to public revenue and monitor and assess all relevant units and officials accordingly. Until then these powers were exercised by either ministers or unit heads on the basis of numerous legal documents, such as ministerial decisions, that had to be amended or abolished (interview, Athens, 4 April 2017). The same provision precludes the subsequent transfer of these powers back to the minister of finance in any way other than through an act of parliament. This is important because it (a) empowered the Greek Parliament whose real role in public revenue has traditionally been limited to rubber-stamping the annual budget and (b) made monitoring far easier for the country's partners in the context of conditionality.

On the other hand, the new arrangement also placed limits on the SGPR's administrative autonomy. Indeed, its head only had the power to *propose* to the finance minister changes in the internal organisation of this body and changes in the internal allocation of personnel. Also, in terms of accountability and reporting, the SGPR's annual report ought to be submitted to parliament via the finance minister (and be made public via the internet). This underlines the SGPR's subordination to the finance minister but also the indirect nature of the accountability chain linking it to parliament.

Finally, in terms of qualifications and broader recruitment criteria for the post of the SGPR's head, the new law underlines the significance of experience in the private sector and the tax system. The term of office would be five years, renewable once, and the appointment process is limited to a Cabinet-level decision on a

[19]See Introduction for the key elements of what the IMF and the EU consider good practice. It is important to note that this practice was not confined to the structure of the revenue administration but included process-related tax matters too, such as a draft bill on the reform of the Code of Tax Procedures (see Kathimerini 2013d).

proposal made by the finance minister. The duration of the term of office is a sign of growing autonomy since it lasts longer than the government's four-year term. Tellingly, for one of the authors of the law, this is 'not unproblematic' because the government of the day—which remained, as he notes, firmly in charge of the appointment process[20]—could appoint someone at the end of its own term of office and thus tie the hands of the next government (Koutnatzis 2016: 235). This statement is a rather stark objection to the very principle of semi-autonomy.

Taken together, the aforementioned provisions show that semi-autonomy is a more apposite description of the public revenue administration's new status, in spite of the second MoU's sporadic references to 'independence'. However, depoliticisation through semi-autonomy does not mean the absence of accountability. Under the new arrangement, the SGPR's head would sign a performance-related contract involving quantitative and qualitative goals (including annual ones), would be potentially paid a significant performance-based bonus and have her contract terminated not only due to standard public sector conditions (such as corruption and gross misconduct) but also failure to meet the agreed goals. This is an important break with standard practices in Greece's public sector and a step in the direction of depoliticisation because it places the assessment of the officeholder (and the accountability which it supports) on a footing that is at least partially objective and this means that loyalty to the minister is no longer a sufficient condition for keeping the officeholder in place. Put in different terms, in a functioning democracy, the new arrangement would mean that it would be harder to keep the officeholder in post if they failed to meet the targets.

At the same time, a joint report by the IMF and the European Commission of November 2012 indicated that the issue of whether it is possible or not to keep the public revenue administration as part of the finance ministry was open (Story et al. 2012: 15). This explains the IMF and EU officials' close supervision of the appointment of the semi-autonomous SGPR's first head. The first head (Secretary General) of the new Secretariat General for Public Revenue was appointed in January 2013 (Greek Cabinet 2013), i.e. nine months after the deadline that appeared in the first version of the second MoU. This appointment followed an open call for applications advertised in November 2012 (Ministry of Finance 2012). The call highlighted several key requirements. Most notable amongst them were (a) the preference for the holder of a postgraduate degree in tax administration 'and the tax system more generally' and significant professional experience, preferably in the private sector, in relation to tax administration and the tax system and (b) significant managerial experience involving HR management, project management, strategic planning, co-ordination and goal-setting. The reference to significant experience in the private sector in particular, certainly stands out and marks a radical departure from past practice but is fully in line with the aforementioned law of November 2012. Three other points in the open call are equally noteworthy, namely (1) the explicit reference to the performance-related contract (involving qualitative and quantitative targets)

[20]This means that this arrangement differs from the one that applies to the heads of independent authorities that are actually mentioned in the Greek Constitution (Koutnatzis 2016: 234).

that the successful applicant would sign with the Minister of Finance, (2) the fact that the officeholder's five-year term of office could end prematurely only in case of resignation or in the very exceptional circumstances stipulated by the law governing the conduct of civil servants[21] and (3) the reference to the possibility of a special annual bonus calculated as a percentage of the extra revenue collected over and above the SGPR's targets.

Approximately 55 applications were received but about a third of them were deemed to not meet basic formal requirements and were excluded (private e-mail, 2 January 2019). This screening was conducted by officials in the ministerial offices of the Minister of Finance and the junior Finance Minister (Koutnatzis 2016: 235). Harry Theoharis was subsequently chosen as the successful candidate and took over immediately, thus ending a period of more than a year during which the country's public revenue administration had remained leaderless (Naftemporiki 2014). He is a software engineer with a degree from Imperial College, who has spent much of his career in start-ups as well as large private sector firms (including Lehman Brothers), prior to working as an adviser in and then head of GGPS, i.e. the Secretariat General for Information Systems, which is the other key part of the Ministry of Finance. Shortly after taking office, he stated that the revenue administration would make much more extensive use of risk analysis[22] so as to better target audits and taxpayers would need to use the banking system to pay their taxes (Kathimerini 2013b). The latter point demonstrates how much political will had been missing in the past from the management of the country's public finances. Making taxpayers pay taxes via their bank accounts would free up significant number of officials who could then be deployed elsewhere, e.g. conducting audits if they had such skills or assisting those in need via the telephone.

Yet Greece's international partners remained cautious. In a report jointly prepared by the IMF and the European Commission in early 2013 they pointedly noted that a declaration is required on the part of the Greek government indicating clearly it intended to give the requisite autonomy to the revenue administration and remove extant administrative barriers to that effect (Story et al. 2013: 8). This was so because they were not convinced by the recent reforms relating to the SGPR and whether the ability of the forthcoming (see below) further transfer of responsibilities from the minister to the head of the semi-autonomous revenue administration would lead to a genuinely semi-autonomous institution that would meet the requirements of the second MoU (Story et al. 2013: 7). Indeed, they stated that the recent reforms (semi-autonomy within the ministry) can only partially satisfy the relevant minimum requirements of functional autonomy (Story et al. 2013: 38). At the same time Poul Thomsen, then deputy director of the IMF's European Department and the fund's leading official in the Greek programme, was speaking publicly of political interference in operational decisions (Thomsen 2013a, b). Moreover, the IMF and the EU

[21]For example, this could happen in case of actions entailing an arrest or imprisonment (Hellenic Parliament 2007, Art. 103).

[22]Senior SDOE staff had voiced their support for this measure (Lampropoulos 2012).

were also facing the unintended consequences of some of the measures that they had imposed. For example, they highlighted the need for further training of revenue officials (both in the institution's HQ and individual tax offices) so as to deal with the loss of experienced staff who left as a result of cutbacks in the public sector (Story et al. 2013: 14).[23] However, the recruitment of 1700 new staff had been planned for 2014 and 2015 (European Commission 2014: 33).

The institutionalisation of the SGPR continued in the course of 2013 (Hellenic Parliament 2013b), with the substantial contribution of experts from the technical assistance teams (Weinzierl 2015: 455). This included the establishment of a five-strong advisory board, including two members with significant international experience in public revenue administration. Its role involved offering expert advice on strategic issues regarding the public revenue administration, including HR management, monitoring performance in relation to the set goals and 'confirming' (as opposed to ascertaining) that the SGPR's head is duly exercising his duties. As one of the authors of this law acknowledged, the fact that these functions were entrusted to an external, technocratic body (as opposed to deploying the legislature's or the executive's control functions) is surely an additional indication of a lack of trust in the country's political system (Koutnatzis 2016: 237). Crucially, the advisory board reported to the minister of finance, who also appointed its members (Ministry of Finance 2015). This means that it could be seen as the minister's watchdog vis-à-vis the head of the public revenue administration. In addition, the finance ministry's internal affairs unit was transferred with its staff and budget to the SGPR, as were the staff and budget of the ministry's directorates for IT applications and data entry.[24] The latter development followed major tensions with the government, which opposed the move (interviews, Athens, 19 December 2016 and 3 April 2017). This was at least partly to do with the government's reluctance to give to the semi-autonomous public revenue administration easy access to the data that would then allow SGPR staff to design better-targeted audits (Reporter.gr 2015). The country's international partners supported the transfer because the SGPR had enough IT work to warrant even command of the entire GGPS (interview, Athens, 4 April 2017). The SGPR's head also obtained (a) more powers in relation to internal organisation matters[25] and (b) the right to propose to the minister the establishment of a special promotion system for the public revenue administration's staff. The SGPR also obtained the formal power to interpret tax law—which is an intrinsic feature of implementing that law, i.e. matching specific cases with abstract provisions—and gained access to banking information so as to better target both risk analysis and audit activity, in line with the provisions of the second MoU (Hellenic Parliament 2013c). However, elements of the sclerotic nature of the entire public

[23]For example, in 2013, 187 new staff were recruited on the basis of meritocratic procedures but 1296 retired, including 883 tax officials, 175 customs officials and 19 financial inspectors. The following year 834 retired (including 574 tax officials) but only 253 were recruited.

[24]These were hitherto parts of GGPS.

[25]See also Hellenic Parliament (2013a).

sector remained intact. Telling in that respect is the fact that the merger of two directorates general of the SGPR required an act of parliament.[26] In September 2013 the SGPR's budgetary autonomy was also increased (Minister of Finance 2013). Moreover, the provision of technical assistance, especially in relation to the conduct of audits, increased significantly since the summer of 2012 (Weinzierl 2015: 454).

Nevertheless, a year later the SGPR's head noted that body's limited administrative autonomy in the organisation's annual report. Indeed, as noted, these limitations relate to staffing, continuous training, personnel management and assessment, budgeting and internal goal-setting and its technology strategy. The SGPR's limited financial autonomy was also noted since, e.g. its procurement programme was carried out by another part of the finance ministry (Secretariat General for Public Revenue 2015: 12).[27]

Moreover, while the European Commission noted the progress made in terms of lifting barriers to transferring powers to the head of the SGPR, it also noted that

> [o]nly 200 SDOE of the 1,000 or so SDOE staff have been transferred to the revenue administration, which was just enough to deal with the 'temporary audit' function. Until the arrival of new staff in the course of 2014 and 2015 the tax administration will not be able to effectively fight major tax evasion (European Commission 2014: 33).

This particular delay had to do with the head of the semi-autonomous SGPR. Theoharis was willing to have SDOE's case load added to SGPR's tasks but he was also very reluctant to see SDOE's staff transferred to the SGPR since he knew that some were thought to be corrupt (interviews, Athens, 3 April 2017 and 9 November 2018). SDOE had, over time, become a hybrid organisation in terms of powers. While formally it was a crime-fighting body, it also had powers that impinged on the collection of public revenues to such an extent that this tended to dominate its public image. Over the years, its political masters ensured via the media that its public profile remained high. This meant that wrestling formal powers away from it was not an easy task, especially under a government that was not that keen on reform. IMF and EU officials pointed out that the country ought to have a single public revenue administration and, as a consequence, SDOE's revenue-related tasks ought to be transferred to the SGPR. Theoharis did not object to this reform. Some of these powers relating to tax and custom duties were transferred through law 4152/2013 (Hellenic Parliament 2013b) but only after a significant row with the government. The latter had support inside SDOE too (interviews, Athens, 19 December 2016 and 9 November 2018).

The aforementioned steps led the country's central bank to hail the progress made in the reform process—singling out the intensification of audits in high-risk groups and the increase in the autonomy of the public revenue administration (Bank of

[26]See Hellenic Parliament (2014).

[27]This kind of function can make a difference when a procurement project has to be carried out quickly. For example, under the first MoU initial steps to merge underutilised tax offices were significantly delayed due to IT problems (see Chap. 3).

Greece 2014: 105)—but the country's international partners remained cautious. Six months after the establishment of the semi-autonomous SGPR and the appointment of its first head, the IMF, aware of implementation problems that had been dogging the programme, noted the centrality of the increase in 'independence of the revenue administration [. . .] to insulate it from what remains *continued political interference*' (added emphasis) and pointed out that

> [i]f these measures—and other measures to modernize the revenue administration's legal framework, operating procedures, and personnel management—fail to deliver, the authorities should consider more fundamental changes, by switching to a revenue agency *outside* [added emphasis] the remit of the civil service.

The IMF also noted the differences between the SGPR and its own preferred model of a Revenue Authority (IMF 2013: 13, 21, 22 and Table 14). The corresponding Table 4.2[28] is reproduced below.

It reiterated its view that political interference in public administration remained a problem in its fifth review of the programme in June 2014 (IMF 2014: 7, 14). During the same period, as was subsequently revealed by Greek media (TVXS 2015a, b), several ministers and MPs of the main ruling party (ND) as well as its official in charge of the party's 'relations with society' were asking (on official paper carrying their party and institutional affiliation logo) Theoharis for specific favours such as (a) moving specific revenue administration officials from one tax or customs office to another, (b) leaving specific officials in the same office, (c) promoting (e.g. from deputy director to director) or (d) assigning key responsibilities (such as head of the audit unit in a large tax office) to a specific individual. The public revenue administration was not unique in that respect. These practices (i.e. appointments, transfers etc. based on party affiliation) were matched across the public sector throughout Prime Minister Samaras' tenure by all of the parties that participated in his government (see, e.g. Eleftherotypia 2013; Vassiliadou 2013; Efimeros 2015; Stagkos 2013; Der Spiegel 2012), not always without support from SYRIZA, the main opposition party.[29]

Speaking in relation to the public revenue administration, one interviewee noted that

> this is where the main methodology for corrupting effectiveness lies. For example, if you go to [the provincial town of] Preveza, they will tell you that there are two [senior] tax officials. One is linked to PASOK, the other to ND. Three months after a change of government, everyone knew that the other person would take over. [. . .] From the moment when 'Dionyssis' takes over, he knows why he took over, who made sure he took over. He knows that he would no longer report to the head of the public revenue administration but to the person who exerted pressure for his appointment to take place and, as a consequence, will

[28]We would normally adapt this table by deleting the last column (current status and timelines) but we chose against doing so in order to demonstrate the intensity of the conditionality regime under which this reform was promoted (see also Chap. 2).

[29]The latter case involved a change in the law to facilitate the rehiring of staff that were found to have been recruited (for partisan gain) illegally just before the 2009 legislative election (Telloglou 2014b).

Table 4.2 Greece: autonomy of the tax administration (revenue agency vs. General Secretariat for Public Revenue)

Major autonomy requirements	Semi-autonomous agency	General Secretariat for Public Revenue	Current status and timelines
1. *Tax administration must be a separate and dedicated body including all tax administration functions* to prevent overlap and duplication. The tax administration needs to be accountable for all of its core businesses functions	Tax administration comprises: (1) a management board; (2) a chief executive officer; (3) the employees; and (4) the various organisational units of a single agency	Tax administration incorporates multiple administrative units: several Directorates General; local offices (DOYs); and other organisational units that are supervised by the SGPR	IAD and parts of GSIS to be transferred to SGPR by July; parts of SDOE to be transferred by October. April 28 Omnibus Bill establishes an Advisory Council of the SGPR, to be set up by July 2013
2. *For operational autonomy the head of the administration must be empowered to administer and enforce the revenue laws*. These powers must be carried out without political interference	Tax administration is responsible for all tax administration functions. Taxes administered by the agency are listed in the enabling legislation	Tax administration assesses and collects taxes and duties and administers and enforces the revenue laws. Minister of Finance has this mandate under law and powers are delegated to the SGPR. Admin powers are delegated to SG	Delegations from Minister and DM to SG have taken place, but their completeness needs to be confirmed. A comprehensive review of the revenue laws that apply powers to the Minister or to specific officials or units must be done to assign them to the SG
3. *The head of the tax administration must be a non-political appointment* for a 5-year term responsible for and with full control over the entire organisation, including all DOYs	CEO appointed by the government, on the recommendation of the Board; responsible for the operational and administrative execution of the agency's mandate. Non-political appointee, for a 5-year term	Secretary General appointed by the government; with responsibilities as per SGPR law, other instruments of delegation, general rules applying to SG in Public service. Non-political appointee, for a 5-year term	No further action required
4. *Authority to design and change organisational structure* to be able to react quickly. Management must have flexibility to design its internal structure	Determines its own structure Board of management approves. May grant considerable leeway to CEO for most organisational changes	The internal structure of the SGPR only up to directorate level may be determined, set up or abolished by decision of the SG upon non-binding opinion of MAREG within 14 days	By end-October 2013, the SG will approve the new organisational structure of the SGPR
5. *Adequate budget* with reasonable management controls with flexibility to	A single budget executed flexibly within a parliamentary appropriation. Funds	A unified budget allocation covers tax administration functions, subject	Budget allocations of IAD and from IAD to be transferred to SGPR by July 2013,

(continued)

Table 4.2 (continued)

Major autonomy requirements	Semi-autonomous agency	General Secretariat for Public Revenue	Current status and timelines
re-allocate funds across budget lines. Control over the budget is the major tool for ensuring that priorities can be accomplished	received on the basis of general budget rules or a percentage of collection formula. The agency may move funds across major budget lines. Management board approves budget request and ensures adherence to financial policy	to same budget rules and as other General Secretariats in MoF. A small financial management unit in the SGPR: (1) coordinates the preparation of the budget; (2) follows up its implementation; and (3) proposes reallocations of non-wage recurrent spending in line with the organic budget law	those of SDOE to be transferred by October. By end-2013, 2014 revenue administration budget will be established with full flexibility for the SGPR to reallocate funds amongst non-wage recurrent spending
6. *The tax administration has authority to undertake at least 90% of its own recruitment, promotion and dismissal.* This enables the tax administration to operate with maximum efficiency	Agency has authority to recruit, promote, dismiss through enabling legislation. The agency sets up fair and transparent processes in all these areas, and provides procedures for redress	SGPR enabled to determine the conditions for hiring under the control of ASEP. All cases of potential dismissal must go to Disciplinary Council, and the SG implements the decision	By end-October 2013, the SGPR will approve staffing numbers and appointment processes of the revenue administration
7. *Tax administration determines its grade structure and has a strong influence over compensation levels.* Due to unique requirements for specialised staff, tax administration is in direct competition with the private sector	Agency determines grading structure subject to overall budget level. This is a decision of the managing board	SGPR empowered—subject to ministerial approval—to determine a special system for grade qualifications, promotions and evolution through grades, and rules relating to promotion and relocation of employees. The SGPR has authority to implement the system	By end-October 2013, the SG approves the grading system and classification of the revenue administration

Source: IMF (2013: 37–39)

call him directly. [. . .] This is the method of completely bypassing the independent secretary general. This is the first step in the direction of the fall [of the new system]. OK, the secretary general does not have to get involved when it comes to small cases, unless it is a huge case. In a huge case [they will call on the secretary general] because it is hard to resolve. But in local ones, of person X, or Y, or the local MP, [it will not involve the secretary general] (interview, Athens, 19 December 2016).

On one occasion the junior finance minister openly made proposals regarding the thorny issue of staff mobility after meeting staff union officials while also playing a key role in the transfer of a senior SDOE official away from the frontline duties reportedly after several of those he audited had complained to the finance minister and even the Prime Minister's office (To Vima 2014; Telloglou 2014a). Moreover, during the first year of its operation, the advisory board did not perform its role in a substantial way and fell in oblivion after the summer of 2014 (Koutnatzis 2016: 237).

These developments indicate that—in light of the Samaras administration's foot-dragging which also related to matters of policy with a direct impact on tax collection (esp. the collection of VAT) and the fight against tax evasion (Kathimerini 2013d) or, indeed, outright opposition—the country's international lenders were beginning to carry out a broader plan in a step-wise manner, as the second MoU openly stated (see supra). It had to face opposition from segments of the bureaucracy (Weinzierl 2015: 451) and the staff unions as well. In March 2013 the staff union called on its members to boycott the effort to increase the institution's audit capability through the creation of a new type of posts (POE-DOY 2013c). They also denounced goal-setting as arbitrary (POE-DOY 2013b). In 2014 the union also opposed and called on its members to boycott staff assessment procedures (POE-DOY 2014). There was (by tradition too) also opposition to external advice (POE-DOY 2013b). Theoharis agreed with the unions (as well as IMF and EU officials) that more staff was needed to carry out more audits, as did senior officials of SDOE [who had noted the ministers' reluctance and responsibility on that front (Lampropoulos 2012)] but also underlined bureaucratic resistance—e.g. in the form of auditors' insistence on a full audit as opposed to settling for a less onerous audit and moving on, which could yield better results (Daley 2013).

The aforementioned measures can be construed as a way to prepare the ground for much more far-reaching reforms which took a more detailed and much more specific form after the elections of 2015, which led—as we demonstrate in Chap. 5—to further steps in the depoliticisation process. However, it is important to underline the fact that the Samaras administration had done a lot to generate the troika's distrust in relation to the reform of the public revenue mechanism. The troika had noted delays in the adoption of ministerial decisions and the issuing of circulars necessary for the reform of the system, and has had to make repeated calls for SDOE's merger with the SGPR and the appointment of new tax inspectors, while European Commissioner Algirdas Šemeta (in charge of taxation matters) pointedly and publicly (speaking in Parliament in June 2013) noted the country's slow progress in the fight against tax evasion and highlighted the need for political will to actually carry out the measures that were being enacted (Kathimerini 2013c). Delays were also noted in March 2013 by MPs of DIMAR (the smallest of the three ruling parties) who went as far as to call for the enhancement of the autonomy of the SGPR (Kathimerini 2013a).

A significant—as subsequent developments indicate—incident that marked this period was the forced resignation of Harry Theoharis, the first head of the semi-autonomous SGPR in June 2014. Theoharis himself attributed it to the fact that the Samaras-led ND/PASOK coalition government did not want to go after certain individuals (Zacharakis 2015; Kathimerini 2014a). As a politician from the then-ruling ND-PASOK coalition reportedly (Süddeutsche Zeitung 2015) told him, tax evaders are voters too. Finance Minister Stournaras asked for and subsequently obtained Theoharis' resignation.[30] This was in line with the wishes of both PM Samaras and several MPs from the two ruling parties. It was not in line (in fact, quite the obverse is true) with the relevant provisions since the SGPR had met[31] the targets for tax collection and had not actually committed an offence. But this begs the question as to why a finance minister who actually supported the principle of depoliticisation and had been supportive of Theoharis as head of the SGPR (interviews, Athens, 2 June 2017 and 9 November 2018) did this.

This key incident relates directly to both the unintended and the intended consequences of depoliticisation. Theoharis was accused of spreading confusion[32] amongst private investors literally days after they had invested in Greek government bonds based on the belief that their investment would receive favourable tax treatment at a time when the Greek government was beginning to test the market (interviews, Athens, 2 June and 3 April 2017). He was also accused of not consulting finance ministers when they felt he should, e.g. when he called for the postponement of the implementation of a major piece of new legislation, namely the Code of Tax Procedure, days before it was meant to enter in force (interviews, Athens, 4 April 2017). He was also accused of lacking a sense of proportion in exercising his duties by no lesser a figure than Prime Minister Samaras who, speaking at a party rally in central Athens (literally a few meters away from the SGPR's HQ) days before the 2014 European elections, said 'we will take immediate action to humanise the revenue administration. We cannot go after people, treating in the same way professional tax evaders and ordinary folk who have trouble coping [with tax increases],' a point which related to the increasing use of asset confiscations[33] for unpaid taxes and the SGPR's new operational plan which entailed more audits in an effort to increase public revenue (Kathimerini 2014b).[34] Of course, this is precisely the point behind the establishment of semi-autonomous or independent public revenue administrations (and non-majoritarian institutions more broadly), i.e. the willingness to ensure they operate *without* being affected by the exigencies of the

[30]In formal terms Theoharis did not have to resign. In fact, he could have rejected this request but how would he then work with the Finance Minister who had made that request on behalf of the government? This incident illustrates the limits of formal arrangements (see also Chap. 5 on the current institutional set-up) but also the relevance of personalities (interviews, Athens, 4 April and 2 June 2017).

[31]The progress was noted by the Commission later in the year, although there was room for further improvement (European Commission 2014: 33). Finance Minister Stournaras publicly acknowledged that Theoharis had 'systematically exceeded the targets set', in the press release issued on the occasion of Theoharis' departure (see Naftemporiki 2014).

[32]It also led to a rise in the cost of borrowing. His circular in question was subsequently withdrawn (Dimitrelis 2014; Kathimerini 2014b).

[33]This task was undermined by the fact that Greece, a member of the Eurozone since 2001, still does not have a complete land register. It is meant to be completed by the early 2020s.

[34]Even after the European elections, PM Samaras spoke of 'errors in the public revenue mechanism that must be corrected' (Naftemporiki 2014).

electoral cycle.[35] The timing of Theoharis' ostracisation demonstrated that Prime Minister Samaras was not willing to risk his party's electoral prospects in the run-up to the likely early legislative election that was expected to take place a year later. Theoharis was effectively dismissed days after the two then ruling parties suffered a major defeat in the 2014 European elections, which SYRIZA (then the main opposition party) won. Noteworthy is the fact that the Parliament's Budget Office (another semi-autonomous new institution) castigated Theoharis' ostracisation in very explicit terms, arguing in its termly report of July 2014 that this event shows the country has a problem of institutional stability, any effort to curtail the discretionary interference of ministers faces major obstacles and, implying that the country's politicians do not want interference to cease, and noted that this reform had been introduced 'under great pressure from the Troika' (Parliamentary Budget Office 2014: 8–9).

Theoharis' departure was not an isolated incident in terms of the then government's opposition to the depoliticisation agenda. As we noted in Chap. 3, back in 2011 prosecutors had started an investigation against Andreas Georgiou, the first head of another key institution that had been drastically reformed along the lines of the depoliticisation model, namely ELSTAT. He stood accused of artificially inflating the country's deficit allegedly in order to help justify the austerity measures taken under the first MoU. This investigation led to charges being actually brought against him in 2013, i.e. a year into Antonis Samaras' tenure as prime minister and a year before he caused Theoharis' departure. As indicated above, Samaras had, as leader of the opposition, provided political cover to these accusations against Georgiou. EU and IMF officials and the leaders of other Eurozone countries were aware of this. Georgiou's case attracted widespread attention from the international media (Harford 2013; Batzoglou 2013; Schlötzer 2013; Frankfurther Allgemeine Zeitung 2013; Die Presse 2013; Les Echos 2013; Kefalas 2013) and contributed to the belief (interview, Athens, 3 April 2017) that the depoliticisation agenda had committed enemies in the top tier of the Greek political élite, despite the fact that—as was noted in numerous reports by the IMF and the EU—every time the public revenue administration did not meet its targets, the country took a step closer to deeply unpopular additional spending cuts and/or tax rises.

The damage that Theoharis' ostracisation did to the credibility of the Greek political class in the eyes of the country's international partners was significant (Papaconstantinou 2016: 346–347) and continued to produce consequences in the period that followed (see Chap. 5). First, it led the European Commission to issue a public and stern rebuke (Kathimerini 2014c; Varvitsioti 2016).[36] In fact, the Commission went further than that. It indicated that Theoharis' removal from office was a

[35]Theoharis himself pointed out that his job was to carry out legislation enacted by others (Kathimerini 2014d).

[36]This is significant if one considers the differences between that institution and the IMF (see also Chap. 5). As was rightly noted at a meeting held in London in January 2018 under the Chatham House rule, 'The IMF is here for three years and then gone. For [the EU, Greece is] part of the family'.

cause of 'serious concern' (Associated Press 2014) not least because he had increased tax collection rates (a matter of both economic efficiency and social justice) and played a key role in reforming and digitising the country's public revenue administration that had remained 'semi-autonomous within the Ministry of Finance'. As a consequence, the Commission would, alongside the ECB and the IMF, keep monitoring the Greek government's commitment to a more autonomous revenue administration as well as more robust, transparent and meritocratic selection of senior public sector managers and was looking forward to a similar process for the selection of Mr Theoharis' successor so as to maintain high standards of integrity and transparency (Eleftherotypia 2014). The Commission's concern was not confined to this particular reform. Rather, it related to the programme's broader sustainability since—as it had noted in the past—the fight against tax invasion related to both fiscal consolidation and the social acceptability of the programme as a whole, given the widespread belief 'that tax evasion, while pervasive, is graver among the most affluent' (European Commission 2012a: 9). As we will show in Chap. 5, the real consequences of Theoharis' ostracisation in institutional terms played out to a greater extent in the subsequent stages of the depoliticisation process.

Second, in the short term it reinforced the view amongst key actors (including the German government) that a much tougher stance was required. This incident made such a negative impression amongst government officials in Germany that it was raised with a delegation of Greek parliamentarians (including MPs from opposition parties) who were visiting Germany at the time (interview, Athens, 9 November 2016). The incident appeared to confirm in the eyes of Greece's partners the view that the country is 'unreformable' and—as a consequence—a hard line was required in future negotiations with the Greek government, irrespective of its ideological orientation. This goes a long way towards explaining the very detailed and specific nature of the third MoU's requirements in relation to the reform of Greece's public revenue mechanism (see Chap. 5). It also played into the hands of the IMF, which has been pushing for more radical changes.[37] Indeed, the fund's leading official in the Greek programme subsequently claimed that Theoharis' ostracisation was a turning point because both the IMF and the governments of some North European countries (beyond Germany) lost faith in the Samaras administration's commitment to the adjustment programme (Varvitsiotis and Telloglou 2015; see also Dixon 2015; Financial Times 2015).

[37] Staff union officials went as far as to accuse the IMF of favouring the collection of taxes by private firms in Greece (ASKI Eforiakon 2013; POE-DOY 2013a). This accusation relates to the IMF's aforementioned point about the possibility of 'switching to a revenue agency outside the remit of the civil service' (IMF 2013: 22). On the other hand, a former ministerial adviser noted that he felt that an independent agency was the IMF's preferred model all along and 'from the beginning there was an effort to find one pretext or another so as to end up where we finally ended up' (interview, Athens, 4 April, 2017).

The open call for applications for Theoharis' replacement was swiftly[38] published and was virtually identical to the previous one (Minister of Finance 2014b). Amongst the 75 applications that were submitted numerous did not meet basic formal requirements and were subsequently excluded (private e-mail, 2 January 2019). What was different was the attitude of Greece's international partners. The five-strong panel that was involved in the next stage of the process was not based on the law that governed the remainder of the process (supra; Hellenic Parliament 2012). It was chaired by the Minister of Finance but (1) one of the four members was a senior official (chief inspector) at the French Ministry of Finance and a member of the European Commission's Task Force for Greece, while (2) the remaining three included two Greek university professors specialising in management and Greece's former top public prosecutor (Naftemporiki 2015). In other words, as a precautionary measure and an indication of the lack of trust vis-à-vis the government of the day, the EU and the IMF had direct access to the details of the applications and the operation of the panel, unlike what happened 18 months earlier when Theoharis was appointed. Katerina Savvaidou was subsequently chosen and appointed by the Cabinet on the finance minister's proposal (Greek Cabinet 2014).

Four elements of her experience stand out in her publicly available curriculum vitae (Savvaidou n.d.). First, she is an academic at the University of Thessaloniki specialising in tax law. Second, she was a member of the SGPR's advisory board since its establishment in 2013. Third, she has considerable experience in the private sector, including firms such as PriceWaterhouseCoopers (senior manager) and Arthur Andersen (legal and tax adviser) that specialise in 'tax optimisation' for large companies and/or wealthy individuals.[39] Finally, she was by no means an outsider in relation to the country's political system. In fact, since the mid-2000s she had held several posts (including in the Ministry of Finance) advising governments of ND, in a country where party political affinity is a *de rigueur* requisite for occupying such posts. So, at the time of her appointment as head of the SGPR, in Katerina Savvaidou they were choosing someone who knew very well Greece's tax law and public revenue administration but also someone who was not exactly a sworn enemy of the main ruling party,[40] i.e. the party that was evidently opposed to semi-autonomy. This happened nearly a month after the IMF had (once again) noted 'continued political interference' in the operation of the public revenue administration (IMF 2014: 7). This view was shared (including in public) by senior officials of the staff union (Daley 2013; interview, Athens, 13 February 2017). It is not a

[38]In the short intervening period (a) the law was amended so as to enable the government to appoint a senior SGPR official as interim secretary general and (b) an interim secretary general was appointed accordingly (Hellenic Government 2014; Minister of Finance 2014a).

[39]Indeed, one can argue that this is a classic case of a poacher who has turned into a gamekeeper. Her predecessor subsequently stated that she had repeatedly acted as representative of various companies while he was head of the SGPR (Zafiropoulos 2015).

[40]When the long list of the top ten candidates was created, a report in the Greek media noted that a delay was caused by an unnamed strong candidate's close links to the country's political system (Pappous 2014).

coincidence that the Bank of Greece too echoed—albeit in more diplomatic language—this view by encouraging the government to increase the autonomy and effectiveness of the public revenue administration so as to lock in the progress[41] made in terms of the country's public finances (Bank of Greece 2015: 26).

Concluding Remarks

The second MoU marks a key stage in the reform of Greece's public revenue administration in general and the central question of depoliticisation in particular. Semi-autonomy is a halfway house between the status quo ante and a fully independent agency and, like many halfway houses, it is not devoid of problems. Semi-autonomy means that, while the revenue administration has remained part of the Ministry of Finance, it has obtained the power to operate in a way that has taken it some way away from the direct control of the minister in terms of key elements of its operation such as the use of the budget and the deployment of staff. On the other hand, in terms of political accountability, the minister in question remained formally accountable to parliament—a picture of apparent responsibility without power. The head of the public revenue administration could not and did not account to parliament directly but the advent of performance-based contracts coupled with the possibility of a bonus payment opens up space (and increases incentives) for the public debate on effectiveness, including in parliament, especially in conditions of systemic crisis caused largely by ineffective tax collection. There is a flipside to this. The revenue administration's semi-autonomy allowed politicians to lay at its door the blame for unpopular decisions, although the legislation that it carried out was actually made by the parliamentary majority (i.e. effectively the government) of the day. In a country where government ministers rarely resign and which was also in the midst of a very harsh adjustment programme, this led an international official to rightly point out that Greek politicians were effectively being handed a gift at the insistence of the IMF, in particular, and the EU (interview, Athens, 3 April 2017). This begs the question: why did they not want this 'gift'? The implication of resistance to this reform is that effective revenue collection is—as it has always been—a matter of political will, not least because the lack of resources, including know-how, can only be a temporary problem, at least in a member state of the EU, as the provision of technical assistance (much of it free of charge) clearly shows. Harry Theoharis' effective dismissal demonstrates beyond doubt the primacy of short-termism amongst the ruling *élite*. The exigencies of the political cycle prevailed, albeit temporarily, despite the fact that—as the European Commission's statement at the time of his dismissal shows—he had actually met the targets. The choice of his

[41]For example, the VAT gap is estimated to have dropped to 26.68% in 2014 from the pick of 33.04% in the previous year but it still remained one of the highest in the EU (CASE and IEB 2018: 80).

successor also shows that Greece's international partners were not, at that point in time, prepared to push the government even further.

In theoretical terms, semi-autonomy is the result of external pressure in line with the first of the three models outlined in Chap. 2. This argument does not relate so much to the turbulent months between the end of the first programme in late 2011 and elections of June 2012—though the absence of real progress during this period shows how incapable the Greek public administration is of operating without direct ministerial input. Rather, our argument relates predominantly to the period that followed the elections of June 2012. In line with the literature on conditionality (see Chap. 2), the amount and the specificity of the details contained in the second MoU grew precisely because of the lack of trust in the Greek ruling *élite* and the country's international partners' determination to bring about change, even in the face of domestic opposition. Just like most of the period covered by the first MoU, the lack of programme ownership that is at the heart of the second model means that social learning did not apply during the period discussed in this chapter. A key minister's support could not and did not amount to programme ownership, especially when opposition to the depoliticisation agenda comes from the very top of the government (unlike the period before November 2011). Similarly, the third model (lesson-drawing) did not apply during this period because the domestic equilibrium remained dominated by those who opposed a departure from the status quo. Indeed this included staff unions that opposed key planks of the reform programme.

As the IMF subsequently noted, the establishment of the SGPR in late 2012 and the appointment of its first head were milestones in the reform process, which extended to other aspects of the organisation and operation of the institution. Further

> [s]ubstantive reforms were implemented in 2013 and the first half of 2014 due to the strong commitment from the [Secretary General] in progressing the reform agenda. However, political commitment to respect the fixed-term appointment and provide leadership stability to the revenue administration was absent from mid-2014 (IMF 2017: 43).

How the implications of this development played out will be discussed in the next chapter, where the focus is on the developments that followed the change of government in early 2015 and the advent to power of two parties that made a lot of political capital on the basis of their severe criticism of the adjustment programme.

References

2012a. Greece - Memorandum of Economic and Financial Policies, December 2012.

2012b. Greece - Memorandum of Understanding on Specific Economic Policy Conditionality. December 2012.

ASKI Eforiakon. 2013. The IMF raises again the issue of privatisation of the public revenue administration. Athens: ASKI Eforiakon (in Greek).

Associated Press. 2014. "EU: 'serious concern' as Greece's tax czar quits." Associated Press, 5 June.

Bank of Greece. 2013. The Governor's report for 2012. Athens: Bank of Greece (in Greek).

Bank of Greece. 2014. The Governor's report for 2013. Athens: Bank of Greece (in Greek).

Bank of Greece. 2015. The Governor's report for 2014. Athens: Bank of Greece (in Greek).
Batzoglou, Ferry. 2013. "Ein Statistiker auf der Anklagebank." *Berliner Zeitung*, 14 February. https://www-nexis-com.ezproxy.lib.bbk.ac.uk/docview/getDocForCuiReq?lni=57RK-0X11-DYJR-N19T&csi=5949&oc=00240&perma=true.
CASE and IEB. 2018. Study and Reports on the VAT Gap in the EU-28 Member States: 2018 Final Report, TAXUD/2015/CC/131. Warsaw.
Daley, Suzanne. 2013. "Greece's Aggressive Pursuit of Tax Evaders Appears to Collect More Anger Than Money." *The New York Times*, 28 October, Europe. Accessed 1 November 2018. https://www.nytimes.com/2013/10/29/world/europe/greeces-aggressive-pursuit-of-tax-evaders-.
Der Spiegel. 2012. "Jobs für gute Freunde." 22 October. http://www.spiegel.de/spiegel/print/d-89234409.html.
Die Presse. 2013. "Unterstützung für griechischen Statistikchef." 8 February. https://www-nexis-com.ezproxy.lib.bbk.ac.uk/docview/getDocForCuiReq?lni=57P8-YP91-JBKK-P4JC&csi=5949&oc=00240&perma=true.
Dimitrakopoulos, Dionyssis G. 2011. "Leaving the eurozone would be a disaster for Greece." *The Guardian*, 22 September, 35.
Dimitrelis, Spyros. 2014. "They 'undid' the circular regarding taxation on Greek government bonds." Capital.gr, 16 May, accessed 30 December 2018. http://www.capital.gr/oikonomia/2017128/-xilosan-tin-egkuklio-gia-ti-forologisi-ton-ellinikon-omologon.
Dixon, Hugo. 2015. "Tsipras shocks again.", Reuters Breaking Views. Reuters, 22 October, accessed 29 November 2018. https://www.breakingviews.com/considered-view/tsipras-shoots-himself-in-foot-by-firing-tax-boss/ - .VikZfUtag9Y.twitter.
Efimeros, Kostas. 2015. "Revealed: the scandal of percentages." The Press Project, 15 April (in Greek), accessed 12 March 2019.
Eleftherotypia. 2010. "Ant. Samaras: PASOK has 'inflated' the deficit." 1 February (in Greek). Accessed 26 December 2018. http://www.enet.gr/?i=news.el.politikh&id=127601.
Eleftherotypia. 2011. "Absurdities relating to the letters." 29 November (in Greek). Accessed 20 December 2018. http://www.enet.gr/?i=issue.el.home&date=29/11/2011&id=329069.
Eleftherotypia. 2013. "Partisan transaction." 28 January (in Greek). http://www.enet.gr/?i=arthra-sthles.el.columns&s=politika-paraskhnia&id=339253.
Eleftherotypia. 2014. "Theoharis, Stournaras and the European Commission." 6 June (in Greek). http://www.enet.gr/?i=news.el.article&id=434139.
Eurogroup. 2012. Statement, 21 February.
European Commission. 2011. Statement by President Barroso following his meeting with Lucas Papademos, Prime Minister of Greece, SPEECH/ 11/778. Brussels.
European Commission. 2012a. The Second Economic Adjustment Programme for Greece. First review. Directorate-General for Economic and Financial Affairs. Brussels.
European Commission. 2012b. The Second Economic Adjustment Programme for Greece. March. Directorate-General for Economic and Financial Affairs. Brussels.
European Commission. 2014. The Second Economic Adjustment Programme for Greece. Fourth review. Directorate-General for Economic and Financial Affairs. Brussels.
European Commission. n.d.-a. "Financial assistance to Greece." European Commission, accessed 5 January 2019. https://ec.europa.eu/info/business-economy-euro/economic-and-fiscal-policy-coordination/eu-financial-assistance/which-eu-countries-have-received-assistance/financial-assistance-greece en - secondeconomicadjustmentprogrammeforgreece.
European Commission. n.d.-b. A new chapter for Greece: further details on the implementation of debt measures (factsheet). Brussels: European Commission.
European Commission, and Hellenic Republic. 2012. Memorandum of understanding between the European Commission acting on behalf of the euro-area member states and the Hellenic Republic, 15 February 2012.
European Commission and European Council. 2011. Statement by President Barroso and President Van Rompuy on the designation of Lucas Papademos as Prime Minister of Greece. Brussels.
Financial Times. 2015. "Greece's top tax collector sacked by Tsipras." 22 October. https://www.ft.com/content/61b20754-78d1-11e5-a95a-27d368e1ddf7.

Frankfurther Allgemeine Zeitung. 2013. "Klage gegen Chef der griechischen Statistikbehörde." 23 January. https://www.faz.net/suche/?offset=&cid=&index=&query=andreas+georgiou&offset=&allboosted=&boostedresultsize=%24boostedresultsize&from=01.01.2013&to=31.12.2013&BTyp=redaktionelleInhalte&author=&username=&sort=date&resultsPerPage=20.

Greek Cabinet. 2013. Act 1 of 16 January: selection and appointment of the Secretary General for Public Revenue. Government Gazette 18, 17 January, 61 (in Greek).

Greek Cabinet. 2014. Act 20 of 25 June: selection and appointment of the Secretary General of the Secretariat General for Public Revenue at the Ministry of Finance. Government Gazette 360, 25 June, 1597 (in Greek).

Harford, Tim. 2013. "Lies, damned lies and Greek statistics." *Financial Times*, 25 January. https://www.ft.com/content/fc5e295a-663b-11e2-b967-00144feab49a.

Heads of state or government of the members of the Eurozone. 2011. Euro summit statement, 26 October. Brussels: European Council.

Hellenic Government. 2014. Legislative act regarding the replacement of SGPR due to the early end of his term of office. Government Gazette, A136, 11 June (in Greek).

Hellenic Parliament. 2007. Law 3528/2007: Civil service code. Government Gazette, A26, 9 February (in Greek).

Hellenic Parliament. 2012. Law 4093/2012: approval of the medium-term financial framework 2013-2016; urgent measures implementing Law 4064/2012 and the medium-term financial framework 2013-2016. Government Gazette, A222, 12 November (in Greek).

Hellenic Parliament. 2013a. Law 4141/2013: investment instruments, provision of credit and other provisions. Government Gazette, A81, 5 April (in Greek).

Hellenic Parliament. 2013b. Law 4152/2013: urgent measures implementing laws 4046/2012, 4093/2012 and 4127/2013. Government Gazette, A107, 9 May (in Greek).

Hellenic Parliament. 2013c. Law 4174/2013: tax procedures and other provisions. Government Gazette, A170, 26 July (in Greek).

Hellenic Parliament. 2014. Law 4254/2014: support and growth measures for the Greek economy in the context of the implementation of Law 4046/2012 and other provisions. Government Gazette, A85, 7 April (in Greek).

IMF. 2012. Greece: Request for Extended Arrangement Under the Extended Fund Facility—Staff Report; Staff Supplement; Press Release on the Executive Board Discussion; and Statement by the Executive Director for Greece. IMF Country Report No. 12/57. March. Washington, D.C.: IMF.

IMF. 2013. Greece: Third Review Under the Extended Arrangement Under the Extended Fund Facility. Washington, D.C.: IMF.

IMF. 2014. Greece: Fifth review under the extended arrangement under the extended fund facility and request for waiver of nonobservance of performance criterion and rephasing of access. IMF Country Report No. 14/151. 16 May. Washington, D.C.: IMF.

IMF. 2017. Greece: ex-post evaluation of exceptional access under the 2012 extended agreement. Washington, D.C.: IMF.

IMF. 2018. IMF conditionality factsheet. Washington D.C.: IMF.

Karkagiannis, Kostas. 2011. "Barroso: "No" political games." *Kathimerini*, 22 November (in Greek). http://www.kathimerini.gr/443475/article/epikairothta/politikh/mparozo-oxi-se-politika-paixnidia.

Kathimerini. 2011a. "Open line between the PM's office and ND in relation to the letter." 27 November (in Greek). Accessed 20 December 2018. http://www.kathimerini.gr/443973/article/epikairothta/politikh/anoixth-grammh-ma3imoy%2D%2D-nd-gia-thn-epistolh.

Kathimerini. 2011b. "Samaras writes to the EU." 24 November (in Greek). Accessed 20 December 2018. http://www.kathimerini.gr/443649/article/epikairothta/politikh/epistolh-apo-samara-pros-ee.

Kathimerini. 2012. "New head for SDOE." 10 August (in Greek). http://www.kathimerini.gr/10336/article/oikonomia/ellhnikh-oikonomia/neos-eidikos-grammateas-sto-sdoe.

Kathimerini. 2013a. "DIMAR MPs request the enhancement of the new SGPR's powers." 28 March (in Greek). Accessed 28 December 2018. http://www.kathimerini.gr/33157/article/epikairothta/politikh/enisxysh-armodiothtwn-toy-neoy-grammatea-dhmosiwn-esodwn-zhta-th-dhmar.

Kathimerini. 2013b. "H. Theoharis: Tax audits to be based on risk analysis." 29 January (in Greek).

Kathimerini. 2013c. "The SGPR's independence exists only on paper." 5 June (in Greek). http://www.kathimerini.gr/490086/article/epikairothta/politikh/sta-xartia-h-ane3arthsia-ths-grammateias-esodwn.

Kathimerini. 2013d. "Troika pushes for tax changes." 22 June (in Greek). http://www.kathimerini.gr/491311/article/oikonomia/ellhnikh-oikonomia/systaseis-apo-troika-gia-thn-epispeysh-twn-allagwn-sth-forologia.

Kathimerini. 2014a. "H. Theoharis: "My departure from the SGPR is a political move"." 10 June (in Greek). http://www.kathimerini.gr/771015/article/epikairothta/politikh/x-8eoxarhs-politikh-kinhsh-h-apoxwrhsh-moy-apo-th-gg-dhmosiwn-esodwn.

Kathimerini. 2014b. "How Mr H. Theoharis was led to resign." 7 June (in Greek). http://www.kathimerini.gr/770838/article/epikairothta/politikh/pws-odhgh8hke-o-k-x-8eoxarhs-sthn-paraithsh.

Kathimerini. 2014c. "She does not want to turn into Theoharis...", 30 July (in Greek). http://www.kathimerini.gr/778216/article/oikonomia/epixeirhseis/den-8elei-na-ginei-8eoxarhs.

Kathimerini. 2014d. "Theoharis resigns." 6 June (in Greek). http://www.kathimerini.gr/770534/article/epikairothta/politikh/paraithsh-x-8eoxarh-me-aixmes.

Kefalas, Alexia. 2013. "La Grèce enquête sur le maquillage de ses comptes publics." *Le Figaro*, 6 February, International. https://www-nexis-com.ezproxy.lib.bbk.ac.uk/docview/getDocForCuiReq?lni=57NW-63S1-F0C5-82T4&csi=5826&oc=00240&perma=true.

Koutnatzis, Stylianos-Ioannis G. 2016. "Auf dem Weg zu einer semi-autonomen Steuerverwaltung? Bestandsaufnahme und Perspektiven aus verfassungsrechtlicher Sicht." In *Staatsreform für ein besseres Europa*, edited by Georgios Dimitropoulos, Athanasios Gromitsaris and Martin Schulte, 227-245. Berlin: Duncker & Humblot.

Lampropoulos, Vassilis. 2012. "SDOE could save the salaries." *To Vima*, 17 December (in Greek). https://www.tovima.gr/2012/12/17/society/to-sdoe-mporoyse-na-swsei-toys-misthoys/.

Les Echos. 2013. "Les statistiques grecques de nouveau contestées, Bruxelles s'inquiète." 4 June. https://www-nexis-com.ezproxy.lib.bbk.ac.uk/docview/getDocForCuiReq?lni=58K7-TCR1-F066-M4C0&csi=5826&oc=00240&perma=true.

Minister of Finance. 2013. Transfer of power to the Secretary General of the Secretariat General for Public Revenue of the Ministry of Finance, Δ6A 1145867 ΕΞ2013. Government Gazette, B2417, 27 September (in Greek).

Minister of Finance. 2014a. Decision regarding the appointment of a DG at the SGPR as its head, Δ1A 1088546 ΕΞ 2014. Government Gazette 338, 11 June, 1503 (in Greek).

Minister of Finance. 2014b. Open call for expression of interest in the position of Secretary General for Public Revenue, 6 June. Athens: Ministry of Finance (in Greek).

Ministry of Finance. 2012. Open call for expression of interest in the position of Secretary General for Public Revenue, 29 November. Athens: Ministry of Finance (in Greek).

Ministry of Finance. 2015. Call for expression of interest for the appointment of members of the advisory board of the SGPR at the Ministry of Finance, 5 June. Athens: Ministry of Finance (in Greek).

Naftemporiki. 2014. "Harry Theoharis resigns." 5 June (in Greek), accessed January 1st, 2019. https://www.naftemporiki.gr/finance/story/817214/paraitithike-o-xaris-theoxaris.

Naftemporiki. 2015. "Who will assess the applications for the SGPR." 8 June (in Greek), accessed 30 December 2018. https://www.naftemporiki.gr/finance/story/818151/poioi-tha-aksiologisoun-tis-upopsifiotites-gia-ti-ggde.

Papaconstantinou, George. 2016. *Game Over: The Truth about the Crisis*. Athens: Papadopoulos (in Greek). Original edition, Game Over: Η Αλήθεια για την Κρίση.

Pappous, Yorgos. 2014. "The list of ten candidates for replacing H. Theoharis reaches the Maximos mansion." *iefimerida*, 21 June (in Greek). Accessed 17 December 2017. https://www.iefimerida.gr/news/160220/στο-μαξίμου-η-λίστα-των-10-υποψήφιων-διαδόχων-του-χάρη-θεοχάρη.

Parliamentary Budget Office. 2014. Quarterly report April-June 2014. Athens: Hellenic Parliament.

POE-DOY. 2013a. Press release number 299/2013, 6 June. Athens: POE-DOY (in Greek).

POE-DOY. 2013b. Press release number 200. Athens (in Greek).

POE-DOY. 2013c. Statement Nr. 205 of 12 March. Athens (in Greek).

POE-DOY. 2014. Decision of the General Council of 18 July 2014 in relation to staff assessment. Athens: POE-DOY (in Greek).

Reporter.gr. 2015. "Tender and stormy relations between SGPR and SGIT/GGPS?", 28 July (in Greek). https://www.reporter.gr/Eidhseis/Oikonomia/266006-Scheseis-«storghs-kai-orghs»-metaxy-GGDE-kai-GGPS.

Samaras, Antonis. 2010. Speech by the President of Nea Demokratia on the occasion of the presentation of ND's economic programme 'Strategy of hope for exit from the crisis', Zappeio, Athens, 7 July (in Greek).

Savvaidou, Katerina. n.d. "Curriculum vitae." Personal page on the website of the Faculty of Law, Aristotle University of Thessaloniki, accessed 20 December 2018. https://www.law.auth.gr/en/staff-public-savvaidou.

Schlötzer, Christiane. 2013. "Griechen klagen Statistikchef an." *Tages-Anzeiger*, 13 February, Wirthschaft. https://www-nexis-com.ezproxy.lib.bbk.ac.uk/docview/getDocForCuiReq?lni=57RC-G9H1-DYJJ-C3BW&csi=5949&oc=00240&perma=true.

Secretariat General for Public Revenue. 2015. "Annual report for 2014 and action plan for 2015." Ministry of Finance (in Greek).

Spanou, Calliope. 2018. "External influence on structural reform: did policy conditionality strengthen reform capacity in Greece?" *Public Policy and Administration*:1-23. doi: https://doi.org/10.1177/0952076718772008.

Stagkos, Aggelos. 2013. "The political class is shooting itself." *Kathimerini*, 6 June (in Greek). http://www.kathimerini.gr/735426/opinion/epikairothta/arxeio-monimes-sthles/h-politikh-ta3h-aytopyrovoleitai.

Story, T., T. Byrd, W. Crandall, J. Leamy, J. Nagy, I. Petrova, B. Russell, E. Empl, F. Van Driessche, P. Weinzierl, S. Weinzierl, and C. Wendling. 2013. Greece - fourth joint assessment by the IMF and the European Commission: revenue management and institutional reforms. IMF/European Commission.

Story, T., G. Harrison, J Leamy, A. Sorensen, J. Bussink, P. Vandenberghe, F. Van Driessche, S. Weinzierl, and C. Wendling. 2012. Greece - administrative reform state of affairs and report on VAT (3rd joint review by the IMF and the European Commission). Washington, D.C.: IMF/European Commission (in Greek).

Süddeutsche Zeitung. 2012. "Welche Zumutungen die Griechen nun ertragen müssen." *Süddeutsche Zeitung*, 13 February. https://www.sueddeutsche.de/wirtschaft/nach-dem-ja-zum-sparpaket-welche-zumutungen-die-griechen-nun-ertragen-muessen-1.1282482.

Süddeutsche Zeitung. 2015. "Der Mann, der den Griechen 130 Milliarden Euro geliehen hat." 5 July. http://www.sueddeutsche.de/wirtschaft/griechenland-der-mann-der-den-griechen-milliarden-euro-geliehen-hat-1.2550801.

Ta Nea. 2012. "Who is Stelios Stasinopoulos." 3 October (in Greek). Accessed 14 May 2018. http://www.tanea.gr/news/greece/article/4756657/?iid=2.

Telloglou, Tassos. 2014a. "Quietly, during August." Protagon, 23 August (in Greek), accessed 12 March 2019. https://www.protagon.gr/epikairotita/ellada/athoryva-mesa-ston-avgousto-35992000000.

Telloglou, Tassos. 2014b. "Useless? Re-hired!" Protagon, 27 December (in Greek), accessed 12 March 2019. https://www.protagon.gr/epikairotita/ellada/den-kanei-gia-tipota-proslamvanetai-pali-38533000000.

Thomas Jr., Landon, and Stephen Castle. 2011. "The Denials That Trapped Greece." *New York Times*, 5 November, Global Business. Accessed 20 December 2018. https://www.nytimes.com/2011/11/06/business/global/europes-two-years-of-denials-trapped-greece.html.

Thomsen, Poul. 2013a. Interview with the Deputy Director of the IMF's European Department and Mission Chief for Greece, published in Greek in Real News, 27 January. Washington, D.C.: IMF. Original edition, Real News, Athens.

Thomsen, Poul. 2013b. Interview with the Deputy Director of the IMF's European Department and Mission Chief for Greece, originally published in Greek in Ta Nea, 26 January 2013. Washington D.C.: IMF.

To Vima. 2014. "Proposal for the free transfer of tax officers between SDOE and SGPR." 27 February (in Greek), Economy. Accessed 28 December 2018. https://www.tovima.gr/2014/02/27/finance/protasi-gia-eleytheri-metakinisi-twn-eforiakwn-metaksy-sdoe-ggde/.

TVXS. 2015a. "Exclusive: blue favours Inc. ND's success story." TVXS.gr, 31 March (in Greek), accessed 28 December 2018. https://tvxs.gr/news/ellada/tvxs-apokleistiko-galazia-roysfetia-ae-success-story-tis-nd.

TVXS. 2015b. "Exclusive: Blue favours Inc. part 2." TVXS.gr, 1 April (in Greek), accessed 28 December 2018. https://tvxs.gr/news/ellada/tvxs-apokleistiko-galazia-roysfetia-meros-deyteron.

Varvitsioti, Eleni. 2016. "Samaras and Tsipras parallel lives...déjà vu." *Kathimerini*, 7 July (in Greek). http://www.kathimerini.gr/848555/article/epikairothta/politikh/vioi-parallhloi-tsipra%2D%2D-samara-se-deja-vu.

Varvitsiotis, Eleni, and Tassos Telloglou. 2015. "The review that never ended." *Kathimerini*, 7 June (in Greek), Investigations. http://www.kathimerini.gr/818336/article/epikairothta/ereynes/h-a3iologhsh-poy-den-ekleise-pote.

Vassiliadou, Nadia. 2013. "Partisan transfers into the civil service inspection corps." *Kyriakatiki Eleftherotypia*, 17 March (in Greek). http://www.enet.gr/?i=news.el.article&id=351018.

Weinzierl, Sebastian. 2015. "Die EU-Task-Force für Griehcenland: internationale Beratung am Beispiel der griechischen Steuerverwaltung." In *Die Krise in Griechenland: Ursprünge, Verlauf, Folgen*, edited by Ulf-Dieter Klemm and Wolfgang Schultheiß, 448-460. Frankfurt/New York: Campus.

Zacharakis, Zacharias. 2015. "Griechenlands schwieriger Kampf gegen Steuerbetrug." *Die Zeit*, 13 February. http://www.zeit.de/wirtschaft/2015-02/griechenland-steuern-tsipras/komplettansicht

Zafiropoulos, Costas. 2015. "Triangular exchanges and the questions that they raise." *Efimerida Ton Syntakton*, 30 October (in Greek), Justice. http://www.efsyn.gr/arthro/oi-trigonikes-synallages-kai-ta-erotimata-poy-prokyptoyn.

Chapter 5
The Third MoU and the Establishment of the Independent Authority for Public Revenue

The Context

When SYRIZA (Coalition of the Radical Left—until then the main opposition party) won the first of the two general elections of 2015 in January of that year, it formed a coalition government with the Independent Greeks (ANEL), a small, right-wing, nationalist, populist party. Their ideological differences notwithstanding, their common thread was (a) vehement opposition to the terms of the first two bailout agreements signed by previous governments in 2010 and 2012, but also (b) a rather aggressive populist rhetoric (on SYRIZA and populism see Mudde 2016; Katsambekis and Stavrakakis 2014), pitching 'the people' on the one hand against the 'lenders' and their 'domestic allies' in the country's *élite* on the other, including the centre-right ND[1] and the centre-left PASOK, i.e. the two parties that had been governing Greece since 1974.

By the time the SYRIZA-ANEL coalition took office in January 2015 the extent and intensity of the lenders' involvement in the management of the country (based on the first two bailout agreements) had gone far beyond the requirements of a time-limited debt crisis. As a consequence, it would be an understatement to say that an incoming government that had won an election on the basis of a promise to 'tear up' the Memorandums of Understanding (MoUs) and renegotiate new and better terms was facing an uphill struggle. In a multi-faceted negotiation between fundamentally unequal parties credibility and good preparation can be valuable assets for the weaker party. However, the new Greek government was lacking both in relation to the country's revenue administration.

Indeed, the SYRIZA-led government had inherited a very deep sense of distrust that previous Greek administrations had done so much to generate in the eyes of the International Monetary Fund (IMF) as well as the country's partners within the

[1] Little did it matter that SYRIZA's coalition partner was led by a career politician who had been a government minister in ND governments.

D. Dimitrakopoulos, A. Passas, *The Depoliticisation of Greece's Public Revenue Administration*, https://doi.org/10.1007/978-3-030-23213-9_5

European Union (EU) at least since the onset of the crisis. Little did it matter that SYRIZA was a new party and only one of its frontbenchers had some (very limited) ministerial experience.[2] This enabled SYRIZA to vehemently denounce the corruption and clientelism of the past and promise to lead a determined fight against tax evasion. This was very important since around a quarter (i.e. three billion euros) of the cost of their anti-austerity measures (known as the 'Thessaloniki programme') would be funded in that way (Guillot 2015). Although this could (in theory) have presaged the development of concrete plans to deal with this issue that had dogged the modern Greek state practically since its establishment in 1830, SYRIZA had no such plans whatsoever, at least with regard to the country's public revenue administration[3] (but see Varoufakis 2017: 173, 219–220, 527–528 on his own plans for tackling tax evasion). The lack of such plans appears even more striking if one considers that academic economists close to or within SYRIZA believed that a significant part of the country's primary deficit at the onset of the crisis was due to poor tax collection (Tsakalotos 2010: 10, Figs. 2 and 3; Koutentakis 2018). It also speaks directly to a key feature of the prevailing Greek political culture, i.e. an emphasis on sloganeering instead of the preparation of concrete plans on some key issues that a new government knows it will have to face (see Chap. 1). The lack of ministerial experience, coupled with the Greek civil service's inability to think on its feet (see Chap. 1), rendered the lack of concrete plans a far bigger problem for the new government that also had to cope with a major crisis.

Moreover, the first two bailout agreements covered such a vast array of issues that an inexperienced government faced with (1) an acute crisis and (2) an overwhelmingly powerful counterpart needed to prioritise ruthlessly amongst the multiple potential objectives. Ahead of the 2015 elections SYRIZA's substantive critique of the bailout agreements had focused largely on

(a) the size of the primary budget surpluses they stipulated as targets (for they were 'choking' demand and the Greek economy's ability to recover) and
(b) the abolition of various forms of workers' rights protections.

At the same time, the precise status of the country's public revenue administration and in particular, whether or the extent to which it would report directly to the Finance Minister or not, was neither an issue that could make the headlines, nor a matter capable of making a difference in the electoral arena. After all, for many Greeks their local tax office was a place where they often had their time wasted, or a

---

[2]That was Yannis Dragassakis, the Tsipras administration's effective number 2 but this experience dated back in 1989–1990.

[3]Equally striking is the fact that the agreement with its junior partner did not take the form of a text entailing specific policies that the two parties had agreed to carry out in a range of policy sectors. This contrasts markedly with the detailed written text whereby participating parties commit to specific policies in a whole range of policy sectors in advanced liberal democracies in Europe such as the 185-page coalition agreement between the German Christian Democrats and Social Democrats (CDU et al. 2013) or the 35-page agreement reached by the Conservatives and the Liberal Democrats in the UK in 2010 (HM Government 2010).

place that exemplified (alongside municipal authorities, planning offices and hospitals) the country's corruption problem (Public Issue 2010, Figs. 16, 17, 2013, Fig. 5).

Finally, in early 2015 SYRIZA was far from being united on the key issue of Greece's continuing membership of the Eurozone. Indeed, there was a sizeable and rather vocal group of SYRIZA MPs[4] as well as several government ministers[5] who favoured the return to the drachma. SYRIZA's parliamentary party was united in its determination to try to renegotiate the terms of Greece's adjustment programmes but in the absence of major progress on that front, some (unlike others) were willing to opt for default and what became colloquially known as 'Grexit'.

Despite the fresh popular mandate that the first Tsipras-led government had received, these internal divisions on this fundamental issue further weakened the government's negotiating position for two reasons. First, in early 2015 the Eurozone was certainly not as devoid of crisis management tools as it was at the start of the crisis. Second, in the meantime European banks' exposure to Greek government debt had been drastically reduced due to the second bailout agreement (2012) with the 'official sector' replacing them as the main holder of Greek debt. This goes a long way towards explaining the new government's opening gambit in the negotiations that soon followed.

Negotiating the Third MoU

Upon taking office in January 2015 new Finance Minister Yanis Varoufakis—a colourful and internationally known professor of economics at the University of Athens who was a vocal critic of the hitherto management of the crisis and a co-author of an alternative plan for the handling of the crisis in the Eurozone (see Varoufakis et al. 2013) stated that around 60–70% of the adjustment programme's content was appropriate and fully compatible with the new government's mandate (Varoufakis 2015a: 2–3). However, the programme had 'failed to "tackle the worst excesses of corruption and rent-seeking"' (Wagstyl et al. 2015) and he wanted to negotiate a viable deal on the remainder, with a focus on alleviating the austerity-induced pressure on the economy.[6]

Increasing the autonomy of the public revenue administration was amongst the measures on which the new Greek government could agree with the country's

[4]One of the most prominent amongst them was Costas Lapavitsas, a professor of economics at London University's School of Oriental and African Studies who had been campaigning over many years for the country's exit from the Eurozone (see, e.g. Lapavitsas 2011; cf. Dimitrakopoulos 2011).

[5]These included Energy, Environment and Reconstruction Minister Panayiotis Lafazanis, Alternate Finance Minister Nadia Valavani (whose remit included tax collection), Alternate Foreign Minister Nikos Khountis, Alternate Defence Minister Costas Isykhos and Alternate Health and Social Security Minister Dimitris Stratoulis. All were also MPs, except Khountis who was a member of European Parliament (MEP).

[6]At that point in time the official target was primary surplus of 4.5% of GDP.

partners. At his first Eurogroup meeting Varoufakis declared that the new government wanted 'to discuss legislative proposals to reinforce the legal framework for an independent tax authority' and called for (further) technical assistance on these issues (Varoufakis 2015a: 3). In the corresponding non-paper the new government stated that it was ready 'to discuss legislative proposals to reinforce the legal framework for an *independent* tax authority *within* the Ministry of Finance' (Hellenic Government 2015: 12; our emphasis, see also his public statement reported on Antenna News 2015). A clearer signal was given at the following meeting of the Eurogroup when Varoufakis stated the government's commitment to 'tax authority reforms towards greater independence, propriety and transparency' (Hellenic Government 2015: 12; our emphasis, see also Varoufakis' public statement on Antenna News 2015) and (under pressure from the country's partners[7]) included acceptance of the prospect of establishing a management board that would take over key internal functions, including personnel-related ones, away from the influence of politicians (Varoufakis 2015b: 16).

This acceptance, however, did not reflect genuine agreement. Varoufakis, an expert in game theory, was well aware of the uneven distribution of power between Greece and its lenders and this is why he opted to 'make all the compromises upfront and then stick to one's guns without bluffs or stratagems' (Varoufakis 2017: 227). At that point in time Greece was formally committed to an annual primary surplus of 4.5% of gross domestic product (GDP) and also faced major debt payments over the summer of 2015.[8] The idea of greater autonomy was facing opposition within the government. Indeed, Nadia Valavani, then Alternate Finance Minister in charge of tax collection, was vehemently against it (Valavani 2016: 116–117) as was her successor though he came from a different wing of the party (see below). Valavani was also opposed to SDOE's (Financial Crime Squad) merger with the public revenue administration (see below). The tax collectors' union too was vehemently opposed to granting greater autonomy [which they sometimes conflated with privatisation (see Chap. 4)] to the country's public revenue administration (interviews, Athens, 13 February 2017). This opposition existed against a backdrop of a feeling amongst insiders that, during the crisis, the public revenue administration's headquarters in Athens had become something akin to the lenders' playground (interviews, Athens, 15 February, 3 April and 2 August 2017).[9] This is so because of the extensive presence of (especially) IMF officials within the public revenue

[7]This pressure shows that—to a very large extent—European and IMF officials were seeking to address issues created by the previous Greek government. That is a point that government ministers had also made in public at that point in time (see report on Antenna News 2015).

[8]Set against expected annual revenues of around 50 billion euros, these specific liabilities amounted to 5.2 billion euros by the end of June to the IMF and 6.7 billion euros in July and August to the European Central Bank (ECB), as Varoufakis told the Eurogroup on 11 February 2015. The financial pressures were acute—as the government acknowledged—and this is why Varoufakis asked the Eurogroup for bridging finance while negotiations on a new agreement were taking place.

[9]Varoufakis who shared this view also asked German Finance Minister Wolfgang Schäuble to choose the head of Greece's public revenue administration (Varoufakis 2017: 211).

administration's headquarters in central Athens. So, since the proposal to further increase the public revenue administration's autonomy came from the lenders, to some this symbolised the country's perceived[10] broader loss of 'sovereignty'.

This opposition reflected several considerations. A major part of SYRIZA's opposition to the depoliticisation of Greece's public revenue administration is couched in the argument that not all politicians are corrupt and prone to interfering in operational (or other) decisions of the public revenue administration (but of course this begs the question of how the public interest is protected against those who are prone to this behaviour). On the contrary—and this is the second point of SYRIZA *cadres*' critique of increased autonomy or independence—democracy is not served when the public revenue administration operates at arm's length from the government of the day. Indeed, whom will the public blame if or when that administration fails to meet its targets? If the line of accountability ends at the Finance Minister's office, voters can punish or reward the government at the ballot box but the same cannot be done with the head of a body that operates at arm's length from the government (interviews, Athens, 9 November 2016, 15 February 2017). Third, while there was support at the highest *échelon* of the first Tsipras administration for the 'departification' of the civil service (see Dragassakis 2015), i.e. doing away with the enduring practices (and consequences) of appointing, promoting or demoting civil servants not on merit but on the basis of their party affiliation, the same officials claimed that 'cleaning up' the public revenue administration (i.e. tackling the issues of corruption and partitocracy) had to be the priority (interview, Athens, 9 November 2016). There is merit to this idea. Increasing the autonomy of the public revenue administration entailed the risk of packaging away its corrupt part too. Doing so during a period of acute economic crisis—i.e. a time when the incentives for tax evasion and avoidance had multiplied—was even riskier and a reason why George Papaconstantinou (Greece's first Finance Minister to face the crisis) did not opt for radical reform (see Chap. 3). Moreover, the idea that the fight against corruption should precede other reforms, reflects the aforementioned notion that not all politicians are the same (i.e. corrupt), which is true, and implies the need for direct political oversight. On the other hand, cleaning up the public revenue administration required concrete plans that the new (SYRIZA-ANEL) government did not have. So, from the perspective of the lenders, the new government's critique could be seen as an attempt to kick reform into the long grass.

Another major critique of independence relates directly to the nature of a public revenue administration's work. As a former senior official of the tax collectors' union noted (interview, Athens, 15 February 2017), a government that seeks to reduce the illicit trade on fuels can do so either by focusing on (a) oil refineries or (b) petrol stations. The choice between the two is not technical but political. This means that in the second case the target would be a potentially large number of individuals who are not well connected to the country's political establishment,

---

[10]This begs the question as to how sovereign a country really is when it owes as much as Greece did at that point in time.

while in the first case the target would be a handful of very wealthy, powerful and well-connected individuals. This, however, begs three questions:

1. Why does one have to choose between the two routes?
2. How often does a public revenue administration actually face this type of dilemma?
3. Who is better placed to make this call? The head of an independent public revenue administration or the head of one that reports to the finance minister?

Finally, as regards the officials of the tax collectors' union, two key factors help explain their opposition to this reform. First, they stood to lose a tried and tested channel of influence (i.e. via the minister) over key decisions, especially in terms of human resource management. Second, a depoliticised public revenue administration was much more likely (than its predecessor) to operate in a goal-orientated manner, especially at a time of an acute crisis which had revealed the consequences of the status quo ante, including the centrality of poor tax collection as a cause of the country's huge public debt, and had brought about the pervasive presence of EU and IMF officials. Yet, just like Greece's other traditionally powerful public sector unions, tax collectors' union officials too were vehemently opposed to staff assessment (see Chap. 4), a key management tool that the leadership of any depoliticised public revenue administration was bound to use.

Nevertheless, the Tsipras-led administration retained its focus on the efforts to improve the terms of the increasingly necessary new bailout agreement that it had prioritised. While an interim deal was reached in February 2015 to extend the (still unfinished) second adjustment programme by 4 months, a more enduring agreement was needed. This agreement had become an absolute necessity because the adjustment programme that had been attached to the second MoU had not been completed and, as a consequence, the corresponding funds had been released. Moreover, during the negotiations of spring and early summer of that year, the Greek government had to make use of emergency measures so as to pay pensions and public sector wages but was rapidly running out of funds and the bond markets were off bounds. Despite opposition within the Ministry of Finance, the Greek government confirmed its willingness to pursue the depoliticisation of the country's public revenue administration in its proposals of 1 June 2015 (interviews, Athens, 15 February and 2 August 2017) thus confirming that this issue has not a deal-breaker.

These negotiations ended in acrimony on 26 June 2015 as the Greek government was unwilling to agree to the other side's final proposals largely on grounds of the austerity measures that they entailed. Prime Minister Tsipras called a referendum on these proposals and asked the Greek people to vote against them so as to send a clear signal to the other side in the negotiations that (he claimed) would follow. On the EU's side, the referendum was presented as a Greek decision to retain or drop the Euro. A direct consequence of these tensions and the instability that they generated was the imposition of capital controls in Greece aimed at preventing the Greek banks from collapsing after months of capital flight. The Greek people clearly rejected the proposed deal (61–39% on 62.5% turnout) and Tsipras replaced Varoufakis with Euclid Tsakalotos—an Oxford-educated professor of economics at the University of

Athens who had been a SYRIZA MP since 2012 and was also opposed to the public revenue administration's full independence[11] (Antenna News 2015). The negotiations that followed ended on 13 July 2015 with an agreement on the new (third) bailout agreement and programme. The large group of Grexit supporters within SYRIZA opposed it in Parliament or abstained[12] and left the party soon after the deal was approved by a large cross-party majority of 222 out of a total of 300 MPs. In the subsequent elections that PM Tsipras called for September 2015, SYRIZA won 145 seats forming a parliamentary party that was much more coherent than the previous one on the central issue of the country's membership of the Eurozone. SYRIZA then formed another coalition government with the right-wing, nationalist populist ANEL.

The third MoU was much more detailed—in terms of the reform of Greece's public revenue administration—than the first two had been, but was not deprived of a degree of ambiguity. The relevant passage indicated that the Greek authorities, with the help of technical assistance would, inter alia,

> *strengthen the independence of the revenue administration.* The authorities will by October 2015 adopt legislation (key deliverable) to establish an autonomous revenue agency, that specifies: (a) the agency's legal form, organization, status, and scope; (b) the powers and functions of the CEO and the independent Board of Governors; (c) the relationship to the Minister of Finance and other government entities; (d) the agency's human resource flexibility and relationship to the civil service; (e) budget autonomy, with own GDFS [General Directorate for Financial Services] and a new funding formula to align incentives with revenue collection and guarantee budget predictability and flexibility; (f) reporting to the government and parliament. The authorities will by December 2015 (key deliverable) appoint the Board of Governors and adopt priority secondary legislation of the law (key human resource, budget) on the autonomous revenue administration agency, so that it can be fully operational by June 2016 (European Commission, Hellenic Republic, and Bank of Greece 2015: 11).

The amount of detail that this passage contains is quite impressive and indicates the EU and the IMF's determination to pursue the reform of the public revenue administration of a country where even the governor of its central bank[13] was arguing that the depoliticisation of the civil service had to be pursued (Bank of Greece 2016: 26). The EU and the IMF's determination also shows they had learned the lesson of the post-2010 past which—as the effective dismissal of the public revenue administration's first semi-autonomous head H. Theoharis shows—was not deprived of attempts (on the part of the Greek political *élite*) to revert to the status quo ante. The increasing amount of detail contained in the (by now) contract-like MoU is a

[11]Earlier in the year, speaking as Alternate Foreign Minister, Tsakalotos argued that 'those who work for independent agencies have their own views' and the management of public finances cannot be independent of the will of the people (Antenna News 2015).

[12]From a total of 149 SYRIZA MPs, 32 opposed it and 11 abstained.

[13]Ironically, that was Professor Yannis Stournaras who (a) had actually served as Finance Minister of the previous administration prior to being appointed Governor of the Bank of Greece and (b) had effectively sacked the first head of the semi-autonomous SGPR in the summer of 2014.

Table 5.1 Disbursements under the third programme (in billion Euros)

Date of disbursement	Amount	Maturity
20/08/2015	13	Amortisation from 2034 to 2057
24/11/2015	2	Amortisation from 2034 to 2057
01/12/2015	2.7	Amortisation from 2055 to 2059
08/12/2015	2.7	
23/12/2015	1	Amortisation from 2034 to 2057
21/06/2016	7.5	Amortisation from 2034 to 2058
26/10/2016	2.8	Amortisation from 2034 to 2058
10/07/2017	7.7	Amortisation from 2034 to 2059
30/10/2017	0.8	Amortisation from 2034 to 2059
28/03/2018	5.7	Amortisation from 2051 to 2054; 2060
15/06/2018	1	Amortisation from 2034 to 2060
06/08/2018	15	Amortisation from 2043 to 2060
Total	61.9	

Source: Adapted by the authors from ESM (n.d.)

response to these attempts.[14] On the other hand, the ambiguity in the third MoU's terminology is also striking. With regard to the institutional status of the country's public revenue administration, the text of the MoU refers to both independence and autonomy. In terms of the organisational form, it refers to revenue administration, revenue agency and revenue administration agency. Finally, in terms of accountability, it refers to reporting to both the government and parliament. This ambiguity appears to indicate that there was some room for negotiations between the EU and the IMF on the one hand and the Greek government on the other on the details of the future of the country's public revenue administration. This does not negate the fact that Greece's partners remained in the driving seat as demonstrated by the structuring of disbursements (which of course remained conditional on the programme's progress) over time—a key feature of conditionality—as Table 5.1 indicates.

So, how did we get from the third MoU to the law that established the Independent Authority for Public Revenue?

Drafting the Law Establishing the Independent Authority for Public Revenue

At that point in time, the politician leading the negotiation on the Greek side was Alternate Finance Minister Tryfon Alexiadis. He had been an employee of the Ministry of Finance since 1987 and had also served in senior posts in the tax

[14]It is also important to note that the first MoU was signed in conditions of acute crisis requiring quick action. As an international official put it, 'when you come during a crisis, you go for quick wins; you cannot write a long thing. You have to be short and efficient' (interview, Athens, 30 March 2017).

collectors' union (Alexiadis 2015). Alexiadis was vehemently opposed to increasing the autonomy of the public revenue administration despite acknowledging that (a) the principle of politicians' non-interference in the operation of the public administration and tax collection in particular was sound and (b) it had been violated on numerous occasions in the past. When asked—upon taking office in July 2015—by the press why tax collection is so hard in Greece, Alexiadis ascribed it to interference by politicians and others and the lack of political will to give the public revenue administration the means (including staff and equipment) it needed, but was also quick to note that he had not been put under pressure to interfere in any of the last 5300 tax inspections and this showed the public's awareness that the new government's senior officials were very different (L'Echo 2015). This speaks directly to SYRIZA's views that 'not all politicians are the same' but leaves open the question of what happens once a minister who is prone to interfering has taken over.

With Alexiadis in charge of this part of the portfolio of the Ministry of Finance, the process that followed was unsurprisingly eventful. Two of his closest collaborators and an official from the Finance Minister's office met officials from the (still semi-autonomous) Secretariat General for Public Revenue with a view to creating—with the technical assistance of the European Commission's Structural Reform Support Service—a roadmap towards the end result. They came up with two scenarios which also exemplified the government's view as to the potential final shape of this key reform though the final decision would be subject to the lenders' approval. One scenario entailed the establishment of an independent authority while the other involved "a more independent [than the hitherto existing] secretariat general", i.e. a structure within the Ministry of Finance (interview, Athens, 2 August 2017).

One major issue that these officials faced was the extent to which the proposed reform was compatible with the Greek Constitution. The issue of constitutionality had two dimensions. First, collecting taxes is a core function of any state. As a consequence, it may not be delegated to an independent authority under the Greek Constitution. Second, the Greek Constitution contains an exhaustive list of independent authorities and a public revenue-related one is not amongst them. This was one of the arguments against the reform used by the tax collectors' union on the basis of legal advice that they commissioned (Karouzos 2016: 2).[15] The aforementioned ministerial officials sought legal advice from various jurists (including academics and a very senior judge of the State Council, the country's top administrative court). Two of these jurists claimed that both solutions were compatible with the country's constitution while one argued that only a structure within the Ministry of Finance would pass the constitutionality test (interview, Athens, 2 August 2017).

[15]The claim of unconstitutionality is also based on the view that the (then draft) law was in breach of the principle of separation of powers, the judicial and parliamentary control of the new authority's decisions was deficient, its powers are not specific (as the Constitution requires) but generic in nature and have been transferred to an institution that is politically irresponsible (which is a breach of the principle of popular sovereignty that is enshrined in the Constitution), the Governor's power in terms of personnel, promotions, and so on breach the principles of transparency and equal treatment (Karouzos 2016: 3–8).

In October 2015—while representatives of government ministries, officials of the EU and the IMF (including those working on providing technical assistance) were trying to give concrete meaning to the third MoU's provisions on the reform of Greece's public revenue administration—the Greek government made a consequential decision. Finance Minister Euclid Tsakalotos asked Katerina Savvaidou, then head of the semi-autonomous public revenue administration (SGPR), to resign but she refused to do so (Kathimerini (English edition) 2015). A few days later (22 October 2015) she was dismissed on a proposal of the finance minister that was endorsed unanimously by the Cabinet, on the basis of the civil service code of conduct. This dismissal was directly linked to senior prosecutors' decision to charge Savvaidou with breach of duty for granting Greek TV channels extra time to pay tax on advertising income[16] and her decision to order a review of the public revenue administration's decision to impose a very large fine (78 million euros) on a Greek company. Savvaidou's former decision related to the country's most powerful media and their owners while the latter decision related to one of the country's wealthiest and most influential entrepreneurs. She strenuously denied both charges (Kathimerini (English edition) 2015) but her critics amongst tax collectors pointed out that (a) in the latter case the law was unambiguous and allowed a review (which she ordered) only if new information had come to the fore (which had not happened) and (b) the strength of the feeling was such that two experienced tax auditors who were involved in this case had resigned after her decision to order a review of the decision to impose the fine despite the fact that the fine had been confirmed by an administrative dispute panel (Efimerida Ton Syntakton 2017b; interview, Athens, 2 August 2017).

Three additional points ought to be noted here. First, as indicated in Chap. 4, Savvaidou's connections with Nea Dimokratia (the centre-right, main opposition party at the time of her dismissal) were well known (Financial Times 2015), as was her work for both Arthur Andersen and PriceWaterhouseCoopers in Greece, i.e. two of the largest firms that offer, inter alia, 'tax optimisation' advice to wealthy clients. Second, given the gravity of the charges that public prosecutors brought against her, it would have been extremely hard for her to remain in post, even in the presence of a supportive government, since senior officials occupying posts like hers should not only be but also appear to be beyond reproach. Third, her decisions that resulted in these charges were made against a specific backdrop of perceived inequality before the law, a point that the government too made at the time (Financial Times 2015). There is a widespread belief amongst ordinary Greeks that as long as the wealthiest members of their society do not pay their taxes, they too are entitled to do the same but there is also evidence that powerful interests had received preferential treatment. Repeated deferrals of taxes due on TV channels' main[17] source of income, i.e. their

[16]She took that decision days before the election of January 2015, as the press revealed at the time but this was not the first deferral of this particular tax (Financial Times 2015; Kanellopoulos 2015).

[17]That is apart from sometimes unsecured bank loans worth several hundred millions.

advertising revenue, was one such example[18] that stood awkwardly next to many ordinary Greeks' loss of upwards of a quarter of their income under the austerity measures taken since 2010. A party like SYRIZA that had made a lot of political capital out of telling voters that, unlike its predecessors in power, it was not tied to such interests and had been elected to fight precisely against this kind of preferential treatment, was always bound to find it extremely hard to renege on at least this promise.[19] Taken together these three points rendered the decision to dismiss Savvaidou politically irresistible for the government.

This decision, however, was also consequential in ways that the Greek government could have foreseen. First of all, the story made it into influential international media outlets (see, e.g. Kitsantonis 2015; Szymanski 2015; Frankfurter Allgemeine Zeitung 2015; Dixon 2015; Financial Times 2015) at a time when the country was struggling to attract international investors and begin to find a degree of normalcy after the acrimonious negotiations earlier in the same year. Irrespective of the merits or otherwise of the charges brought against Savvaidou, it was impossible to convince the country's partners that her dismissal was not politically motivated, since (a) up until that point, i.e. just a few months after the end of an acrimonious negotiation that led to the third bailout, the sense of distrust remained quite strong amongst EU and IMF officials and (b) her association with the main opposition party was not unknown. What mattered to that particular audience was the lack of leadership stability in an evolving institution and the government's credibility in relation to this key reform. As the IMF subsequently noted, 'political commitment to respect [sic] the fixed-term appointment and provide leadership stability to the revenue administration was absent from mid-2014 to early 2016, when reform progress slowed significantly' (IMF 2017: 43). Above all, the image of a country whose political *élite* was still bent on resisting change after not one or two but three bailouts was quite powerful. This latter narrative was supported (interview, Athens, 3 April 2017) by another enduring (and still ongoing) saga, namely various felony charges that public prosecutors brought—as early as January 2013, i.e. under the previous coalition government (Kathimerini 2013b)—against the head of another independent institution, namely the Hellenic Statistical Authority (ELSTAT).[20] Just a few weeks before Savvaidou's dismissal, the country's second most senior public prosecutor had sought to overturn a previous ruling that had exonerated Andreas Georgiou of the charge of falsely stating the country's public finances (Mandrou

[18]Another was the operation (since 1990) of these private channels on the basis of temporary licences. This meant they were using a public resource (the spectrum) without paying the corresponding fee at market rate.

[19]Varoufakis claims that even the IMF's top official on the Greek programme wanted them to do so (Varoufakis 2017: 184).

[20]The investigation that led to these criminal charges commenced in 2011 but had been going on since then (see Chaps. 3 and 4) thus enhancing the impression that Greece's political *élite* is inimical to independent authorities.

2015, for a complete chronology of judicial proceedings see International Statistical Institute 2018).[21]

Two other events that took place in the autumn of 2015 contributed to the strengthening of EU and IMF officials' sense of distrust vis-à-vis the SYRIZA-ANEL government. One was the poor quality of the first draft of the law that Alternate Minister Alexiadis presented to them. The other was personnel-related decisions made by the SGPR's interim head, Ioannis Bakas that appeared to be dictated by internal (political) pressures (interview, Athens, 2 August 2017). More specifically, Bakas—a career official of the public revenue administration who had been appointed interim head of the SGPR by the SYRIZA-ANEL government—devised a special procedure for the appointment of heads of some key units, sub-directorates and directorates so as to deal with pressing needs of the administration (once the incumbents' term of office had expired), as the government replied to critiques from opposition parties with the main difference in comparison to the hitherto applicable procedure being the non-involvement of an advisory board whose opinion was not binding anyway (Christodoulou 2016; Hadjinikolaou 2016). This decision was taken while the appointment of the new head of the entire SGPR was still pending and further contributed to the aforementioned feeling of distrust amongst EU and IMF officials.

Taken together, these developments had a key consequence. They hardened the EU and the IMF's stance (interviews, Athens, 15 February, 3 April and 2 August 2017). In particular, while up until that point the European Commission's staff were not that keen on the IMF's continuing promotion of the idea of an independent agency (preferring more autonomy, in line with the model that prevails in EU member states), the SYRIZA-ANEL government's aforementioned actions significantly undermined its own commitment to depoliticisation and deprived Commission officials of the leeway that they hitherto had in that respect. Both the European Commission and the IMF acknowledged this link in subsequent reports (European Commission 2017b: 55; IMF 2017: 43).

However, it is also important to note that while this was happening, evidence indicates the SYRIZA-ANEL government was beginning to act in good faith, albeit in the shadow of the EU and the IMF's significant local presence and very intrusive oversight which is typical of conditionality-based programmes. The process that led to the appointment of Savvaidou's successor is indicative of both. An international call for applications was followed by the establishment of a seven-strong panel that—unlike the one used for Savvaidou's appointment—included only a minority of government appointees.[22] The other members were the heads of (1) the (independent) Higher Council for Personnel Selection (as its chair), (2) the Parliament's

[21]The Georgiou saga ended in February 2019 with his acquittal (WSJ Europe 2019).

[22]That was Fragkiskos Koutentakis, then Secretary General for Public Finances at the Ministry of Finance.

Budget Office,[23] (3) the country's Fiscal Council,[24] (4) a Greek academic who teaches international political economy[25] and, crucially, two representatives of the European Union (Ministry of Finance 2015). Finally, acting on a proposal of the finance minister, the Cabinet selected and appointed Yiorgos Pitsilis in January 2016 (Greek Cabinet 2016). Pitsilis is a career lawyer who specialises in tax law (like his predecessor) and has worked in one of the most high-profile law firms in Athens (1999–2010). He has also worked as a tax advisor of the Association of Greek Banks (2010–2016).

In addition, the government legislated to merge SDOE with the public revenue administration through the transfer of a) all powers that relate to tax and custom duty collection as well as b) 500 officials to the public revenue administration (Hellenic Parliament 2015). Before SYRIZA's split of the summer of 2015 (see *supra*), Alternate Finance Minister Valavani was opposed to SDOE's merger with the public revenue administration on grounds that it would practically lead to the abandonment (in all but name) of 36,000 cases involving wealthy individuals (Valavani 2016: 226). This stance echoed the views of SDOE's then head too who argued that as, at that point in time, SDOE was dealing with approximately 2500 cases generated by financial prosecutors' investigation orders, and—as a government minister noted, 'we all knew who was involved in several of them' (implying powerful individuals)—the transfer risked delaying their handling beyond the limit set by the statute of limitations, 'who would bear the responsibility for the consequences?' (interview, Athens, 9 November 2016). The limit of this line of reasoning is demonstrated by the fact that, as a ministerial advisor pointed out, when the merger did take place, SDOE officials handed over approximately 100–120 cases each, thus leading him to note: 'Even if each one of these officials had 10 lives—10 lives!—they would still not have had enough time to check all of these cases' (interview, Athens, 9 November 2016).

In theoretical terms, these developments indicate the relevance of the first of the three theoretical models outlined in Chap. 2 (external incentives). For much of 2015 the EU and IMF refrained from providing funding to Greece due to the Greek government's attempt to renegotiate the terms of the previous agreement. This maximised pressure on the Greek government. With domestic public funds almost exhausted and in the face of (a) the priority attached to reduced primary budget surpluses and (b) the protection of some of the domestic labour law and (c) the risk of a catastrophic 'Grexit' (against which there was a robust national majority), the Greek government had to give in.

[23]Panayiotis Liargovas is an academic economist with the University of the Peloponnese.

[24]Panayiotis Korliras is an academic economist with the Athens University for Economics and Business.

[25]Dimitris Sideris of Panteion University of Social and Political Sciences.

The Independent Authority for Public Revenue

Despite vehement opposition from the union of tax collectors (POE-DOY n.d.; in.gr 2016), the Greek Parliament enacted in May 2016 a law (Hellenic Parliament 2016a) that established a new Independent Authority for Public Revenue (IAPR—*Ανεξάρτητη Αρχή Δημοσίων Εσόδων*) which differs radically from the pre-existing institutional arrangements, especially those of the pre-crisis era. The bulk of this section presents the main features of this authority with the focus being on its functional independence, administrative and financial autonomy. As we will show, the key change is the removal of the Greek public revenue administration from the finance minister's direct and unmitigated influence. This is done in a way that reflects central features of the IMF-promoted design considerations and the European Commission's Fiscal Blueprints (see Chap. 1).

However, Greece's partners remain evidently cautious (or even suspicious[26]) and this is reflected in a number of provisions such as those that relate to the committee that chooses some of the authority's key officeholders (see below). These can be seen as '*mésures de confiance*' (interview, Athens, 30 March 2017) that were entirely warranted since the enactment of this reform is not supported by a broad-based consensus within the Greek political class. The lack of this support is clearly demonstrated by the debate in parliament that preceded the establishment of the new Independent Authority for Public Revenue and cannot be concealed by the fact that the new law was enacted by a large majority including, significantly, Kyriakos Mitsotakis,[27] leader of the (then) main opposition party ND (Hellenic Parliament 2016d: 10266) and several other opposition MPs.[28] Two are the most striking features of this debate. First, less than a fifth of the several MPs who took the floor mentioned it.[29] Second, although a few paid lip service to it, none of them made an explicit and detailed statement on the principle on which this key reform is based. Rather, they preferred to bemoan what they see as the loss of sovereignty which, in their eyes, this reform entails for the country[30] with two senior opposition MPs going as far as to say

[26]Spyros Danellis, an opposition MP, rightly pointed out when the bill was being debated in parliament that this measure shows Greece's partners do not trust the country (Hellenic Parliament 2016c: 10112).

[27]He is on record (already since December 2011) as a supporter of a revenue administration that operates 'at a distance' from the government of the day (Kathimerini 2011).

[28]237 of 298 voting MPs voted in favour of the new authority in principle and 228 also supported the principle of the new authority's functional independence.

[29]The debate on IAPR was part of a debate on a broader ('omnibus') bill which largely related to unpopular measures such as tax rises and who controls the nation's assets that were being placed in the portfolio of a new asset holding company.

[30]See, e.g. PASOK MPs Koutsoukos and Baryiotas (Hellenic Parliament 2016c: 10077, 10172 respectively), Skandalidis, Arvanitidis and Konstantopoulos (Hellenic Parliament 2016d: 10184, 10194, 10195 respectively).

that IAPR will not be independent—'it will be controlled more by the foreigners'.[31] The majority's main line of defence was to (a) attack ND and PASOK (i.e. their predecessors) for behaving in the past in ways that made this reform necessary, (b) point out that tax policy (e.g. tax rates, the progressive nature of the tax system and the scope of the tax base) remained under the minister's remit and (c) note that the issue of the new institution's constitutionality had been resolved.[32] This indicates that this major reform is not couched in deep and broad consensus within the Greek political *élite*. Rather, the support it had in Parliament at the point of its enactment was as shallow as it was broad.

Status

Underlining their importance, the new law enunciates, at its very beginning, IAPR's 'functional independence' and its 'administrative and financial autonomy' while the corresponding regulatory impact assessment pointedly notes that the objective of the new system has increased the effectiveness and efficiency of the public revenue administration 'by making it independent from political changes' (Ministry of Finance n.d.: 2). The same provision (Art. 1 para. 2) clearly states that the new authority (a) is not subject to any control or oversight on the part of government institutions, state bodies or other administrative authorities but (b) *is* subject to parliamentary control. Functional independence refers to its actual operation and decisions, while administrative and financial autonomy refers to its internal organisation, structure, human and budgetary resources. The point about functional independence is made repeatedly in various provisions of IAPR's founding law. The new authority has no legal[33] personality (Art. 1 para. 1).

Institutional Set-up

The authority's governing institutions are (1) the management board and (2) the governor. The *Management Board* comprises the chairman and four members. They all serve for a term of 5[34] years that is renewable once and, tellingly, lasts longer than

[31]That was Yannis Koutsoukos (PASOK MP, former employee of the Ministry of Finance and former head of ADEDY, the umbrella organization that covers all public sector unions (Hellenic Parliament 2016d: 10242). His party's leader, Fofi Gennimata shared this view (Hellenic Parliament 2016d: 10271).

[32]To that effect, Finance Minister Tsakalotos introduced an amendment to the bill mainly to indicate that the IAPR has no legal personality, a point which is explicitly made in Art. 1 of IAPR's founding law (see below).

[33]On its precise legal status, see Dimitriou (n.d.: 22–23) and Koutnatzis (n.d.: 14, esp. fn. 43).

[34]The terms of office of the first members of the board are staggered (Art. 8 para. 2).

the government's maximum term of office which is 4 years. Their duty is to promote the achievement of the authority's objectives. They must act on the basis of the principles of objectivity and impartiality (Art. 8 paras 4–5). The members of the management board must be highly qualified and experienced[35] persons of high standing in areas that relate to the authority's activity. The law introduces a very wide range of exclusions[36] crucial amongst which—in yet another break with the past—is the exclusion of any person who is serving or has served (during the current or the previous parliamentary term) as a member of the Greek or the European Parliament, the government or the executive institutions of a political party or has been a parliamentary candidate during the same period (Art. 8 para. 10).

In terms of the authority's operation, the management board offers general guidelines and has veto power over the authority's strategic and operational planning as well as the annual report (Art. 9 para. 1; Art. 22). This shows that it is meant to act as a· veritable check vis-à-vis the authority's powerful head (the governor—see below). This is further highlighted by its veto power over the compatibility of the authority's strategic and operational plans with the governor's performance contract which it is also charged with monitoring. In addition, it has simple opinion rights over the authority's draft budget and monitors its execution. In relation to the authority's internal organisation and personnel, the management board has veto power over the authority's personnel policy and its implementation (which it also monitors) and the authority's internal organisation (including any revisions thereof) and rulebook (Art. 9 paras 2–3). Specifically, its ascent is needed for the development and implementation of the authority's personnel recruitment, its promotion and remuneration[37] systems, the personnel's qualitative and quantitative assessment, the internal reallocation of personnel and the definition and redefinition of appointment criteria. The board also has veto power over the authority's internal organisation and rulebooks as well as their major[38] reforms.

The authority's single most powerful officeholder is its *Governor* (Art. 13) who serves a 5-year term (renewable once if supported by the finance minister as well as a two-thirds majority inside the management board). The governor (the authority's veritable head) is not a member of the board (but attends its meetings) and has no voting rights. The qualifications and other requirements—including the exclusions—that apply to the management board's members also apply to the governor. S/he operates and is remunerated on the basis of a performance contract that includes both qualitative and quantitative goals. Her remuneration can be as high as the remuneration of the country's Supreme Court (Areios Pagos—*Άρειος Πάγος*) chair's (approx. 6000 € gross per month) thus potentially making her one of the highest paid

[35]At least 10 years of experience is the formal requirement.

[36]Predictably, they must also have a strong tax compliance record, should not be amongst the authority's functionaries, must not have been sacked as a result of disciplinary proceedings from any public sector body or have been barred by a professional body. They are also barred from performing any duties or functions that are incompatible with their authority-related duties.

[37]Bonuses included.

[38]As, for example, in the creation or abolition of directorates general and regional units.

public servants in Greece. The magnitude of her powers is demonstrated by the way in which the law defines them: all powers that relate to the operation of the authority except those that have been explicitly granted to its management board (Art. 14 para. 1).

A very significant development is the governor's almost complete freedom of action in relation to the management of the authority's personnel resources. These powers include the right to choose the heads of various units, shape the criteria for personnel recruitment[39] and management (including promotion and bonuses), personnel assessment and the system for internal performance management (Art. 14). The governor also has the power to shape and revise the authority's internal structure (unlike the previous regime; see *supra*, section on the 2nd MoU)—and allocate and reallocate resources—but, crucially, must do so on the basis of modern public management techniques such as specific job descriptions.[40]

Finally, the other major individual officeholder is the *Expert* (*Εμπειρογνώμονας*) who is appointed only during the first 5 years of the authority's life so as to offer to the management board expert advice in relation to best practice on the basis of experience of tax matters that the officeholder has obtained abroad. S/he has the right to attend the meetings of the management board and obtain the information needed for the discharge of her duties but has no voting rights. S/he is subject to the same probity requirements as the other major officeholders and her term of office can be extended once for another 5 years if the finance minister so decides on the management board's proposal.

Selection and Appointment Procedures

Both the management board's members and the governor are—unlike the expert[41]—appointed on the basis of an open competition[42] (Art. 10). The board's members are selected by a high-ranking, independent, special committee where government appointees are in a minority.[43] The committee establishes—on the

[39]Nevertheless, these must be submitted to ASEP, in line with separate extant legislation.

[40]See the subsection on implementation.

[41]The finance minister chooses and appoints one candidate from a short list of three proposed by the European Commission.

[42]As defined by articles 1–6 of Law 3861/2010.

[43]It comprises the head of the Supreme Council for Civil Personnel Selection (ΑΣΕΠ) as chair, the head of the Parliament's Budget Office, the head of the country's Fiscal Council, the Finance Ministry's Secretary General for Public Finance, an academic chosen by the finance minister and (only for the first 7 years of the authority's life) two representatives of the European Commission. Among those, only the head of the Parliament's Budget Office, the Finance Ministry's Secretary General for Public Finance and the academic chosen by the finance minister are very likely to have strong links to the ruling majority. The head (coordinator) of Parliament's Budget Office is nominated by the Speaker (to whom he also reports) after an open call for applications, and is then chosen by Parliament's Internal Rules of Procedure Committee, that is the ruling majority (see Speaker of the Hellenic Parliament 2014, Art. 5).

basis of predetermined and objective criteria—a short list comprising twice the number of posts to be filled. From that list, the finance minister selects his preferred candidates subject to the approval of Parliament's Committee on Institutions and Transparency. If the latter objects with regard to one or more candidates, the finance minister proposes other shortlisted candidates. The members of the management board are subsequently formally appointed by the finance minister. During the first of their regular monthly meetings they elect the board's chair (Art. 12 para. 2).

The same high-ranking special committee leads in the selection of the governor (Art. 15). It establishes a short list of four candidates on the basis of objective, predefined criteria. The management board ranks the top two candidates and makes a recommendation to the finance minister who chooses and appoints the governor and states the factors that led them to that decision.

Members of the management board can be sacked by the Cabinet on a reasoned proposal of the finance minister but the reasons for this decision are restricted.[44] The governor can be dismissed for the same reasons on the basis of 'undisputed' and 'objective' facts (Art. 16) but the process differs. If these facts exist, the management board is required to set the process in motion by making a reasoned proposal to the finance minister who then has the power to make her own proposal to the Cabinet. Only the Cabinet can dismiss the governor. The finance minister has the right to ask (at any time) the management board for its opinion as to whether there is real evidence that constitutes grounds for the governor's dismissal.

Powers

IAPR's powers (Art. 2 paras 1–3) include the totality of its predecessor's powers as well as all those mentioned in other laws (which, curiously, have not been codified on the occasion of this law's enactment) and those that will be granted to it in the future. In particular, the new law highlights—in addition to the standard powers to determine and collect tax and custom revenues and other public revenues, the monitoring of tax collection and the implementation of all relevant laws as well as the power to take and carry out all necessary measures to that effect—the power to

(a) in terms of functional independence

- interpret all relevant applicable tax laws;
- determine its own strategic and operational plans, including goal-setting and performance indicators;

[44]They include conflict of interest, health issues, running for parliament, major misdemeanors such as breach of confidentiality and abuse of position for personal or commercial gain. Any member of the management board who has been sacked can appeal against their dismissal in front of the country's top administrative court.

- oversee, coordinate, monitor and assess the operation of all relevant units in relation to the strategic and operational objectives defined in its own plans;
- plan tax, customs and other relevant controls for the monitoring of all relevant tax laws;
- assess and prioritise any control requests that it receives;
- combat tax evasion, smuggling, illicit trade, tax fraud;
- combat corruption, lack of transparency, inefficiency, low productivity and low-quality service provision encountered in public revenue, custom, and other relevant services;
- propose legislative and other measures aiming to improve tax and customs compliance, including in relation to speeding up the collection of public revenue;
- offer its opinion on draft legislation that relates to its domain of responsibility;
- take any other action that its duties require.

(b) In terms of administrative and financial autonomy, it has the power to

- organise its own services and manage all resources available to it;
- shape and manage its own budget which, crucially for the authority's autonomy, enjoys a significant degree of protection under the new law;[45]
- develop, update, maintain (or purchase) and utilise the IT system that it needs in the context of a broader IT and e-government strategy.

Crucially, the new law repeats the previous law's (see Chap. 4) prohibition of the redistribution of any of these powers from IAPR to government ministers or other government institutions by any means other than an act of parliament (Art. 2 para. 4). This reminder of a key constitutional principle in a major piece of legislation such as this underlines both the creditors' lack of trust vis-à-vis the Greek governments and their awareness of past (inherently unconstitutional) practice.

An entire section of the new law is dedicated to the central issue of the new authority's *functional independence*. Art. 3 reiterates the absence of hierarchical control and administrative oversight on the part of the government or other public or private institutions, and highlights the personal and functional independence that the new authority's key officeholders (Chairman, Governor, Management Board, Expert) enjoy. Indeed, it stipulates that they are bound only by the law and their conscience. A clear line of *accountability* is established in relation to parliament (Art. 4): IAPR's key officeholders are obliged (if asked) to testify in parliament but can also do so on their own initiative. In addition, the authority is obliged to keep the finance minister regularly informed by providing aggregate data so that she can carry out her duties. A major reform introduced by the new law concerns reporting procedures and a new line of accountability. The authority's annual report is adopted on the governor's proposal and needs the management board's assent. It is submitted

[45]The law creates a 'floor' under that budget by stipulating that it cannot be smaller than 95% of the average ordinary appropriations made for the authority during the previous 3 years (Art. 19 para. 3, 3rd indent).

to the prime minister, the finance minister and the parliamentary speaker. It is subject to a debate in the parliament's Finance Committee. Crucially, unlike in the past when the report had to be submitted to parliament by the finance minister, the new arrangement no longer requires the minister's intervention. As a result, the new arrangement establishes a direct line of accountability between the revenue authority and parliament. In addition, the authority's strategic plan is submitted to the Parliament's Speaker. Accountability to parliament is a major innovation introduced in 2016 but also one that is incomplete as we indicate in the next section of this chapter.

The finance minister is explicitly barred from exercising any hierarchical control or oversight. Nevertheless, s/he retains the right to make strategic proposals and offer strategic guidelines for the implementation of the government's tax policy but *not* in relation to organisational, functional or personnel matters. In a clear and significant break with the past,

(a) the finance minister is prohibited from asking for information or providing binding instructions in relation to specific cases[46] and
(b) in case of a disagreement between the minister and IAPR's governor in relation to the implementation of tax policy, the matter is referred to the authority's management board (Art. 5 para. 4), thus underlining IAPR's functional independence.

Government ministers must also inform, in due course, the authority of any draft legislative provisions relating to the authority's remit but the authority's opinion is not binding on the relevant government minister. Conversely, prior to making horizontal decisions and issuing circulars regarding the interpretation and enforcement of tax law, the authority informs the minister so that s/he can issue a non-binding opinion or express her views.

The new authority's functional independence is further enhanced by the fact that its internal operation is based on the internal rulebooks that are issued by its own governor subject to the agreement of the management board (Art. 6 para. 3). The law also provides for an internal institutional arrangement that

(a) seeks to promote the authority's functional independence, administrative and financial autonomy in relation to the rest of the government apparatus;
(b) creates internal checks vis-à-vis
(c) an otherwise very powerful head (governor).

Decision-Making Procedures

The authority's internal rules of procedure determine the details of the decision-making process but the quorum for a meeting of the Management Board is, by law, four, decisions require the support of the absolute majority of present members and

[46]This prohibition applies also to the management board (Art. 9 para. 6).

in case of a tie, the Governor has the casting vote (IAPR 2017b, Art. 5–7, Art. 6 para. 1 respectively). As regards transparency, meetings are minuted but are not public (IAPR 2017b, Art. 5 para. 4θ).

Goal-Setting and Reporting Procedures

Detailed revenue goals are set annually by the finance minister and are indicated in the country's annual budget. Reporting procedures are set out in great detail in the new law (Art. 20). IAPR keeps the finance minister periodically informed via its quarterly reports also with regard to issues that it encounters during its operation. The finance minister has the right to hold regular (monthly) as well as extraordinary hearings with the governor. In addition, the prime minister, the finance minister and the parliamentary speaker have the right to ask for and obtain special reports on issues that fall in the authority's scope (Art. 20 para. 2). The authority must also publish online its strategic and operational plans alongside targets, performance indicators, and monthly developments (including monthly reports on the state of revenue collection). IAPR must also publish a detailed annual report and the corresponding plan which will then feed into its operational plan.

However, IAPR's insulation is not unfettered. Key here is the finance minister's (and various finance ministry units') direct access (under Art. 37) to aggregate data that IAPR holds in its management information system.[47] If further information is needed, IAPR is required to provide it as a matter of priority. This is key both in relation to the minister's ability to set targets (a) that IAPR is required to achieve (which is crucial in the context of the medium-term budgeting that developments in the governance of the Euro area dictate, including the operation of Greece's Fiscal Council (Hellenic Parliament 2014) but also (b) in relation to the content of the governor's employment contract.

In terms of internal goal-setting, the governor sets the qualitative and quantitative goals as well as the priorities of each unit alongside the measurement methodology and the timeframe for their implementation. Linked to the governor's power to set internal goals is her power to select the heads of units and assess them on the basis of their performance. The criteria are set out in detail in the new law (Art. 26) and relate to the selection and term of office of senior officials (e.g. directors general, directors and deputy directors) as well as mid-ranking ones such as heads of unit. They are chosen by the governor of a term of 1–3 years (renewable once). Crucially, the governor has the power to end these officials' term of office on the basis of either their performance or other reasons (Art. 27 para. 3). The authority's personnel are

[47]The law that established IAPR was revised in 2016 so as to compel the Authority to provide individual-level aggregate data but only after individual tax reference numbers have been digitally concealed (Hellenic Parliament 2016b, Art. 105). Access to this sort of data had caused tensions while Harry Theoharis was the head of the then semi-autonomous SGPR since this information would facilitate the design of better-targeted audits (see Chap. 4; Reporter.gr 2015).

either permanent civil servants or contractual agents.[48] Their remuneration is subject to performance-based rewards such as bonus payments.[49]

Implementing the New Institutional Set-up

The implementation of these reforms is well under way. The members of the management board have been appointed, crucially with the support of the (then) main opposition party[50] (Kathimerini 2016b). The Governor has already started using his power to select key post-holders [e.g. the Director General for Tax Administration, whom he chose in March 2017 and to move others who have failed to meet key targets (IAPR 2017c; Kathimerini 2016a; European Commission 2017a: 12)]. Moreover, the Governor has already (a) identified the senior posts where staff needs to rotate across geographical areas so as to ensure that existing close relations between them, tax consultants and taxpayers are broken up as far as possible (IAPR Governor 2017) and (b) started using these powers to rotate this staff, starting from senior officials who had been in the same post for 10 years (CNN Greece 2019). The Governor has already started reporting directly to Parliament (see, e.g. IAPR 2017a). The IAPR has issued its revised medium-term strategic plan as well as its annual operation plans (IAPR 2017d, g). Although the Governor signed his contract in December 2017, it is not a public document (European Commission 2018a: 43) despite the fact that (according to IAPR's founding law[51]) it contains the qualitative and quantitative targets that the Governor must strive to achieve as well as the annual bonus that the Governor will receive if s/he exceeds these targets or meets the public revenue administration's key performance indicators that the same contract stipulates (see below). The IAPR is already working on the basis of quantitative targets but it is also pursuing a rather active media campaign indicating that it is well aware of both the geographical areas,[52] the economic sectors—such as the hotel industry and tourism more broadly (To Vima 2017b, c)—as well as the social groups (e.g. lawyers and doctors) where tax evasion

---

[48]Operating under private law provisions.

[49]Finally, an amendment introduced by Finance Minister Tsakalotos when the bill was being debated in parliament limits to 5% the number of IAPR staff who can be temporarily placed in ministerial offices, political party HQs or in MPs' offices and this decision requires the Governor's assent. This is a very important defence mechanism because politically connected public sector employees often serve in posts that have nothing to do with either real needs or their skills. For example, teachers serve in MP's offices.

[50]C. Kotsogiannis, Professor of Economics at the University of Exeter, is the chairman. G. Theodorakopoulos, a member of the state's legal counselling team is the vice chairman. Two university professors (an economist and a civil law expert) and an economics researcher are its members (IAPR n.d.).

[51]See Art. 13 para. 7.

[52]The islands of Mykonos and Santorini which the Governor visited at the peak of the holiday season in August 2017 exemplify this point (IAPR 2017e).

and avoidance are rife. In response, the IAPR is increasingly using modern techniques (such as risk-based compliance strategies and cross-checking electronically available information from the country's banking system) to better target its activity, while it is also building an e-register of each taxpayer's assets so that the public revenue administration is better able to cross-check cases of potential tax avoidance and evasion (To Vima 2017c, e; Hadjinikolaou 2019a). Moreover, in a significant and long overdue move that seeks to tackle the illicit fuel trade,[53] secondary legislation has been enacted to compel petrol stations to provide IAPR automatically key sales data at the end of each business day (Ministry of Finance 2018). This means that IAPR will possess crucial information that it will then cross-check against other data (e.g. tax returns) and thus capture significant segments of this (lucrative) illicit trade. This is a reform that has been announced more than once by past governments but also one that has been delayed due to lack of political will. Moreover, its internal affairs department has been conducting checks on IAPR staff's finances so as to detect irregularities or cases of unexplained enrichment (Efimerida Ton Syntakton 2017a).

Despite vehement objections and a boycott from staff unions, the Authority has also presented its plans for the initial assessment of its own personnel (combined with concrete job descriptions) which was a requirement under the terms of the third bailout agreement (IAPR 2017f; To Vima 2017a, d). As of 2018, this assessment is to be carried out annually. However, the enabling legislation that is required for the implementation of grading, remuneration and performance assessment tailored to the IAPR has not yet been enacted although—as the Commission points out—'[t]he reform is vital to enhance IAPR's prospects to attract highly-qualified staff and to allow for their development and progression' (European Commission 2018b: 18). Although by the end of 2018 the IAPR had already drafted the corresponding bill and conducted an internal consultation (4–20 December 2018) on it alongside the requisite accompanying materials that relate to the principles and objectives of the Authority's HR management system, job descriptions and so on (see the materials in IAPR 2018), by the time the European Commission published its second report since the end of the third adjustment programme, the legislative changes that are required to carry out this key reform had still not been adopted and, as a consequence, the first step in the process of linking grading to job descriptions had not been taken (European Commission 2019b: 5 and 22, respectively). This is an important aspect of the new authority. So, it deserves greater attention.

The effort to introduce job descriptions started in 2013, when the institution was semi-autonomous, on the basis of self-reform, but this effort bore no meaningful results (Liargova 2018: 56). As the corresponding literature indicates, self-reform is extremely hard or even impossible to carry out. This is so for two principal reasons. First, organisational actors (distinct staff groups in a given organisation) are active participants in the problem that the reform seeks to address. As a consequence, the proposals they make are not deprived of selfish, ulterior motives though this does not

[53]The corresponding primary legislation was enacted in 2009 but very long delays followed (Kathimerini 2013a, e).

necessarily mean that such groups cannot, under certain conditions, play the role of change agents. In any case, intra-organisational perspectives are useful only when they are combined with external ones that are deprived of the biases that are inherent in the internal operation of the organisation. Several scholars underline the fact that both the external and the internal environment of organisations co-define the dynamics of reform policies (Painter and Pierre 2005; Kuhlmann 2006) and more precisely the practice of change management (van Witteloostuijn et al. 2013). Second, organisational reform is a supremely specialised function that requires expertise (Spanou 2018). Often this expertise is not available within the organisation that is being reformed (Pardo del Val and Clara 2003). So, external advice and expertise are normally entirely necessary (Tsekos and Triantafyllopoulou 2018; Monastiriotis and Antoniades 2009). In light of this, it comes as no surprise that, as Liargova (2018: 57–58) concludes, the effort to carry out the mandated job descriptions will continue under the guidance of the IMF and in collaboration with the external partners of the European Commission's DG TAXUD, and will bear real and practical results now that the IAPR has become an independent authority.

There are other problems, besides those that relate to the introduction of job descriptions. There is evidence of delays in relation to other key internal reforms that aim to increase IAPR's effectiveness. As the European Commission noted in its first post-programme report—based on EMU's enhanced surveillance regime—published in November 2018 these relate to the following:

(a) increasing IAPR's staff to the target (for 2018) of 12,000 has not been achieved because of (i) delays in the recruitment of 548 new tax collectors and customs officials through an open competition that started in April 2017 and (ii) delays in recruiting further 250 staff via an ongoing mobility scheme across the Greek civil service;
(b) IAPR's Reform Action Plan had not yet been finalised due to a 'protracted consultation period' with the Ministry of Finance and this delay has had a knock-on effect on key actions such as (1) fostering even further the automation of obligations requiring physical presence at IAPR offices; (2) improving tax compliance by redesigning operation and audit processes and (3) improving the institution's HR Management System and IT infrastructure (European Commission 2018b: 17–19).

The European Commission's second report after the end of the third adjustment programme paints a mixed picture in February 2019, i.e. 2 years after IAPR's formal establishment. On the one hand, the Reform Action Plan was eventually adopted, progress was also made in terms of IT-related reforms, the additional funds that are required for the supplementary remuneration part of the IAPR's HR reform have been included in the 2019 budget and steps have been taken to protect IAPR officials from malicious legal action taken by taxpayers. Moreover, the country's public revenue administration has obtained access to a much greater array of information regarding taxpayers' assets, including deposit boxes, loans and so on and can thus conduct better targeted and more effective audits (Hadjinikolaou 2019b). On the other hand, overall staffing levels actually decreased to 11,492 (from 11,633). This reduction is the result of higher than expected departures (primarily via retirement), delays in ongoing recruitment of tax and customs officials (a delay that is due to other government priorities[54]), 'a relatively high rejection rate of offers extended by IAPR to successful candidates' as well as the fact that the recently established mobility scheme 'has not yet resulted in the expected number of transfers to IAPR' but the government maintains that the target (12,500 staff) will be met by the end of 2019 (an election year) partly through (a) measures aiming to ease the transfer of staff to IAPR via the mobility scheme and (b) finalising the HR reform aiming to enable IAPR to attract and maintain its staff. Despite the higher than expected retirements, the average age of IAPR staff remains rather high and the authority's own estimates indicate that it will not reach the aforementioned target of 12,500 staff by the end of 2019 (European Commission 2019b: 5, 31 and 33).

Finally, in July 2018, the Finance Minister and the Minister for Administrative Reorganisation decided that IAPR staff that fails when appraised will be transferred to the Finance Ministry (Minister of Finance and Minister for Administrative Reorganisation 2018). Under the mobility scheme that is already in operation, the officials who fail to make the grade could—in theory—be reallocated to other segments of the public sector (instead of remaining in a key ministry's HQ) but the electoral costs that this move would entail for the ruling parties, especially in the run-up to the 2019 election, were prohibitive. It is worth noting that these delays occurred despite (a) the fact that progress was a requirement for the disbursal of approximately 700 million euros of funding (Kathimerini 2018) and (b) the discouraging signal it sends to extant effective and well-qualified staff and young graduates who may wish to pursue a career in the civil service in general and IAPR in particular. The fact that several months after the formal end of the third adjustment programme—and despite being subject to the EMU's enhanced surveillance regime—the Greek government needs to be put under pressure to remain in the reform path, indicates the relevance of the external incentives model outlined in Chap. 2.

How Does the Independent Authority for Public Revenue Compare to the Past? Innovations and Pitfalls

Since the core objective of the reform was to sever the link between the government and the country's public revenue administration, to what extent does the new institutional arrangement achieve this objective. Figures 5.1 and 5.2 depict the key stages of the processes whereby IAPR's key officeholders are appointed.

[54]As the Commission reported in February 2019, the delay is due to the government's decision to prioritise the recruitment of permanent personnel to deal with waste management at local and regional levels (European Commission 2019b: 33). Although it can certainly be argued that this decision is in the public interest (public health), it is also true that with European, legislative, regional and local elections due to take place in 2019, the ruling party's electoral prospects were also served by the recruitment of nearly 9000 staff, including from the very large pool of low-skilled unemployed persons who were particularly hit by the crisis.

Open call for applications ↓
A high-ranking, independent committee (where for the first seven years of IAPR's operation government appointees are in a minority) is established ↓
Based on pre-determined and objective criteria, the high-ranking, independent committee draws up a list of the top candidates featuring twice the number of vacant posts ↓
Subject to the agreement (for each individual) of the parliament's committee on Institutions & Transparency, the minister of finance chooses the successful applicants. They must be highly qualified persons of high standing who have at least 10 years of experience in the area of the authority's activity ↓
The successful candidates are formally appointed

Fig. 5.1 The appointment of IAPR's Management Board

Pre-crisis	Post-2017
No call for applications	Open call for applications ↓
The finance minister or the prime minister chose the appointee	A high-ranking, independent committee (where for the first seven years of IAPR's operation government appointees are in a minority) is established ↓
No formal criteria applied, except standard exclusions (e.g. due to past convictions etc.)	Based on pre-determined and objective criteria, the high-ranking, independent committee draws up a list of the top four candidates and submits it to the Management Board. They must be highly qualified persons of high standing who have at least 10 years of experience in the area of the authority's activity (esp. tax or customs law or public finance) ↓
	The Management Board picks the top two candidates and proposes them to the minister of finance in order of priority ↓
	The minister of finance chooses the successful applicant and presents the factors that led to this choice ↓
	The successful candidate is formally appointed

Fig. 5.2 The appointment of the (pre-crisis) head of the revenue administration and (post-2017) IAPR's Governor

The first striking element of the new system is the dramatic reduction of the role of the government in the appointment of the public revenue administration's key officeholders. This is the quintessential characteristic of depoliticisation. The rest (functional independence, administrative and financial autonomy) are its derivatives.

While the finance minister chooses both the members of the Management Board and the Governor, s/he must pick them from a list of candidates that is (1) prepared by a body over which they do not have direct and complete control and (2) that list is established on the basis of objective and predetermined criteria. This dramatically increases the transparency of the new system and clearly delineates it from the past, as does the requirement of an open call which—until the onset of the crisis—was entirely unheard of in this segment of the Greek state apparatus. The purpose of transparency is also served much better under the new system since the finance minister must provide reasons for their choice of governor and (in the case of the Management Board) a parliamentary committee is involved. Indeed, Parliament has veto power in the appointment of the members of the Management Board. On the contrary, it is entirely absent from the process of appointing the Governor (see below).

The role of the Management Board is key in three senses, all of which directly promote the objective of depoliticisation. In addition to the high-ranking, independent committee that is central in both appointment processes, the Management Board intervenes directly in the Governor's appointment *before* the finance minister's ultimate decision. It does so by (a) whittling the top four candidates down to two and (b) ranking the remaining top two candidates thus further channelling the minister's discretion. This means that it has the opportunity to block any candidates who have a party political affiliation (and/or agenda) if such candidates make it on to the initial list (see below) and place the onus on the minister to alter the ranking, a decision that the minister must then explain. Crucially, in case of conflict between governor and minister in the course of the implementation of tax policy (which is when an independent public revenue administration is likely to make decisions that the ruling majority will dislike), the matter is referred to the Management Board which, therefore, has the opportunity to protect the governor from ministerial pressure and can also serve as the source of advice (its other role) in terms of best practice and so on. Finally, the Management Board has veto power over the content of the Governor's annual report to the prime minister, the finance minister and parliament. This means not only that—as indicated above—a new and direct line of accountability is established between the revenue administration and parliament—but also a quasi-filter is created. So, if the governor chooses to 'massage' the report so as to unduly please the ruling majority, the Management Board has an opportunity (and a duty) to intervene and thus protect the revenue administration's functional independence. These powers, composition and appointment process differ markedly from those of its predecessor [the advisory board that was established in 2013 (see Chap. 4)]. The current arrangement goes much further in the direction of (a) depoliticisation and (b) strengthening the organisation's internal capability and overall credibility.

As regards the durability of the depoliticisation agenda, in institutional terms there is cause for concern. The special, high-ranking committee that plays a central role in the appointment of IAPR's top officeholders is currently composed of seven members. Government appointees are currently in a minority but this is certain to last only for the first 7 years of IAPR's operation for that is how long the European Commission's two representatives will sit on the committee in question. Since it is not yet known who (or if) will take their place thereafter, and in light of the fact that—as the rhetoric used by parliamentarians during the enactment of IAPR's founding law (including by those who voted for it) indicates—the authority is likely to remain a symbol of external imposition in the eyes of the country's political *élite*, a future government that wants to reduce the authority's functional independence does not have to do much to achieve that effect. All it has to do is leave the law as it currently stands. In that scenario, the government appointees on the committee (namely the head of the Parliament's Budget Office, the Finance Ministry's Secretary General for Public Finance and the academic who is chosen by the finance minister) will actually form the majority. This means that the ruling majority will have an opportunity to shape the outcomes of the appointment of both the Management Board and the Governor. Arguably, in that eventuality, the risk for the depoliticisation agenda could be fatal. As a consequence, a real test will be the handling of this issue when it arises. Will the future majority that will need to decide whether to replace the two European Commission officials choose officials with credentials of objectivity or not? One alternative way to resolve this issue would be to reduce the size of the committee to four with the chair (ex officio the head of ASEP—the country's Supreme Council for Personnel Selection) having the casting vote. In any case, the endurance of the depoliticisation agenda remains to be tested in a country where, during the crisis and in spite of external pressure for reform and some initial steps aiming to reduce favouritism at the top *échelons* of the civil service, the corresponding scores remain relatively poor and 'the number of political appointees has increased since 2015 reaching close to 60%', totalling 2495 according to the government's own figures (European Commission 2019a: 56).

It is, however, important to note that the aforementioned appointment processes are not the only innovations that promote and may sustain the depoliticisation agenda in the future. The extensive use of quantitative targets and other modern management techniques, including risk-based targeting of audits, the rotation of key personnel, job description and job evaluation within the organisation and so on are necessary complements of and have the capacity to support the efforts of independent-minded members of the Management Board and Governor. These techniques and instruments—if used appropriately and systematically—can inject a large (and in Greece's case desperately needed) degree of objectivity in the operation of the public revenue administration. This objectivity is a key part of the reasoning that underpins the depoliticisation agenda and is meant to act as an antidote to the pressure for 'special treatment'.

As indicated in the preceding section, one of the most significant innovations introduced in 2016 is the new line of accountability that links IAPR directly to the Hellenic Parliament. The new arrangement deals with an anomaly of the previous regime (2012–2016) whereby the minister was accountable to Parliament but was not (frustratingly for at least two former ministers) in a position to direct the public revenue administration (Varoufakis 2017: 163 and 502; interview, Athens, 4 April 2017). The authority's annual report—once adopted on the governor's proposal and with the management board's assent—is submitted (*without* the finance minister's involvement) not only to the prime minister and the finance minister but also the Parliament's Speaker who occupies the third most senior position in the entire Greek polity. The annual report is then subject to a debate in the parliament's Finance Committee in the presence of IAPR's governor who is thus held to account directly by parliamentarians. The publication of the report and the televised debates in the Parliament's Finance Committee certainly serve the purpose of transparency. This is a key requirement in the process of holding to account any authority that operates at arm's length from the elected government of the country. While it is not likely that the public at large will take a direct interest in the figures and other kinds of information that these reports contain, transparency is served because the media, civil society organisations and others can then raise in public, both within parliament and beyond, issues of effectiveness, due process and so on in line with the theoretical arguments used by the supporters of NMIs (non-majoritarian institutions) in advanced liberal democracies (see Chap. 1).

The adversarial or even confrontational nature of Greek politics and political culture and the classification of the Greek parliament amongst the 'talking shops' (as opposed to the 'working parliaments'; Alivizatos 1990; Polsby 1975) are two key traits of representative democracy in Greece. The country's Third Republic is characterised by stable single-party governments, underpinned by robust parliamentary majorities and internally disciplined political parties. Coalition governments are a new (post-2011) phenomenon. The institutional consequences of this new political reality are twofold. First, the conflict between majority and minority has replaced the conflict between the executive and the legislature (Katrougalos and Mavromoustakou 2003) which reproduces the majority's hegemony in the operation of the Greek parliament. Second, parliament has become the main forum for the publicisation and reproduction of political conflict between government and opposition. Parliament's scrutiny of independent authorities in general, and IAPR in particular, has suffered, as a consequence.

Under Parliament's rules of procedure, each independent authority submits its annual report for the purposes of parliamentary scrutiny that is conducted either by the Committee for Institutions and Transparency or any other relevant (sectoral) committee. In addition, each independent authority may also submit (on its own volition) special, topical reports for scrutiny. Parliamentary committees may request these authorities to submit reports on matters 'of general interest'. Parliamentary committees submit their own conclusions to the Speaker who subsequently transmits them to the relevant minister(s) and authority. The same committees also have the power to take evidence from ministers and any other individual or public officeholder (including heads of independent authorities). However, this scrutiny is incomplete because parliament does not have the formal power to sanction these officials, e.g. by dismissing them (Kaminis 2002: 101–102). This applies to IAPR's Governor too. So, it is not apposite to refer to the current institutional arrangement as 'parliamentary scrutiny' but a kind of accountability process aiming to inject a degree of transparency in IAPR's operation (Botsis 2007: 366). In other words, the main aim of this feeble mechanism 'is that agencies inform and communicate with the legislature rather than the latter scrutinizing the former' (Psygkas 2017: 138).

In addition, the Hellenic Parliament does not have the requisite expertise and experience to genuinely hold IAPR to account. Its Scientific Service (the institution's pool of internal, permanent expertise) is dominated by lawyers thus reproducing the legalistic ethos that underpins public policies and public policy making in Greece. Other kinds of expertise are needed since lawyers are not trained, for example, to conduct cost–benefit analyses or measure price or tax elasticities and so on. It is also unclear if Parliament's Budget Office (created in 2011) and the information that the country's Fiscal Council can provide can genuinely enable MPs to play their part in the new arrangement. For example, we know already that committees of the Hellenic Parliament do not produce genuine reports on the operation of independent and regulatory agencies. Rather, they call 'reports' the minutes of their meetings (Passas 2011). Despite these major weaknesses, the current system is not necessarily 'toothless'. Rather, IAPR's founding law creates opportunities for determined and well-informed parliamentarians who are genuinely willing to hold the new institution to account. The prevalence of new, modern management techniques that place emphasis on the use of more objective criteria (e.g. quantitative targets coupled with regular public reporting) for IAPR's operation and internal assessment processes, also offer opportunities to parliamentarians who, armed with this evidence, can hold the Governor to account.

On that front there is a long way to go in two senses. First, the focus of parliamentary scrutiny must shift to the substance, i.e. the protection of the public interest, away from sloganeering and catering for a very particular clientele. Second, given the very significant powers that the Governor has, coupled with the quantitative targets that his contract includes (in addition to the potential payment of performance-based bonuses), it would be apposite to make that contract (or, at least the relevant portions thereof[55]) available to the relevant parliamentary committee so that they can then (a) ascertain whether these targets have been met, (b) indicate what, if anything, needs to be done about them either at the individual or the systemic level and even (c) influence the very same targets that the government has set in the contract. In other words, the new system offers a first class *potential* opportunity to inject a real and desperately needed dose of transparency and accountability. After all, IAPR's founding law stipulates (Art. 9 para. 4) that the Management Board (a) has veto power over the compatibility of these targets with the authority's strategic and operational plans (that ensuring the targets are realistic) and (b) monitors the enforcement of the Governor's performance-based contract. This means that the Management Board has access to the Governor's targets and this information is not private in a strict sense of the term.

Arguably, if Greek parliamentarians take the opportunity and start (a) inquiring into the operation of IAPR from the perspective of the public interest and (b) do so

[55]We cannot see why the portion that contains the targets should not be communicated to them, given public interest at stake. Nor is it conceivable that such targets are not actually contained in it (interview, Athens, 5 November 2018) given that (a) targets are used by the Governor to assess key staff and (b) there is another rather heavily quantitative dataset that can be used, namely the budget itself. One alternative would be to set targets on the basis of the estimated tax gap.

transparently and on the basis of objective criteria, no IAPR Governor found wanting will be able to remain in post in spite of a well-documented report that calls for his resignation even in the absence of the formal power to remove him from his post. In fact, even in the absence of the (implicit or explicit) power to get the Governor sacked, Parliament has the ability—because of the new system's emphasis on transparency and quantitative targets—to shape tax collection in the public interest through the scrutiny of IAPR's operation. For the Governor too, the new line of accountability directly to Parliament offers a potential bulwark against the undue influence of external interests. The better the Parliament becomes at scrutinising IAPR, the smaller the ability of outside influences to place the Governor under undue pressure. Moreover, if Parliament does play its role well, IAPR's independence will be protected because opposition parties too will have a say in target-setting and so on including the protection of the authority's status. In other words, the new system entails the potential of transforming Parliament into IAPR's ally in the fight against tax evasion and avoidance thus promoting the public interest.

Acting in that way, IAPR and Parliament can (together) address another critique of the new arrangement. Indeed, the whole new institutional framework is based on an one-sided understanding of where the threats to fair end effective tax collection come from and that side is 'politics'. The key term used to describe the problem which this important reform seeks to address is 'political interference'. However, private interests are the other elephant in the room. IAPR's founding law is almost entirely silent on that source of undue influence despite the fact that both in the recent[56] and the more distant past, alleged favouritism and corruption were linked to very wealthy, i.e. powerful, individuals (as well as others). Although—according to one account (interview, Athens, 2 August 2017)—this issue was raised with EU and IMF officials, the new arrangement's silence on this issue is definitely striking and leaves it exposed to criticism at least from the left of the political spectrum as well as from a populist's perspective. The point also relates to the selection of key office-holders. Katerina Savvaidou's case is a very telling one and speaks directly to the pervasive issue of 'revolving doors' between private interests (in this case companies that advise wealthy clients on 'tax optimisation' or 'tax planning') and crucial public sector posts (and back). It is not unfair to say that IAPR's founding law is based on a short-sighted assumption about the origin of 'political interference' and does not recognise the fact that ultimately it served *private* interests. In that sense, the new system's one-sided concern with electoral democracy as a source of corruption and ineffectiveness risks simply cutting out the proverbial 'middle man'. In other words, for IAPR's top officeholders, 'the temptations remain in place', as a senior minister rightly noted (interview, Athens, 9 November 2016; also interview, Athens, 5 November 2018).

Finally, there is one additional critique of the reform examined in this book—or, more accurately, the way in which it has been carried out. When the IAPR was established, it took with it the Ministry of Finance staff who had hitherto been

---

[56]Classic examples are those that are associated with Katerina Savvaidou's dismissal (see *supra*).

working in the unit that dealt with issues of legislative initiative, i.e. the minister's (even now) key role. This group of officials had accumulated a significant amount of expertise and experience in drafting as well as interpreting key legal texts (varying from decrees to ministerial decisions and circulars interpreting extant law). Given that the interpretation of legal provisions is one of IAPR's core functions (since interpretation is a necessary task for any implementing body), having this expertise made sense from the new institution's perspective but, at the same time, this move significantly curtails the minister's ability to exercise his duties, especially in an area of public policy (taxation) where extant legal provisions are dense and complex. One may well argue that this represents no major loss since Greece's autonomy in making tax policy remains significantly circumscribed as long as the country operates under EMU's enhanced surveillance. However, the transfer of this staff also contradicts one of the key tenets of the depoliticisation paradigm, namely the idea that elected politicians remain in charge of making policy—only its implementation is hived off [for reasons of credibility, efficiency etc. (see Chap. 2)] to a depoliticised body. The ministry may well rebuild its capacity in this area but this is likely to take a lot of time, after this major loss of institutional memory.

This development speaks to a broader theme, i.e. the reality of IAPR's relation with the ministry in terms of policy making. In formal terms, the former is the implementor while the latter is the policy maker. In the medium term though, reality is likely to be quite different, as the example of the Next Steps Agencies in Britain demonstrates. As Rhodes pointed out more than 20 years ago,

> [g]iven that the 'Next Steps' agencies will develop a near monopoly of expertise in their policy area, given that policy often emerges from many small decisions, it is conceivable the agency tail will wag the departmental dog (Rhodes 1996: 10).

This risk clearly exists in IAPR's relationship with the Ministry of Finance. This is so because every year the latter must prepare the country's annual budget. Any such budget involves not only the choice of objectives (e.g. to collect X amount from tax Y) but also the making of forecasts (e.g. if the rate for a given tax is A, it will yield amount B). IAPR, as the implementing agency, is likely to have a major input in this kind of decision. If the Ministry of Finance does not possess its own capacity to make this type of assessment, IAPR may well end up being the tail that will wag the dog. Even if the Ministry of Finance does possess this capacity, it will always be vulnerable to IAPR's argument in relation to its own capability saying, for example, 'we do not have enough staff (or any other resource) to achieve this target'. In other words, the relationship between the two institutions is likely to be much more balanced (not just symbiotic) than this model's proponents would want us to believe.

The next, final chapter of this book draws on the empirical material presented in Chaps. 3–5 to draw conclusions about (a) the ability of each of the theoretical models outlined in Chap. 2 to shed light on the depoliticisation of Greece's public revenue administration, (b) Greece's reform capacity and (c) the link between conditionality and the operation of the European Union.

References

Alexiadis, Tryfon. 2015. "Curriculum vitae (in Greek)." Tryfon Alexiadis' blog, 17 July, accessed 1 November 2018. http://alexiadistrifon.blogspot.com/2015/07/blog-post.html.

Alivizatos, Nikos. 1990. "The difficulties of "rationalization" in a polarized political system: the Greek Chamber of Deputies." In *Parliament and Democratic Consolidation in Southern Europe*, edited by U. Liebert and M. Cotta, 131-153. London/New York: Pinter.

Antenna News. 2015. "Tsakalotos: no to SGPR's full independence." 4 March (in Greek). Accessed 1 November 2018. http://www.antenna.gr/news/Economy/article/392079/tsakalotos-oxi-se-pliri-anexartisia-tis-ggde.

Bank of Greece. 2016. The Governor's report for 2015. Athens: Bank of Greece (in Greek).

Botsis, Foivos. 2007. "Parliamentary Control of the Constitutionalized Independent Authorities." *Efimerida Dimosiou Dikaiou/Journal of Public Law* (3):361-367 (in Greek).

CDU/CSU/SPD. 2013. Deutschlands Zukunft gestalten. Koalitionsvertrag zwischen CDU, CSU und SPD, 18. Legislaturperiode. Berlin: CDU.

Christodoulou, Marios. 2016. "The truth about the selection process of the S.G. for Public Revenue." *Efimerida Ton Syntakton*, 21 January (in Greek). http://www.efsyn.gr/arthro/i-alitheia-gia-ton-tropo-epilogis-toy-gg-dimosion-esodon.

CNN Greece. 2019. "System for cyclical transfers in tax and customs offices." CNN Greece, 9 January (in Greek), accessed 24 March 2019. https://www.cnn.gr/oikonomia/story/161154/systima-kyklikon-metatheseon-se-efories-kai-teloneia.

Dimitrakopoulos, Dionyssis G. 2011. "Leaving the eurozone would be a disaster for Greece." *The Guardian*, 22 September, 35.

Dimitriou, Spyros. n.d. "The quest for an administrative reform model and its limits: the case of the independent authority for public revenue." https://www.constitutionalism.gr/. Forthcoming in *To Syntagma*, accessed 24 March 2019 (in Greek). https://www.constitutionalism.gr/dimitriou-arhi-dimosion-esodon/.

Dixon, Hugo. 2015. "Tsipras shocks again." Reuters Breaking Views. Reuters, 22 October, accessed 29 November. https://www.breakingviews.com/considered-view/tsipras-shoots-him self-in-foot-by-firing-tax-boss/ - .VikZfUtag9Y.twitter.

Dragassakis, Yiannis. 2015. Live TV interview with Vice President of the Tsipras Government, Intriga, hosted by Elli Stae, Alpha TV, 18 March, https://youtu.be/4UCGlwCrqm8.

Efimerida Ton Syntakton. 2017a. "Nine tax inspectors and customs officers with 'peculiar' tax returns." 27 July (in Greek). Accessed 1 December 2018. http://www.efsyn.gr/arthro/ennea-eforiakoi-teloneiakoi-me-perierga-pothen-eshes.

Efimerida Ton Syntakton. 2017b. "Prosecutors propose to put K. Savvaidou on trial." 11 May (in Greek). Accessed 27 November 2018. http://www.efsyn.gr/arthro/eisaggeliki-protasi-gia-parapompi-tis-k-savvaidoy-se-diki.

ESM. n.d. "Programme timeline - Greece." European Stability Mechanism, accessed 18 February 2019. https://www.esm.europa.eu/assistance/greece.

European Commission. 2017a. Compliance Report. The Third Economic Adjustment Programme for Greece. Second Review. 16 June. Directorate-General for Economic and Financial Affairs. Brussels.

European Commission. 2017b. The ESM Stability Support Programme for Greece: First & Second Reviews. July 2017 Background Report. *European Economy Institutional Papers*. Luxembourg: European Commission.

European Commission. 2018a. Compliance Report. ESM Stability Support Programme for Greece. Third Review, March 2018. Directorate-General for Economic and Financial Affairs. Brussels: European Commission.

European Commission. 2018b. Greece: Enhanced Surveillance Report, Greece, November 2018. *European Economy Institutional Papers*. Brussels: European Commission.

European Commission. 2019a. Commission staff working document: Country Report Greece 2019 including an in-depth review on the prevention and correction of macroeconomic imbalances, accompanying the document Communication from the Commission to the European Parliament, the European Council, the Council, the European Central Bank and the Eurogroup 2019 European Semester: assessment of progress on structural reforms, prevention and correction of macroeconomic imbalances, and results of in-depth reviews under Regulation (EU) No 1176/2011, COM(2019) 150 final, SWD(2019) 1007 final, 27.2.2019. Brussels.

European Commission. 2019b. Enhanced Surveillance Report – Greece, February 2019. *European Economy Institutional Papers*. Brussels: European Commission.

European Commission, Hellenic Republic, and Bank of Greece. 2015. "Memorandum of Understanding between the European Commission (acting on behalf of the European Stability Mechanism) and the Hellenic Republic and the Bank of Greece (19 August)." http://ec.europa.eu/economy_finance/assistance_eu_ms/greek_loan_facility/pdf/01_mou_20150811_en.pdf.

Financial Times. 2015. "Greece's top tax collector sacked by Tsipras." 22 October. https://www.ft.com/content/61b20754-78d1-11e5-a95a-27d368e1ddf7.

Frankfurter Allgemeine Zeitung. 2015. "Griechische Regierung entlässt Chefin der Steuerbehörde." 22 October.

Greek Cabinet. 2016. Act 1 of 20 January: selection and appointment of the Secretary General of the Secretariat General for Public Revenue at the Ministry of Finance. Government Gazette 18, 20 January (in Greek).

Guillot, Adéa. 2015. "Greece struggles to address its tax evasion problem." *The Guardian*, 24 February. Accessed 1 November 2018. https://www.theguardian.com/world/2015/feb/24/greece-collecting-revenue-tax-evasion.

Hadjinikolaou, Prokopis. 2016. "The appointment of tax office heads without assessment." *Kathimerini*, 20 January (in Greek), Economy. http://www.kathimerini.gr/846377/article/oikonomia/ellhnikh-oikonomia/diey8yntes-stis-efories-xwris-a3iologhsh.

Hadjinikolaou, Prokopis. 2019a. "Asset register for all." *Kathimerini*, 4 January (in Greek). http://www.kathimerini.gr/1003061/article/oikonomia/ellhnikh-oikonomia/po8en-esxes-gia-oloys.

Hadjinikolaou, Prokopis. 2019b. "The tax office to audit bank deposit boxes, cards and loans." *Kathimerini*, 22 February (in Greek).

Hellenic Government. 2015. Eurogroup meeting, 11 February 2015, Brussels. Non-paper from the Greek Government. Mimeo.

Hellenic Parliament. 2014. Law 4270/2014: authorities for public financial management and surveillance (transposition of Directive 2011/85/EU) - public accounting and other provisions. Government Gazette A143, 28 June (in Greek).

Hellenic Parliament. 2015. Law 4336/2015: ratification of the draft agreement on economic assistance from the European Stability Mechanism and provisions for the implementation on the financing agreement. Government Gazette A94, 14 August (in Greek).

Hellenic Parliament. 2016a. Law 4389/2016: urgent provisions for the implementation of the agreement on public financial targets and structural reforms and other provisions. Government Gazette A94, 27 May (in Greek).

Hellenic Parliament. 2016b. Law 4446/2016: bankruptcy code, administrative justice, duties, voluntary disclosure of past taxable income, electronic transactions, amendments to Law 4270/2014 and other provisions. Government Gazette A240, 22 December (in Greek).

Hellenic Parliament. 2016c. Minutes of parliamentary proceedings, Saturday 21 May. Athens: Hellenic Parliament (in Greek).

Hellenic Parliament. 2016d. Minutes of parliamentary proceedings, Sunday 22 May. Athens: Hellenic Parliament (in Greek).

HM Government. 2010. The coalition: Our programme for government - freedom, fairness, responsibility. London: HM Government.

IAPR. 2017a. Activity report on 2016. Athens: IAPR (in Greek).

IAPR. 2017b. Internal Rules of Procedure of the IAPR. Decision of the Governor Δ.ΟΡΓ.Α 1063470 ΕΞ 2017. Government Gazette B1579, 9 May (in Greek).

IAPR. 2017c. New Director General for Revenue Administration. Press release, 14 March. Athens (in Greek).
IAPR. 2017d. Operational plan for 2017. Athens: IAPR (in Greek).
IAPR. 2017e. Press release, 1 August. Athens: IAPR (in Greek).
IAPR. 2017f. Press release, 25 September. Athens: IAPR (in Greek).
IAPR. 2017g. Revised strategic plan for 2017-20. Athens: IAPR (in Greek).
IAPR. 2018. "Human resource management." IAPR web site, accessed 7 January 2019. https://www.aade.gr/menoy/aade/diacheirise-anthropinoy-dynamikoy.
IAPR. n.d. "The Management Board." IAPR. Accessed 7 January 2019 (in Greek). https://www.aade.gr/dioikisi.
IAPR Governor. 2017. Decision on the organisation of the Independent Authority for Public Revenue ΔΟΡΓ.Α.1036960/10-3-2017. Government Gazette B968, 22 March (in Greek).
IMF. 2017. Greece: ex-post evaluation of exceptional access under the 2012 extended agreement. Washington, D.C.: IMF.
in.gr. 2016. "The Ministry of Finance occupied due to the SGPR's new status." in.gr, 19 May (in Greek), accessed 14 February 2018. http://news.in.gr/greece/article/?aid=1500078241.
International Statistical Institute. 2018. Court proceedings against Andreas Georgiou, former President of ELSTAT (the Hellenic Statistical Authority).
Kaminis, Giorgos. 2002. "The Independent Authorities Between Independence and Parliamentary Control." *Nomikon Vima* 50:95-105 (in Greek).
Kanellopoulos, Dimitris. 2015. "Risk-free parrots." *Efimerida ton Syntakton*, 21 January (in Greek). https://www.efsyn.gr/politiki/ekloges/ekloges-ianoyarios-2015/12047_papagaloi-me-azimioto.
Karouzos, Yannis. 2016. Legal opinion memo for the attention of POE-DOY. Athens (in Greek).
Kathimerini. 2011. "Urgent preliminary inquiry into corrupt tax inspectors." 15 December (in Greek), Economy. Accessed 18 December 2018. http://www.kathimerini.gr/445452/article/oikonomia/ellhnikh-oikonomia/epeigoysa-prokatarktikh-e3etash-gia-to-grhgoroshmo-twn-eforiakwn.
Kathimerini. 2013a. "Data gathering service to host information from petrol stations." 3 December (in Greek). http://www.kathimerini.gr/505269/article/oikonomia/ellhnikh-oikonomia/yphresia-ypodoxhs-dedomenwn-apo-ta-prathria.
Kathimerini. 2013b. "Greece's statistics chief faces charges over claims of inflated 2009 deficit figure." 22 January (English edition). http://www.ekathimerini.com/147870/article/ekathimerini/news/greeces-statistics-chief-faces-charges-over-claims-of-inflated-2009-deficit-figure.
Kathimerini. 2013c. "Petrol station owners accuse the Ministry of Finance of inaction against whopping illicit trade in fuel." 19 November (in Greek), Business. http://www.kathimerini.gr/60113/article/oikonomia/epixeirhseis/prathrioyxoi-adranei-to-ypoyrgeio-oikonomikwn-sto-orgio-toy-la8remporioy-kaysimwn.
Kathimerini. 2016a. "New heads for tax enforcement centres." 9 November (in Greek). http://www.kathimerini.gr/882691/article/oikonomia/ellhnikh-oikonomia/neoi-epikefalhs-se-elegktika-kentra.
Kathimerini. 2016b. "Parliament approves IAPR's Management Board." 6 September (in Greek). http://www.kathimerini.gr/873643/article/epikairothta/politikh/egkri8hke-h-systash-toy-symvoylioy-dioikhshs-ths-aade.
Kathimerini. 2018. "Key report by the lenders due in February." 1 December (in Greek), Economy. http://www.kathimerini.gr/997906/article/oikonomia/ellhnikh-oikonomia/krisimh-h-ek8esh-twn-daneistwn-ton-fevroyario.
Kathimerini (English edition). 2015. "Tax official refuses to quit over charges." 20 October. http://www.ekathimerini.com/202689/article/ekathimerini/news/tax-official-refuses-to-quit-over-charges.
Katrougalos, George, and Ivi Mavromoustakou. 2003. "The Greek party system and the recent organisational and functional changes of the Vouli (Parliament)." In *The Future of Political Parties*, edited by Dimitris Tsatsos and Xenophon Kontiades, 149-174. Athens: Papazissis (in Greek).

Katsambekis, Giorgos, and Yannis Stavrakakis. 2014. "Left-wing populism in the European periphery: the case of SYRIZA." *Journal of Political Ideologies* 19 (2):119-142.

Kitsantonis, Niki. 2015. "Top Greek Tax Official Is Dismissed." *New York Times*, 22 October. https://www.nytimes.com/2015/10/23/business/international/top-greek-tax-official-is-dismissed.html.

Koutentakis, Fragkiskos. 2018. Financial stability is a basic condition for economic recovery. Interview with the Athens News Agency, 13 May. Athens: Athens News Agency (in Greek). https://www.amna.gr/home/article/256642/Fr-Koutentakis-I-dimosionomiki-statherotita-einai-proupothesi-gia-tin-anakampsi--

Koutnatzis, Stylianos-Ioannis G. n.d. "The independence of the public revenue administration: testing the limits of parliamentarism." https://www.constitutionalism.gr, accessed 24 March 2019 (in Greek). http://tinyurl.com/y2vb3n74.

Kuhlmann, Sabine. 2006. "Local government reform between 'exogenous' and 'endogenous' driving forces." *Public Management Review* 8 (1):67-86.

L'Echo. 2015. "Tryfon Alexiadis: "Je serai aussi jugé sur ma capacité, ou incapacité, à récolter l'impôt"." *L'Echo*, 11 août. https://www.lecho.be/actualite/archive/Tryfon-Alexiadis-Je-serai-aussi-juge-sur-ma-capacite-ou-incapacite-a-recolter-l-impot/9663861.

Lapavitsas, Costas. 2011. "Greece must default and quit the euro. The real debate is how." *The Guardian*, 20 September, 32.

Liargova, Pelagia. 2018. "Change management in a modern public administration." Dissertation, National School of Public Administration and Local Government. Athens (in Greek).

Mandrou, Ioanna. 2015. "Supreme Court: judicial reconsideration of former ELSTAT head's case." *Kathimerini*, 14 September (in Greek). http://www.kathimerini.gr/830849/article/epikairothta/ellada/areios-pagos-dikastikh-epane3etash-ths-ypo8eshs-toy-prwhn-epikefalhs-ths-elstat.

Minister of Finance, and Minister for Administrative Re-organisation. 2018. Joint Ministerial Decision (number 2/58459/0004) on the definition of the procedure and ways and other issues relating to the transfer of staff of the Independent Authority for Public Revenue that will fail their assessment during the Authority's first year of operation. edited by Ministry of Finance and Ministry for Administrative Re-organisation. Government Gazette B3294, 8 August (in Greek).

Ministry of Finance. 2015. Appointment of the panel for the assessment of applications for the post of Secretary General of the SGPR. Athens: Ministry of Finance (in Greek).

Ministry of Finance. 2018. Cross-checking data on trade in fuel. Press release, 8 November. Athens (in Greek).

Ministry of Finance. n.d. Regulatory impact assessment report on the bill entitled 'Urgent provisions for the implementation of the agreement on public financial targets and structural reforms and other provisions'. Athens (in Greek).

Monastiriotis, Vassilis, and Andreas Antoniades. 2009. Reform that! Greece's failing reform technology: beyond 'vested interests' and 'political exchange', *Hellenic Observatory Papers on Greece and Southeast Europe, GreeSE Paper No 28*. London: LSE/Hellenic Observatory.

Mudde, Cas. 2016. *SYRIZA: The Failure of the Populist Promise. Reform and Transition in the Mediterranean* book series. Basingstoke: Palgrave.

Painter, Martin, and Jon Pierre. 2005. "Unpacking policy capacity." In *Challenges to state policy capacity: global trends and comparative perspectives*, edited by Martin Painter and Jon Pierre, 1-18. Basingstoke: Palgrave.

Pardo del Val, M., and Martínez Fuentes Clara. 2003. "Resistance to change: a literature review and empirical study." *Management Decision* 41 (2):148–155.

Passas, Argyris. 2011. "National parliaments in the EU's policy process: from formal competence to a political role. The case of the Hellenic Parliament." In *The Future of the Hellenic Parliament: Constitutional and Political Dimensions*, edited by Xenophon Kontiadis and Philippos Spyropoulos, 253-285. Athens: Sideris (in Greek).

POE-DOY. n.d. Submission of opinion by Eirini Yfanti, leader and on behalf of POE-DOY, to the Committee on Economic Affairs of the Hellenic Parliament on the bill establishing the Independent Authority for Public Revenue. Athens: mimeo (in Greek).

Polsby, N. W. 1975. "Legislatures." In *Handbook of Political Science*, edited by Fred I. Greenstein, Nelson W. Polsby, 257-319. Reading, MA: Addison-Wesley.

Psygkas, Athanasios. 2017. *From the democratic deficit to a democratic surplus: constructing administrative democracy in Europe*. New York: Oxford University Press.

Public Issue. 2010. National survey on corruption in Greece (2009) carried out on behalf of Transparency International - Greece. Athens: Public Issue (in Greek).

Public Issue. 2013. National Survey on Corruption in Greece (2013) conducted on behalf of Transparency International Greece. Summary presentation of survey results. Athens: Public Issue and Transparency International Greece.

Reporter.gr. 2015. "Tender and stormy relations between SGPR and SGIT/GGPS?", 28 July (in Greek). Accessed 1 December 2018. https://www.reporter.gr/Eidhseis/Oikonomia/266006-Scheseis-«storghs-kai-orghs»-metaxy-GGDE-kai-GGPS.

Rhodes, Rod A. W. 1996. *The New European Agencies - Agencies in British Government: Revolution or Evolution?* Florence: European University Institute.

Spanou, Calliope. 2018. "External influence on structural reform: Did policy conditionality strengthen reform capacity in Greece?" *Public Policy and Administration*:1-23. doi: https://doi.org/10.1177/0952076718772008.

Speaker of the Hellenic Parliament. 2014. Amendment of the Speaker's decision number 16074/10803 of 20 December 2010 entitled 'Entry in force of the Special Internal Rules of Procedure of Parliament's Budget Office'. Government Gazette 309B, 12 February (in Greek).

Szymanski, Mike. 2015. "Tsipras streitet mit seiner obersten Steuereintreiberin." *Süddeutsche Zeitung*, 21 October. https://www.sueddeutsche.de/wirtschaft/griechenland-tsipras-streitet-mit-seiner-obersten-steuereintreiberin-1.2701819.

To Vima. 2017a. "Consultation on IAPR's staff appraisal." 25 September (in Greek), Economy. Accessed 1 December 2017. http://www.tovima.gr/finance/article/?aid=903214&wordsinarticle=%CE%91%CE%91%CE%94%CE%95.

To Vima. 2017b. "Hotels in IAPR's pincers." 27 July (in Greek). Accessed 1 December 2018. https://www.tovima.gr/2017/07/27/finance/stin-tsimpida-tis-aade-ta-ksenodoxeia/.

To Vima. 2017c. "Panic as tax evasion exceeds 77 per cent." 15 July (in Greek). Accessed 1 December 2018. http://www.tovima.gr/finance/article/?aid=892051&wordsinarticle=%CE%91%CE%91%CE%94%CE%95.

To Vima. 2017d. "Tax collectors and customs officers to boycott staff appraisal." 18 October (in Greek). Accessed 1 December 2018. http://www.tovima.gr/society/article/?aid=909000&wordsinarticle=%CE%91%CE%91%CE%94%CE%95.

To Vima. 2017e. "Tax compliance checks based on breaches and collectability." 25 April (in Greek). Accessed 1 December 2018. http://www.tovima.gr/finance/article/?aid=875972&wordsinarticle=%CE%91%CE%91%CE%94%CE%95.

Tsakalotos, Euclid. 2010. Contesting Greek exceptionalism: The political economy of the current crisis. Unpublished mimeo. Athens.

Tsekos, T. N., and A. Triantafyllopoulou. 2018. "Policy Evaluation Capacity in Greek Local Government: Formal Implementation and Substantial Failures." In *Evaluating Reforms of Local Public and Social Services in Europe*, edited by I. Kopric, H. Wollman and G. Marcou, 315-331. Basingstoke: Palgrave.

Valavani, Nadia. 2016. *The third memorandum - The reversal of a reversal. Personal proofs of a collective denial.* Athens: A. A. Livanis (in Greek).

van Witteloostuijn, Arjen, Gabriele Jacobs, and Jochen Christe-Zeyse. 2013. "A theoretical framework of organizational change." *Journal of Organizational Change Management* 26 (5):772-792.

Varoufakis, Yanis. 2015a. Talk in the 11th February 2015 Eurogroup meeting. Mimeo.

Varoufakis, Yanis. 2015b. Talk in the 16th February 2015 Eurogroup meeting. Mimeo.

Varoufakis, Yanis. 2017. *Adults in the room: my battle with Europe's deep establishment.* London: The Bodley Head.

Varoufakis, Yanis, Stuart Holland, and James K. Galbraith. 2013. *A Modest Proposal for Resolving the Eurozone Crisis, Version 4.0.* https://varoufakis.files.wordpress.com/2013/07/a-modest-proposal-for-resolving-the-eurozone-crisis-version-4-0-final1.pdf.

Wagstyl, Stefan, John Aglionby, Mark Odell, and Michael Hunter. 2015. "Greece's rift with Germany deepens." *Financial Times*, 5 February. https://www.ft.com/content/fb828c8c-ad11-11e4-a5c1-00144feab7de.

WSJ Europe. 2019. "Man Who Revealed the Depth of Greece's Financial Quagmire Is Cleared." 1 March, Europe.

Chapter 6
Conclusion

We set out to examine the process of depoliticisation of Greece's public revenue administration, i.e. the gradual switch from it being an integral part of the bureaucracy of the Greek Ministry of Finance reporting directly to the minister to a separate authority that is functionally independent and administratively and financially autonomous vis-à-vis the government of the day. The first section of this chapter discusses the three hypotheses as to why this reform has happened. These are drawn from the study of the European Union's (EU) enlargement (Schimmelfennig and Sedelmeier 2005a) but their logic is applicable here due to the similarities that we discussed in Chap. 2.

In a nutshell, we argue that while the first hypothesis which highlights the essence of conditionality—i.e. *power asymmetry* between Greece on the one hand and its partners on the other—clearly explains the choice of the direction of travel (i.e. less ministerial control), it does not account for the ultimate destination, i.e. how far the reform went; rather, the extent of the reform is the result of the priorities of the government in the final stages of the negotiations as well as, more importantly, successive Greek governments' reactions to external pressure for reform. These reactions exacerbated the problem of credibility and lack of trust in the eyes of the country's partners who, in turn, pushed the reform even further. This is why the reform went as far as it did.

External Pressure, Social Learning or Lesson-Drawing?

The first model reflects the logic of consequences. The *external incentives model* is couched in rationalist bargaining where domestic actors operate as strategic utility maximisers who are keen to preserve or enhance their welfare. The outcome of the bargaining process reflects the relative bargaining power of the two sides. In turn, this power mirrors the uneven distribution of (a) information and (b) the benefits that are expected to derive from a specific agreement (Schimmelfennig and Sedelmeier

D. Dimitrakopoulos, A. Passas, *The Depoliticisation of Greece's Public Revenue Administration*, https://doi.org/10.1007/978-3-030-23213-9_6

2005b: 10). The more and better information one side has, the more able it is to shape the outcome of bargaining and the less need one side has to reach a specific agreement, the more power it has to achieve its objective by threatening to withhold cooperation. In the context of the EU's enlargement (the study of which is the basis of these models), the rewards range from assistance to full membership of the EU. The EU provides them if the conditions are met but withholds them in the opposite case (reactive reinforcement or reinforcement by reward). In the presence of a mismatch between the domestic status quo, on the one hand, and EU rules on the other, conditionality is deployed so as to alter the incentives that support the domestic status quo, either directly through intergovernmental bargaining, or indirectly, i.e. through the differential empowerment of the domestic actors that wanted but were hitherto unable to bring about change. This leads to the first hypothesis: '*a government adopts EU rules if the benefits of EU rewards exceed the domestic adoption costs*' (Schimmelfennig and Sedelmeier 2005b: 12). The balance between costs and benefits depends on (1) the determinacy of conditions, (2) the size and speed of rewards, (3) the credibility of threats and promises and (4) the size of adoption costs (Schimmelfennig and Sedelmeier 2005b: 12–17).

In the context of the crisis that engulfed Greece at the end of the 2000s, the country desperately needed and ultimately obtained unprecedented amounts of funds in exchange for institutional and policy reforms. This means that Greece's relationship with its partners started from conditions of power asymmetry. This is the reason why the process of depoliticisation started in the first place. Although there was both a) the need for this specific reform and b) some (limited) domestic support for it, the issue of depoliticisation did not make it on to the agenda until Greece's partners placed it there in early 2012. Until then, the country's first minister of finance to face the crisis had not even tried to place it on the agenda, largely because he knew it would be opposed within the government. Subsequent events demonstrate that opposition and reluctance were present throughout this period (2009–2019). Our empirical evidence suggests that in the absence of conditionality, this reform would not have materialised. Throughout the period examined in this book, domestic political support for the principle of this reform was confined to two finance ministers. On the other hand, the conditions set were quite specific. When semi-autonomy was introduced in 2012, the law had to comply with a checklist provided by the country's international partners and in 2015, the MoU itself became even more specific. The fact that, since 2012, this reform *ensemble* was designated as either a prior action or a structural benchmark—i.e. a formal condition that had to be met prior to the provision of funding—also shows that the rewards too were determinate. The fact that funding was repeatedly withheld—indeed the programme that was attached to the second MoU was never formally completed and the associated funding was accordingly withheld (though for reasons that related to other aspects of the programme)—also demonstrated clearly the credibility of the threat. Greece's partners also took precautions in the form of direct involvement in the selection process of the second and third heads of the semi-autonomous public revenue administration. Finally, in terms of adoption costs, they were identical to the status quo in financial terms (since the public revenue administration would remain funded by the state budget) and dwarfed in comparison to the expected rewards. In political terms, they were limited to those (largely in the senior *échelons* of the staff union) who felt very strongly about depoliticisation, but could easily be countered with reference to power asymmetry and the fact that the public revenue administration's depoliticisation is not an issue that could mobilise larger segments of Greek society, and certainly not as much as further pension and wage cuts or job losses would be.

External pressure (i.e. power asymmetry) alone can only account for the commencement as well as the direction of the reform, not how far the reform ended up going. The broader context has had an impact in relation to timing, the nature of the external constraint and the priorities of the government. Depoliticisation became a requirement after the first MoU, although it was a potential reform model way before it. The requirement was significantly amplified in the course of 2012 but especially after the two consequential removals from office of the first and second heads of the (then still) semi-autonomous public revenue administration. Both hugely amplified the Greek political *élite's* credibility problem in the eyes of the country's partners and also made the European Commission change its stance on the issue of full independence. The view that, in the absence of constant political interference on the part of the Samaras administration, semi-autonomy was quite likely (possibly with some fine tuning that all major institutional reforms need in the early stages of their life) to have become the end result of the reform process is plausible. After all, semi-autonomy is the model that prevails amongst the members of the Euro area. If it had been allowed to operate and produce the intended result (which is higher rates of collection of the taxes that had been legislated for), there is no a priori reason to suggest that full independence would have followed. On the contrary, introducing semi-autonomy and then acting against it generated a significant incentive for the International Monetary Fund (IMF) and the EU to push the reform process further, as well as to take the extra precautions by means of their involvement in the appointment of the second and third heads of Greece's public revenue administration (post-2012). Under the SYRIZA-ANEL government, though opposition to this reform was clear, it was not as hard. The priority was to reduce the targeted primary budget surplus and defend the country's employment protections. However, there is no doubt that the dismissal of the second head of the (then still) semi-autonomous public revenue administration gave the final push towards further reform and the establishment of an independent authority. This is so because the dismissal of the semi-autonomous revenue administration's second head effectively (coupled with public statements against independence) equated the SYRIZA-ANEL government to its ND-PASOK predecessor in the eyes of the country's partners, leading the IMF's officials to conclude that 'political commitment to respect the fixed-term appointment and provide leadership stability to the revenue administration was absent from mid-2014 to early 2016, when reform progress slowed significantly' (IMF 2017: 43).

The logic of appropriateness informs two alternative models. The *social learning model* is couched in the impact of internalised identities and shared norms (Schimmelfennig and Sedelmeier 2005b: 18–20). Since the EU is a formal organisation of a European international community that is defined by a specific underlying common identity and is underpinned by a concrete *ensemble* of common values and norms, non-members (in the case of enlargement) adopt these rules if they regard them as appropriate, i.e. corresponding to a collective set of values, norms and identity (Schimmelfennig 2003: 83–90). This leads to the second hypothesis: '*a state adopts EU rules if it is persuaded of the appropriateness of EU rules*' (Schimmelfennig and Sedelmeier 2005b: 18). Unlike the previous model which relies on bargaining about conditions and rewards, coercion and mere behavioural adaptation, under this model adaptation depends on the legitimacy and the appropriateness of rules, persuasion and complex learning. If such rules exist and are clear and specific, their legitimacy determines the likelihood of their adoption. Engagement of target governments in a deliberative process and the association of reforms with more abstract, legitimate principles and norms that underpin the community to which applicant states aspire to belong is a way to avoid reform being associated with foreign imposition and the problems that are associated with the lack of domestic programme ownership. Legitimacy is also boosted when these rules are seen to be equitable and do not conflict with the rules of other bodies such as international organisations. Finally, social learning is also affected by resonance. Under this model discourse is likely to be the starting point of the process of adaptation, but the key test is formal and behavioural change (Schimmelfennig and Sedelmeier 2005b: 20).

The crucial element of this model is programme ownership, in line with the literature [including reports of IFI (international financial institutions) officials] on conditionality (see Chap. 2). This is also the reason why this model is not applicable here. The support of two finance ministers (under the first and second MoUs—see Chaps. 3 and 4) does not amount to genuine programme ownership that cuts across government and has explicit backing from the head of the government. Particularly telling in that respect is the Samaras administration: it legislated semi-autonomy but also (a) appointed a PM's confidant as head of the Financial Crime Squad, (b) ostracised the first head of the semi-autonomous SGPR (Secretariat General for Public Revenue) when the PM felt this would be politically expedient and (c) went on to appoint as head of the revenue administration certainly an expert but also someone who was very close to the main ruling party. The Tsipras administration was also quick to seize the opportunity and sack the very same person when this opportunity arose. In that sense, both the ND-PASOK and the SYRIZA-ANEL governments failed the key test that underpins this reform: how to react when the semi-autonomous public revenue is headed by or operates in a way that is not to the government's liking. This, in and of itself, proves beyond doubt the absence of programme ownership in relation to depoliticisation. There are two additional reasons why this model is not applicable here. First, while within the EU several states have semi-autonomous public revenue administrations, others (including France and Germany) do not (see Chap. 1). Second, the norms that were embodied in both semi-autonomy and full independence did not resonate with the ethos that prevails within the Greek political *élite* in a country where very few public officials resign (as Katerina Savvaidou's case also shows). Semi-autonomous or independent bodies (irrespective of their precise legal status) are either contested or criticised in public or, quite often understaffed or otherwise undermined.[1] The two main parties—SYRIZA and ND, on either side of the centre of the political spectrum—behaved in a very similar way when in power: seeking (when the opportunity arose) to place in key posts as heads of these bodies individuals who often have the requisite expertise but are also close to them.[2] This is de facto contestation of the norms embodied in the principle of depoliticisation because if expertise and the prospect of effectiveness were the key criteria as the notion of depoliticisation implies, proximity to political views would not come into play at all. Put in another way, this is the first step towards undermining depoliticisation. The risk remains in place.

Finally, social learning also relies on persuasion. The provision of technical assistance could, in theory, become a channel through which persuasion could occur, largely because it is provided and received by specialists. However, in Greece's case technical assistance too became a victim (in terms of rhetoric and perception) of the febrile atmosphere generated by the crisis leading even influential individuals who should know better to refer to the country's public revenue administration as the 'troika-dominated tax office' (Varoufakis 2017: 479), not distinguishing between technical assistance (whose provision was asked for and started being provided *before* the first MoU was concluded) and the remainder of the adjustment programme. In other words, this highlights the continuing relevance and impact of clientelism as a central feature of the Greek political and administrative culture.

The final model (*lesson-drawing*) is couched in domestic dissatisfaction with extant policy and/or institutions that generates a search for arrangements that operate elsewhere. The rationalist variant of this model involves simple learning (i.e. a change in means but not ends, as a result of new information) while the sociological variant involves complex learning and a change of goals. This model's key difference from the other two models is that in this case the EU does not play the decisive role in bringing about domestic change (Schimmelfennig and Sedelmeier 2005b: 21). Rather, conditionality can shape domestic change by setting boundaries to the range of options that domestic actors consider or by offering a menu of acceptable models. Consequently, (a) adaptation is a domestic decision that results—not from adjustment costs—but from the perceived utility of imported solutions or (b) the external incentives model may explain the commencement and overall direction of change and lesson-drawing the specific form that has been chosen. So, the third hypothesis is as follows: '*a state adopts EU rules if it expects these rules to*

[1]In recent times one such example was ND's use of parliamentary procedures to block the appointment of members to the board of the National Broadcasting Council in an effort to prevent the implementation of a media law that ND opposed.

[2]The appointment of Yannis Stournaras as governor of the Bank of Greece in 2014 and the appointment of Vassiliki Thanou as head of the country's Competition Commission in late 2018 are emblematic examples. Both had the requisite expertise (the former as both an academic economist and minister of finance, the latter as former chair of the country's Supreme Court and then as the prime minister's senior legal adviser) but both were close to the views of the governments that chose them.

solve domestic policy problems effectively' (Schimmelfennig and Sedelmeier 2005b: 22). This model presupposes dissatisfaction with existing domestic arrangements. Proximity of and similarities with the EU and the systems of its member states inform the search for solutions but the transferability of rules is key. This model takes as its starting point 'a domestic disequilibrium in which the balance of domestic pressures favours a departure from the status quo' (Schimmelfennig and Sedelmeier 2005b: 24) and in that sense it differs from the external incentives model which starts from a domestic equilibrium that is upset through the provision of the incentives that conditionality entails.

The balance of domestic forces did not favour a departure from the status quo since 2010, even when the supporters of depoliticisation included the country's finance minister (as was the case for most of the period between 2009 and the end of 2014). The finance minister's support for the model of the IRS (Internal Revenue Service) (i.e. independence) even before the conclusion of the first MoU is the only evidence of lesson-drawing we have. As a consequence, the model did not apply for most of the period under consideration. On the other hand, some evidence points in the direction of support under the SYRIZA-ANEL government since its officials accepted that interference in operational and other decisions is a cause of poor tax collection and they (correctly) note that it is not confined to the political segment of the country's establishment. However, their critique of the democratic credentials of full independence (and in particular the fact that, although the public revenue administration is now accountable to parliament, the latter does not have the formal power to sack the governor) indicates dissonance, at least at the level of discourse, as does the notion that *who* is in government matters most.

So, we conclude that the single most important institutional reform introduced under the bailout agreements reflects the impact of conditionality in the sense that power asymmetries explain both the start of the reform and the direction of its travel. In the absence of Greece's overwhelming need for financial assistance, none of the aforementioned reforms (especially depoliticisation) would have occurred. Nevertheless, the final outcome of the reform process, i.e. an operationally independent, and financially and administratively autonomous public revenue authority, was also shaped by successive Greek governments that actually opposed that reform. In other words, the weaker party in that unbalanced relationship made consequential choices thus shaping the outcome more than its share of the distribution of power would normally lead us to expect. This consequential domestic reaction owes much to Greece's deficient reform capacity. We turn to it in the next section.

Greece's Reform Capacity

In our review of the literature (see Chap. 1), we highlighted the presence of several factors that act as effective barriers to reform and thus, when combined, contribute to what is almost unanimously portrayed, in that literature, as Greece's limited reform capacity. In this section, we argue that most of these factors were at play in the reform process that we have analysed in this book and this is why we remain rather pessimistic about the prospect of its survival in the medium term.

In light of the fact that the notion of political cost is the single biggest barrier to reform, one would expect this reform to materialise more quickly and in a far less problematic manner than it did in the end. This is so because in the context of a major crisis and the country's desperate need for financial assistance, one could argue that it was very easy for politicians to shift blame to the IMF and the country's European partners. Since Greeks became acutely aware of the country's status of utmost dependence on its partners for the provision of financial assistance, it would also be easy to shift the blame for tax rises too. In other words, the material conditions were perfect for domestic political actors to shift blame and thus significantly limit the political price (cost) they stood to pay for the introduction of this reform. This argument could be taken a step further. Having unelected individuals in key parts of the state apparatus could be beneficial for the government of the day by distancing it from the ever unpopular collection of taxes. Indeed, as one official reported, she made this point to IMF staff:

> Do you have any idea about the kind of gift you are giving to the minister? They are foolish to reject it. In this country [where ministers rarely resign] they ought to say "yes, take the problem off my back" (interview, Athens, 3 April 2017).

The problem with this line of reasoning is that it presupposes that the collection of taxes is something that Greek politicians actually want to pursue, irrespective of its links to the electoral cycle. Yet, if there is a simple truth that our analysis shows, it is that the Greek political *élite* is unwilling to dissociate the electoral cycle from the process of tax collection. This is the only logical conclusion that we can draw from the fact that—even in the midst of this very severe economic crisis—political proximity remained a key consideration (positively in the first of the two consequential removals from office, negatively in the second one) in relation to who should head the country's public revenue administration. Given semi-autonomy, the other route that was available to these two governments would be to change tax policy—since the revenue administration can only implement the policy made by the majority of the day. In the main, they opted to attack the officeholder instead. This largely reflects another key factor that undermines Greece's reform capacity.

In Greece much of the political process relates to and evolves around individuals, rather than impersonal systems, structures and institutions that are built on trust. Although Greece started from a low base, trust in impartial institutions dropped even further during the crisis (Ervasti et al. 2018). In that sense, the politicians' rejection of impartiality in the form of a semi-autonomous or independent public revenue administration is a reflection of broader society's predominant modus operandi.

The reform process also reveals the enduring relevance of the state's weak capacity as demonstrated by the civil service's inability to think, especially in conditions of crisis, without constant, direct input from its political masters. Although the bulk of civil servants enjoy the perks of a job for life the permanence of which is guaranteed by the Constitution, they do not operate accordingly. In other West European countries where the same status applies, it was fostered as a way of promoting the common good against the whim of the rulers, including elected ones. Yet in Greece the prevailing ethos amongst the central government's civil servants is one of total inaction in the absence of direct political input from ministers. The fact that reforms stalled towards the end of the first adjustment programme and until the second elections of 2012 is also the consequence of the fact that ministers themselves either do not want a genuine independent civil service or do little to foster it, when in power. This does not make much sense for those who care about rational policy making in light of the other key barrier to reform that permeates the Greek political system, namely the total unwillingness and inability of the main political parties to prepare anything that resembles an action plan in relation to specific issues *prior* to winning an election. For the main parties, this is definitely not a matter of resources since they remain—even now—well funded. Rather, this unwillingness reflects (a) a particular understanding of what democratic politics is about and (b) a disdain for evidence (see Chap. 1).

The prevailing view of democratic politics in Greece is built on sloganeering and inflammatory rhetoric that portrays political opponents as enemies, rather than the articulation of carefully considered alternative plans for action. The use of slogans as if they had the character of actions or plans goes hand in hand with disdain for evidence and is clearly reflected in the weakness of the national parliament in holding the executive to account. The critique of the public revenue administration's new line of accountability exemplifies this logic. It is limited to the fact that parliament lacks the *formal* power to sack the governor but those who articulate this critique—including MPs of (then) ruling parties—have not done anything to improve the new institution's accountability to parliament and do not even try to engage in creative thinking, preferring instead to criticise and denounce it. For example, it is hard to see how the governor could retain their post if a large majority of the relevant parliamentary committee came up with carefully researched and considered evidence presented in a report, backed up by expert opinion, indicating that much more could have been done to increase public revenues but the governor had failed to take action.

Invoking the absence or presence of specific legal rules is another barrier to reform, especially in the case of the public revenue administration. This means that little effort is made, especially by the civil service but also politicians, to think about outcomes when designing or assessing public policy. Indeed, if one reads what was said in parliament during the debate on the establishment of the Independent Authority for Public Revenue (see Chap. 5), one will not find any reference to arguments in favour or against it couched in terms of effectiveness. This culture though, is not a top-down phenomenon. Rather it complements the clientelism that is prevalent in Greek society.

The reliance on slogans and the absence of a culture of evidence-based policy making (which is not confined to Greece amongst European countries) is in Greece's case also associated with a climate of polarisation. This is not confined to the period in the run-up to elections but permeates contemporary political discourse. The single biggest expression of this phenomenon in the reform process that we have examined is the language used in the Greek parliament.

Conditionality and Membership of the European Union

This conclusion has important implications for the EU since it is making increasing use of conditionality not only externally but also internally as the ongoing reform of EMU (Economic and Monetary Union) shows. Just like membership of the EU more broadly, conditionality requires a significant degree of programme ownership at the domestic level. In the presence of a domestic political *élite* that is lacking reform capacity either in terms of political will or alternative plans, a case can be made for a less wide-ranging adjustment programme and a slower speed of reform. Jeroen Dijsselbloem, former Finance Minister of the Netherlands and chair of the Eurogroup, acknowledged this need when he said that

> the programmes were overloaded, there were so many measures, so many reforms at the same time, even if you have a perfect, brilliant civil service it will be hard to do all those things at the same time (Dijsselbloem 2018).

On the other hand, in Greece's case the magnitude of the country's problems and the pressing needs generated by the financial crisis made this task immeasurably hard for policy makers. One point in particular that deserves to be highlighted was called 'the MoU's double-edged sword' by one of our interviewees, by which he referred to the idea that 'in the absence of MoU-enshrined obligations, none of these things would have happened, while many [of these reforms] faced difficulties precisely because they were MoU-enshrined obligations' (interview, Athens, 2 June 2017).

Nevertheless, the reforms that we describe in the empirical chapters—especially in Chaps. 4 and 5 and, in particular, job description and job evaluation within IAPR and linking petrol stations to the Ministry of Finance so as to record transactions and thus fight against the illicit fuel trade, are things that are taken for granted in any West European country. Yet in Greece, it took three MoUs and plenty of arm-twisting on the part of the EU and the IMF—after almost four decades of EU membership—to make them happen. This is a heavy indictment on the Greek political class that had been accustomed to running the country on borrowed money.

This has implications for the process of European integration. Both the operation of conditionality and the process of European integration more broadly require a significant degree of 'ownership', i.e. genuine and consistent adherence to the logic that permeates the objectives that integration and conditionality are meant to achieve. From that perspective, this book shows how shallow the Greek political *élite's* pro-Europeanism (i.e. support for European integration) really is. For decades, vocal support for European integration was not coupled with the effective, consistent, fair (i.e. European) way of budgeting and collecting taxes on the part of the Greek state. On the contrary, for decades amateurish methods of public budgeting went hand in hand with lax, corrupt, inconsistent and ineffective ways of collecting taxes. Greek politicians could talk the European talk (as they did), but were unwilling and/or unable to walk the European walk when it came to managing the country's public finances. When the easy access to cheap borrowing dried out, the need for reform became evident. In other words, reality forced the Greek political *élite* to deal with the reform of tax collection. There was no spontaneous domestic realisation that this issue had to be dealt with anyway. Only a handful of those who were in a position of power actually tried to do something about it. This 'story' is very similar to the country's accession to the Euro area. The domestic reforms that made this possible happened due to a small group of people that did not touch any issues that required them to expend major political capital (Dimitrakopoulos and Passas 2003). This relates in particular to the state apparatus which, as subsequent developments clearly show, needed root and branch reform, although this reform was—and remains—a condition for sustaining Greece's participation in European integration.

Given the justifiable lack of trust in the Greek political *élite*, the scale of the problems and the funds required, the use of conditionality on the part of Greece's international partners was the inevitable foundation of the reform programmes. However, the successful operation of conditionality requires credibility on both sides but it was in short supply on the Greek side in relation to the public revenue administration. This lack of credibility is demonstrated by two successive governments' attitudes towards this reform.

In other words, conditionality requires credibility which, in turn, requires domestic reform capacity. That reform capacity was—as this research demonstrates—lacking either in terms of political will (which shows the objective of reform was not shared) or in terms of concrete alternative plans. The lack of alternative plans is as far-reaching as the lack of political will. For decades (indeed even during the crisis) Greek politicians were happy to promise to fight tax evasion but were unwilling to put in place a key tool—namely a full and functioning Land Registry which Greece was lacking at the onset of the crisis. Just like an efficient public revenue administration, it is another cornerstone of any modern European state, yet Greece is still striving to build one by 2022, again under the impulse of its international partners. In other words, this episode shows that Greece is far from being—despite its involvement in European integration for nearly four decades—a normal European state.

Finally, the reform examined in this book also shows the enduring implications of key characteristics of the European Union. First, the EU is an organisation that operates on the basis of a more or less specific distribution of formal power. Its formal competence in terms of tax matters is rather limited. This has hampered the role of European Commission officials in situ in Greece because of the prevailing view amongst them that this is a matter where member states ought to take the lead. Second, the issue of reform capacity was not confined to Greece. It related to the European Commission too and that is a point used by those—especially in the German government—that were determined to push for the IMF's involvement in crisis management. While the European Court of Auditors has voiced some criticism of the European Commission's involvement in the handling of the crisis in Greece (European Court of Auditors 2015, 2017), the Commission has institutionalised a new mechanism—in the form of the Structural Reform Support Service that it did not possess at the beginning of the crisis. In a typical EU fashion, this is a case of crisis-induced institutionalisation of capacity at EU level. This, however, cannot negate the fact that European integration is like a chain: it is only as strong as its weakest link. This link will remain weak as long as inconvenient reforms are domestically opposed.

References

Dijsselbloem, Jeroen. 2018. Some governments did not want to fight against vested interests. Interview with the former head of Eurogroup published in Greek weekly *Documento*, 6 September (in Greek).

Dimitrakopoulos, Dionyssis G., and Argyris G. Passas, eds. 2003. *Greece in the European Union, Europe and the Nation State Series*. London: Routledge.

Ervasti, Heikki, Antti Kouvo, and Takis Venetoklis. 2018. "Social and Institutional Trust in Times of Crisis: Greece, 2002–2011." *Social Indicators Research*. https://doi.org/10.1007/s11205-018-1862-y

European Court of Auditors. 2015. Special report: Financial assistance provided to countries in difficulties. Luxembourg: Publications Office of the European Union.

European Court of Auditors. 2017. The Commission's intervention in the Greek financial crisis. Report No. 17 (pursuant to Article 287(4), second subparagraph, TFEU). Luxembourg: European Court of Auditors.

IMF. 2017. Greece: ex-post evaluation of exceptional access under the 2012 extended agreement. Washington, D.C.: IMF.

Schimmelfennig, Frank. 2003. *The EU, NATO and the Integration of Europe*. Cambridge: Cambridge University Press.

Schimmelfennig, Frank, and Ulrich Sedelmeier, eds. 2005a. *The Europeanization of Central and Eastern Europe. Cornell Studies in Political Economy Series*. Ithaca, NY: Cornell University Press.

Schimmelfennig, Frank, and Ulrich Sedelmeier. 2005b. "Introduction: conceptualizing the Europeanization of Central and Eastern Europe." In *The Europeanization of Central and Eastern Europe*, edited by Frank Schimmelfennig and Ulrich Sedelmeier, 1-28. Ithaca, N.Y.: Cornell University Press.

Varoufakis, Yanis. 2017. *Adults in the room: my battle with Europe's deep establishment*. London: The Bodley Head.

Index

D. Dimitrakopoulos, A. Passas, *The Depoliticisation of Greece's Public Revenue Administration*, https://doi.org/10.1007/978-3-030-23213-9

MIX
Papier aus verantwortungsvollen Quellen
Paper from responsible sources
FSC® C105338

If you have any concerns about our products,
you can contact us on
ProductSafety@springernature.com

In case Publisher is established outside the EU,
the EU authorized representative is:
Springer Nature Customer Service Center GmbH
Europaplatz 3, 69115 Heidelberg, Germany

Printed by Libri Plureos GmbH
in Hamburg, Germany